Get the eBook FREE!

(PDF, ePub, Kindle, and liveBook all included)

We believe that once you buy a book from us, you should be able to read it in any format we have available. To get electronic versions of this book at no additional cost to you, purchase and then register this book at the Manning website.

Go to https://www.manning.com/freebook and follow the instructions to complete your pBook registration.

That's it!
Thanks from Manning!

AI Agents in Action

AI Agents in Action

MICHEAL LANHAM

MANNING
SHELTER ISLAND

For online information and ordering of this and other Manning books, please visit
www.manning.com. The publisher offers discounts on this book when ordered in quantity.
For more information, please contact

    Special Sales Department
    Manning Publications Co.
    20 Baldwin Road
    PO Box 761
    Shelter Island, NY 11964
    Email: orders@manning.com

Manning Publications Co.
20 Baldwin Road
PO Box 761
Shelter Island, NY 11964

Development editor:	Becky Whitney
Technical editor:	Ross Turner
Review editor:	Kishor Rit
Production editor:	Keri Hales
Copy editor:	Julie McNamee
Proofreader:	Katie Tennant
Technical proofreader:	Ross Turner
Typesetter:	Dennis Dalinnik
Cover designer:	Marija Tudor

ISBN: 9781633436343
Printed in the United States of America

I dedicate this book to all the readers who embark on this journey with me. Books are a powerful way for an author to connect with readers on a deeply personal level, chapter by chapter, page by page. In that shared experience of learning, exploring, and growing together, I find true meaning. May this book inspire you and challenge you, and help you see the incredible potential that AI agents hold— not just for the future but also for today.

brief contents

contents

preface

My journey into the world of intelligent systems began back in the early 1980s. Like many people then, I believed artificial intelligence (AI) was just around the corner. It always seemed like one more innovation and technological leap would lead us to the intelligence we imagined. But that leap never came.

Perhaps the promise of HAL, from Stanley Kubrick's *2001: A Space Odyssey*, captivated me with the idea of a truly intelligent computer companion. After years of effort, trial, and countless errors, I began to understand that creating AI was far more complex than we humans had imagined. In the early 1990s, I shifted my focus, applying my skills to more tangible goals in other industries.

Not until the late 1990s, after experiencing a series of challenging and transformative events, did I realize my passion for building intelligent systems. I knew these systems might never reach the superintelligence of HAL, but I was okay with that. I found fulfillment in working with machine learning and data science, creating models that could learn and adapt. For more than 20 years, I thrived in this space, tackling problems that required creativity, precision, and a sense of possibility.

During that time, I worked on everything from genetic algorithms for predicting unknown inputs to developing generative learning models for horizontal drilling in the oil-and-gas sector. These experiences led me to write, where I shared my knowledge by way of books on various topics—reverse-engineering Pokémon Go, building augmented and virtual reality experiences, designing audio for games, and applying reinforcement learning to create intelligent agents. I spent years knuckles-deep in code, developing agents in Unity ML-Agents and deep reinforcement learning.

Even then, I never imagined that one day I could simply describe what I wanted to an AI model, and it would make it happen. I never imagined that, in my lifetime, I would be able to collaborate with an AI as naturally as I do today. And I certainly never imagined how fast—and simultaneously how slow—this journey would feel.

In November 2022, the release of ChatGPT changed everything. It changed the world's perception of AI, and it changed the way we build intelligent systems. For me, it also altered my perspective on the capabilities of these systems. Suddenly, the idea of agents that could autonomously perform complex tasks wasn't just a far-off dream but instead a tangible, achievable reality. In some of my earlier books, I had described agentic systems that could undertake specific tasks, but now, those once-theoretical ideas were within reach.

This book is the culmination of my decades of experience in building intelligent systems, but it's also a realization of the dreams I once had about what AI could become. AI agents are here, poised to transform how we interact with technology, how we work, and, ultimately, how we live.

Yet, even now, I see hesitation from organizations when it comes to adopting agentic systems. I believe this hesitation stems not from fear of AI but rather from a lack of understanding and expertise in building these systems. I hope that this book helps to bridge that gap. I want to introduce AI agents as tools that can be accessible to everyone—tools we shouldn't fear but instead respect, manage responsibly, and learn to work with in harmony.

acknowledgments

I want to extend my deepest gratitude to the machine learning and deep learning communities for their tireless dedication and incredible work. Just a few short years ago, many questioned whether the field was headed for another AI winter—a period of stagnation and doubt. But thanks to the persistence, brilliance, and passion of countless individuals, the field not only persevered but also flourished. We're standing on the threshold of an AI-driven future, and I am endlessly grateful for the contributions of this talented community.

Writing a book, even with the help of AI, is no small feat. It takes dedication, collaboration, and a tremendous amount of support. I am incredibly thankful to the team of editors and reviewers who made this book possible. I want to express my heartfelt thanks to everyone who took the time to review and provide feedback. In particular, I want to thank Becky Whitney, my content editor, and Ross Turner, my technical editor and chief production and technology officer at OpenSC, for their dedication, as well as the whole production team at Manning for their insight and unwavering support throughout this journey.

To my partner, Rhonda—your love, patience, and encouragement mean the world to me. You've been the cornerstone of my support system, not just for this book but for all the books that have come before. I truly couldn't have done any of this without you. Thank you for being my rock, my partner, and my inspiration.

Many of the early ideas for this book grew out of my work at Symend. It was during my time there that I first began developing the concepts and designs for agentic systems that laid the foundation for this book. I am deeply grateful to my colleagues at

Symend for their collaboration and contributions, including Peh Teh, Andrew Wright, Ziko Rajabali, Chris Garrett, Kouros, Fatemeh Torabi Asr, Sukh Singh, and Hanif Joshaghani. Your insights and hard work helped bring these ideas to life, and I am honored to have worked alongside such an incredible group of people.

Finally, I would like to thank all the reviewers: Anandaganesh Balakrishnan, Aryan Jadon, Chau Giang, Dan Sheikh, David Curran, Dibyendu Roy Chowdhury, Divya Bhargavi, Felipe Provezano Coutinho, Gary Pass, John Williams, Jose San Leandro, Laurence Giglio, Manish Jain, Maxim Volgin, Michael Wang, Mike Metzger, Piti Champeethong, Prashant Dwivedi, Radhika Kanubaddhi, Rajat Kant Goel, Ramaa Vissa, Richard Vaughan, Satej Kumar Sahu, Sergio Gtz, Siva Dhandapani, Annamaneni Sriharsha, Sri Ram Macharla, Sumit Bhattacharyya, Tony Holdroyd, Vidal Graupera, Vidhya Vinay, and Vinoth Nageshwaran. Your suggestions helped make this a better book.

about this book

AI Agents in Action is about building and working with intelligent agent systems—not just creating autonomous entities but also developing agents that can effectively tackle and solve real-world problems. The book starts with the basics of working with large language models (LLMs) to build assistants, multi-agent systems, and agentic behavioral agents. From there, it explores the key components of agentic systems: retrieval systems for knowledge and memory augmentation, action and tool usage, reasoning, planning, evaluation, and feedback. The book demonstrates how these components empower agents to perform a wide range of complex tasks through practical examples.

This journey isn't just about technology; it's about reimagining how we approach problem solving. I hope this book inspires you to see intelligent agents as partners in innovation, capable of transforming ideas into actions in ways that were once thought impossible. Together, we'll explore how AI can augment human potential, enabling us to achieve far more than we could alone.

Who should read this book

This book is for anyone curious about intelligent agents and how to develop agentic systems—whether you're building your first helpful assistant or diving deeper into complex multi-agent systems. No prior experience with agents, agentic systems, prompt engineering, or working with LLMs is required. All you need is a basic understanding of Python and familiarity with GitHub repositories. My goal is to make these concepts accessible and engaging, empowering anyone who wants to explore the world of AI agents to do so with confidence.

Whether you're a developer, researcher, or hobbyist or are simply intrigued by the possibilities of AI, this book is for you. I hope that in these pages you'll find inspiration, practical guidance, and a new appreciation for the remarkable potential of intelligent agents. Let this book guide understanding, creating, and unleashing the power of AI agents in action.

How this book is organized: A road map

This book has 11 chapters. Chapter 1, "Introduction to agents and their world," begins by laying a foundation with fundamental definitions of large language models, chat systems, assistants, and autonomous agents. As the book progresses, the discussion shifts to the key components that make up an agent and how these components work together to create truly effective systems. Here is a quick summary of chapters 2 through 11:

- *Chapter 2, "Harnessing the power of large language models"*—We start by exploring how to use commercial LLMs, such as OpenAI. We then examine tools, such as LM Studio, that provide the infrastructure and support for running various open source LLMs, enabling anyone to experiment and innovate.
- *Chapter 3, "Engaging GPT assistants"*—This chapter dives into the capabilities of the GPT Assistants platform from OpenAI. Assistants are foundational agent types, and we explore how to create practical and diverse assistants, from culinary helpers to intern data scientists and even a book learning assistant.
- *Chapter 4, "Exploring multi-agent systems"*—Agentic tools have advanced significantly quickly. Here, we explore two sophisticated multi-agent systems: CrewAI and AutoGen. We demonstrate AutoGen's ability to develop code autonomously and see how CrewAI can bring together a group of joke researchers to create humor collaboratively.
- *Chapter 5, "Empowering agents with actions"*—Actions are fundamental to any agentic system. This chapter discusses how agents can use tools and functions to execute actions, ranging from database and application programming interface (API) queries to generating images. We focus on enabling agents to take meaningful actions autonomously.
- *Chapter 6, "Building autonomous assistants"*—We explore the behavior tree—a staple in robotics and game systems—as a mechanism to orchestrate multiple coordinated agents. We'll use behavior trees to tackle challenges such as code competitions and social media content creation.
- *Chapter 7, "Assembling and using an agent platform"*—This chapter introduces Nexus, a sophisticated platform for orchestrating multiple agents and LLMs. We discuss how Nexus facilitates agentic workflows and enables complex interactions between agents, providing an example of a fully functioning multi-agent environment.
- *Chapter 8, "Understanding agent memory and knowledge"*—Retrieval-augmented generation (RAG) has become an essential tool for extending the capabilities

of LLM agents. This chapter explores how retrieval mechanisms can serve as both a source of knowledge by processing ingested files, and of memory, allowing agents to recall previous interactions or events.

- *Chapter 9, "Mastering agent prompts with prompt flow"*—Prompt engineering is central to an agent's success. This chapter introduces prompt flow, a tool from Microsoft that helps automate the testing and evaluation of prompts, enabling more robust and effective agentic behavior.
- *Chapter 10, "Agent reasoning and evaluation"*—Reasoning is crucial to solving problems intelligently. In this chapter, we explore various reasoning techniques, such as chain of thought (CoT), and show how agents can evaluate reasoning strategies even during inference, improving their capacity to solve problems autonomously.
- *Chapter 11, "Agent planning and feedback"*—Planning is perhaps an agent's most critical skill in achieving its goals. We discuss how agents can incorporate planning to navigate complex tasks and how feedback loops can be used to refine those plans. The chapter concludes by integrating all the key components—actions, memory and knowledge, reasoning, evaluation, planning, and feedback—into practical examples of agentic systems that solve real-world problems.

About the code

The code for this book is spread across several open source projects, many of which are hosted by me or by other organizations in GitHub repositories. Throughout this book, I strive to make the content as accessible as possible, taking a low-code approach to help you focus on core concepts. Many chapters demonstrate how simple prompts can generate meaningful code, showcasing the power of AI-assisted development.

Additionally, you'll find a variety of assistant profiles and multi-agent systems that demonstrate how to solve real-world problems using generated code. These examples are meant to inspire, guide, and empower you to explore what is possible with AI agents. I am deeply grateful to the many contributors and the community members who have collaborated on these projects, and I encourage you to explore the repositories, experiment with the code, and adapt it to your own needs. This book is a testament to the power of collaboration and the incredible things we can achieve together.

This book contains many examples of source code both in numbered listings and in line with normal text. In both cases, source code is formatted in a `fixed-width font like this` to separate it from ordinary text. Sometimes, some of the code is typeset `in bold` to highlight code that has changed from previous steps in the chapter, such as when a feature is added to an existing line of code. In many cases, the original source code has been reformatted; we've added line breaks and reworked indentation to accommodate the available page space in the book. In some cases, even this wasn't enough, and listings include line-continuation markers (➥). Additionally, comments in the source code have often been removed from the listings when the code is described in the text. Code annotations accompany many of the listings, highlighting important concepts.

You can get executable snippets of code from the liveBook (online) version of this book at https://livebook.manning.com/book/ai-agents-in-action. The complete code for the examples in the book is available for download from the Manning website at www.manning.com/books/ai-agents-in-action. In addition, the code developed for this book has been placed in three GitHub repositories that are all publicly accessible:

- GPT-Agents (the original book title), at https://github.com/cxbxmxcx/GPT-Agents, holds the code for several examples demonstrated in the chapters.
- GPT Assistants Playground, at https://github.com/cxbxmxcx/GPTAssistants Playground, is an entire platform and tool dedicated to building OpenAI GPT assistants with a helpful web user interface and plenty of tools to develop autonomous agent systems.
- Nexus, at https://github.com/cxbxmxcx/Nexus, is an example of a web-based agentic tool that can help you create agentic systems and demonstrate various code challenges.

liveBook discussion forum

Purchase of *AI Agents in Action* includes free access to liveBook, Manning's online reading platform. Using liveBook's exclusive discussion features, you can attach comments to the book globally or to specific sections or paragraphs. It's a snap to make notes for yourself, ask and answer technical questions, and receive help from the author and other users. To access the forum, go to https://livebook.manning.com/book/ai-agents-in-action/discussion. You can also learn more about Manning's forums and the rules of conduct at https://livebook.manning.com/discussion.

Manning's commitment to our readers is to provide a venue where a meaningful dialogue between individual readers and between readers and the author can take place. It isn't a commitment to any specific amount of participation on the part of the author, whose contribution to the forum remains voluntary (and unpaid). We suggest you try asking the him challenging questions lest his interest stray! The forum and the archives of previous discussions will be accessible from the publisher's website as long as the book is in print.

about the author

MICHEAL LANHAM is a distinguished software and technology innovator with more than two decades of experience in the industry. He has an extensive background in developing various software applications across several domains, such as gaming, graphics, web development, desktop engineering, AI, GIS, oil and gas geoscience/geomechanics, and machine learning. Micheal began by pioneering work in integrating neural networks and evolutionary algorithms into game development, which began around the turn of the millennium. He has authored multiple influential books exploring deep learning, game development, and augmented reality, including *Evolutionary Deep Learning* (Manning, 2023) and *Augmented Reality Game Development* (Packt Publishing, 2017). He has contributed to the tech community via publications with many significant tech publishers, including Manning. Micheal resides in Calgary, Alberta, Canada, with his large family, whom he enjoys cooking for.

about the cover illustration

The figure on the cover of *AI Agents in Action* is "Clémentinien," taken from Balthasar Hacquet's *Illustrations de L'Illyrie et la Dalmatie*, published in 1815.

In those days, it was easy to identify where people lived and what their trade or station in life was just by their dress. Manning celebrates the inventiveness and initiative of the computer business with book covers based on the rich diversity of regional culture centuries ago, brought back to life by pictures from collections such as this one.

Introduction to agents and their world

This chapter covers

- Defining the concept of agents
- Differentiating the components of an agent
- Analyzing the rise of the agent era: Why agents?
- Peeling back the AI interface
- Navigating the agent landscape

The agent isn't a new concept in machine learning and artificial intelligence (AI). In reinforcement learning, for instance, the word *agent* denotes an active decision-making and learning intelligence. In other areas, the word *agent* aligns more with an automated application or software that does something on your behalf.

1.1 Defining agents

You can consult any online dictionary to find the definition of an agent. The *Merriam-Webster Dictionary* defines it this way (www.merriam-webster.com/dictionary/agent):

1

- One that acts or exerts power
- Something that produces or can produce an effect
- A means or instrument by which a guiding intelligence achieves a result

The word *agent* in our journey to build powerful agents in this book uses this dictionary definition. That also means the term *assistant* will be synonymous with *agent*. Tools like OpenAI's GPT Assistants will also fall under the AI agent blanket. OpenAI avoids the word *agent* because of the history of machine learning, where an agent is self-deciding and autonomous.

Figure 1.1 shows four cases where a user may interact with a large language model (LLM) directly or through an agent/assistant proxy, an agent/assistant, or an autonomous agent. These four use cases are highlighted in more detail in this list:

- *Direct user interaction*—If you used earlier versions of ChatGPT, you experienced direct interaction with the LLM. There is no proxy agent or other assistant interjecting on your behalf.
- *Agent/assistant proxy*—If you've used Dall-E 3 through ChatGPT, then you've experienced a proxy agent interaction. In this use case, an LLM interjects your requests and reformulates them in a format better designed for the task. For example, for image generation, ChatGPT better formulates the prompt. A proxy agent is an everyday use case to assist users with unfamiliar tasks or models.
- *Agent/assistant*—If you've ever used a ChatGPT plugin or GPT assistant, then you've experienced this use case. In this case, the LLM is aware of the plugin or assistant functions and prepares to make calls to this plugin/function. However, before making a call, the LLM requires user approval. If approved, the plugin or function is executed, and the results are returned to the LLM. The LLM then wraps this response in natural language and returns it to the user.
- *Autonomous agent*—In this use case, the agent interprets the user's request, constructs a plan, and identifies decision points. From this, it executes the steps in the plan and makes the required decisions independently. The agent may request user feedback after certain milestone tasks, but it's often given free rein to explore and learn if possible. This agent poses the most ethical and safety concerns, which we'll explore later.

Figure 1.1 demonstrates the use cases for a single flow of actions on an LLM using a single agent. For more complex problems, we often break agents into profiles or personas. Each agent profile is given a specific task and executes that task with specialized tools and knowledge.

Multi-agent systems are agent profiles that work together in various configurations to solve a problem. Figure 1.2 demonstrates an example of a multi-agent system using three agents: a controller or proxy and two profile agents as workers controlled by the proxy. The coder profile on the left writes the code the user requests; on the right is a

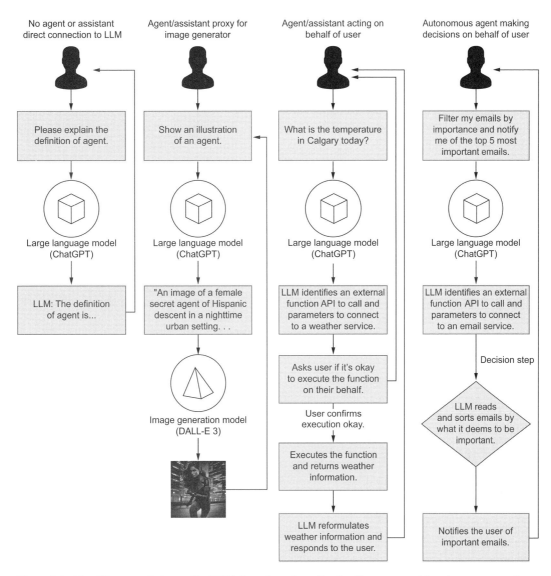

Figure 1.1   The differences between the LLM interactions from direct action compared to using proxy agents, agents, and autonomous agents

tester profile designed to write unit tests. These agents work and communicate together until they are happy with the code and then pass it on to the user.

   Figure 1.2 shows one of the possibly infinite agent configurations. (In chapter 4, we'll explore Microsoft's open source platform, AutoGen, which supports multiple configurations for employing multi-agent systems.)

   Multi-agent systems can work autonomously but may also function guided entirely by human feedback. The benefits of using multiple agents are like those of a single

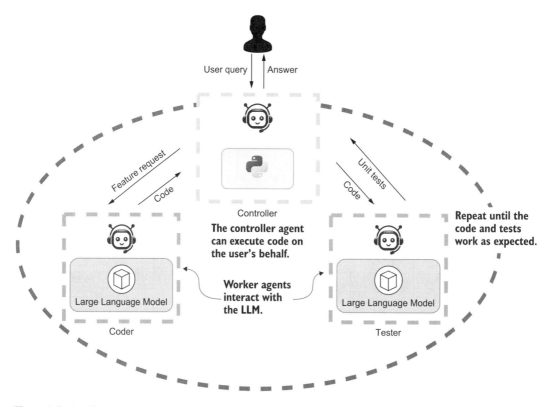

Figure 1.2   **In this example of a multi-agent system, the controller or agent proxy communicates directly with the user. Two agents—a coder and a tester—work in the background to create code and write unit tests to test the code.**

agent but often magnified. Where a single agent typically specializes in a single task, multi-agent systems can tackle multiple tasks in parallel. Multiple agents can also provide feedback and evaluation, reducing errors when completing assignments.

As we can see, an AI agent or agent system can be assembled in multiple ways. However, an agent itself can also be assembled using multiple components. In the next section, we'll cover topics ranging from an agent's profile to the actions it may perform, as well as memory and planning.

1.2   *Understanding the component systems of an agent*

Agents can be complex units composed of multiple component systems. These components are the tools the agent employs to help it complete its goal or assigned tasks and even create new ones. Components may be simple or complex systems, typically split into five categories.

Figure 1.3 describes the major categories of components a single-agent system may incorporate. Each element will have subtypes that can define the component's type, structure, and use. At the core of all agents is the profile and persona; extending from that are the systems and functions that enhance the agent.

Figure 1.3   The five main components of a single-agent system (image generated through DALL-E 3)

The agent profile and persona shown in figure 1.4 represent the base description of the agent. The persona—often called the *system prompt*—guides an agent to complete tasks, learn how to respond, and other nuances. It includes elements such as the background (e.g., coder, writer) and demographics, and it can be generated through methods such as handcrafting, LLM assistance, or data-driven techniques, including evolutionary algorithms.

We'll explore how to create effective and specific agent profiles/personas through techniques such as rubrics and grounding. In addition, we'll explain the aspects of human-formulated versus AI-formulated (LLM) profiles, including innovative techniques using data and evolutionary algorithms to build profiles.

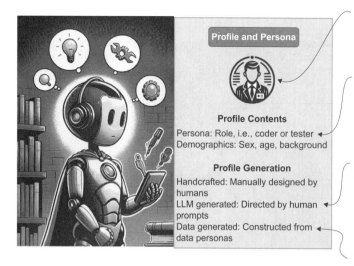

Agent persona: We'll understand how to clearly define the persona, specifying their role and characteristics to guide the agent effectively.

Agent role and demographics: We'll see how relevant demographic and role details can provide agent context, such as age, gender, or background, for a more relevant interaction.

Human vs. AI assistance for persona generation: We'll highlight the role of human involvement in persona generation, whether it's entirely human driven or assisted by LLMs or other agents.

Innovative persona techniques: Prompts generated through data or other novel approaches such as evolutionary algorithms to enhance agent capabilities.

Figure 1.4 An in-depth look at how we'll explore creating agent profiles

NOTE   The agent or assistant profile is composed of elements, including the persona. It may be helpful to think of profiles describing the work the agent/assistant will perform and the tools it needs.

Figure 1.5 demonstrates the component actions and tool use in the context of agents involving activities directed toward task completion or acquiring information. These actions can be categorized into task completion, exploration, and communication, with varying levels of effect on the agent's environment and internal states. Actions can be generated manually, through memory recollection, or by following predefined plans, influencing the agent's behavior and enhancing learning.

Understanding the action target helps us define clear objectives for task completion, exploration, or communication. Recognizing the action effect reveals how actions influence task outcomes, the agent's environment, and its internal states, contributing to efficient decision making. Lastly, grasping action generation methods equips us with the knowledge to create actions manually, recall them from memory, or follow predefined plans, enhancing our ability to effectively shape agent behavior and learning processes.

Figure 1.6 shows the component knowledge and memory in more detail. Agents use knowledge and memory to annotate context with the most pertinent information while limiting the number of tokens used. Knowledge and memory structures can be unified, where both subsets follow a single structure or hybrid structure involving a mix of different retrieval forms. Knowledge and memory formats can vary widely from

Action targets: We'll learn the importance of defining action targets, whether for task completion, exploration, or communication, to clarify the agent's objectives.

Action space and impact: We'll learn the significance of understanding how actions affect task completion and their effect on the agent's environment, internal states, and self-knowledge.

Action generation methods: We'll see the various ways actions can be generated, such as manual creation, memory recollection, or plan following, to illustrate the diversity of agent behaviors.

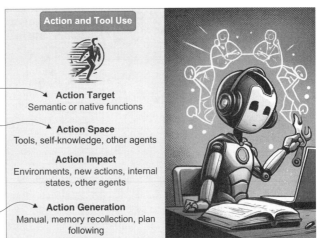

Action and Tool Use

Action Target
Semantic or native functions

Action Space
Tools, self-knowledge, other agents

Action Impact
Environments, new actions, internal states, other agents

Action Generation
Manual, memory recollection, plan following

Figure 1.5   The aspects of agent actions we'll explore in this book

language (e.g., PDF documents) to databases (relational, object, or document) and embeddings, simplifying semantic similarity search through vector representations or even simple lists serving as agent memories.

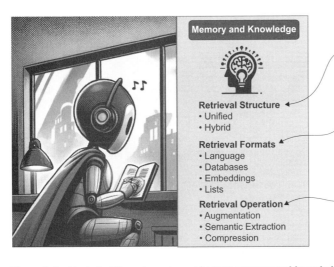

Memory and Knowledge

Retrieval Structure
• Unified
• Hybrid

Retrieval Formats
• Language
• Databases
• Embeddings
• Lists

Retrieval Operation
• Augmentation
• Semantic Extraction
• Compression

Retrieval structure variety: We'll learn about the diverse memory structures agents can employ, including unified and hybrid approaches, enabling flexibility in information storage.

Retrieval formats: We'll explore the various data sources for memory, such as language (e.g., PDF documents), databases (relational, object, or document), and embeddings, offering a rich pool of information to draw upon.

Semantic similarity: We'll learn how embeddings enable semantic similarity searches, facilitating efficient retrieval of relevant data and enhancing the agent's decision-making capabilities.

Figure 1.6   Exploring the role and use of agent memory and knowledge

Figure 1.7 shows the reasoning and evaluation component of an agent system. Research and practical applications have shown that LLMs/agents can effectively reason. Reasoning and evaluation systems annotate an agent's workflow by providing an ability to think through problems and evaluate solutions.

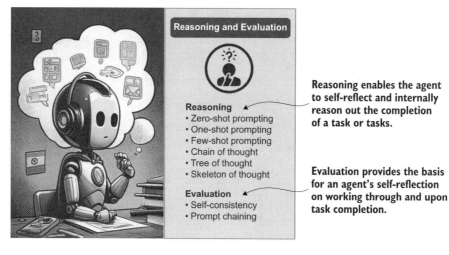

Figure 1.7   The reasoning and evaluation component and details

Figure 1.8 shows the component agent planning/feedback and its role in organizing tasks to achieve higher-level goals. It can be categorized into these two approaches:

- *Planning without feedback*—Autonomous agents make decisions independently.
- *Planning with feedback*—Monitoring and modifying plans is based on various sources of input, including environmental changes and direct human feedback.

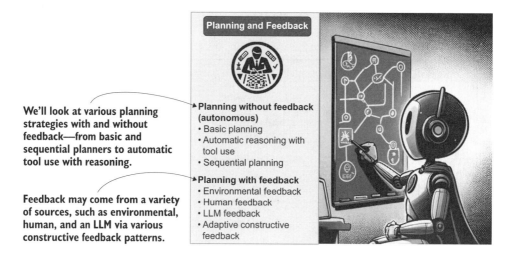

Figure 1.8   Exploring the role of agent planning and reasoning

Within planning, agents may employ *single-path* reasoning, *sequential reasoning* through each step of a task, or *multipath* reasoning to explore multiple strategies and save the efficient ones for future use. External planners, which can be code or other agent systems, may also play a role in orchestrating plans.

Any of our previous agent types—the proxy agent/assistant, agent/assistant, or autonomous agent—may use some or all of these components. Even the planning component has a role outside of the autonomous agent and can effectively empower even the regular agent.

1.3   Examining the rise of the agent era: Why agents?

AI agents and assistants have quickly moved from the main commodity in AI research to mainstream software development. An ever-growing list of tools and platforms assist in the construction and empowerment of agents. To an outsider, it may all seem like hype intended to inflate the value of some cool but overrated technology.

During the first few months after ChatGPT's initial release, a new discipline called *prompt engineering* was formed: users found that using various techniques and patterns in their prompts allowed them to generate better and more consistent output. However, users also realized that prompt engineering could only go so far.

Prompt engineering is still an excellent way to interact directly with LLMs such as ChatGPT. Over time, many users discovered that effective prompting required iteration, reflection, and more iteration. The first agent systems, such as AutoGPT, emerged from these discoveries, capturing the community's attention.

Figure 1.9 shows the original design of AutoGPT, one of the first autonomous agent systems. The agent is designed to iterate a planned sequence of tasks that it defines by looking at the user's goal. Through each task iteration of steps, the agent evaluates the goal and determines if the task is complete. If the task isn't complete, the agent may replan the steps and update the plan based on new knowledge or human feedback.

AutoGPT became the first example to demonstrate the power of using task planning and iteration with LLM models. From this and in tandem, other agent systems and frameworks exploded into the community using similar planning and task iteration systems. It's generally accepted that planning, iteration, and repetition are the best processes for solving complex and multifaceted goals for an LLM.

However, autonomous agent systems require trust in the agent decision-making process, the guardrails/evaluation system, and the goal definition. Trust is also something that is acquired over time. Our lack of trust stems from our lack of understanding of an autonomous agent's capabilities.

> **NOTE**   Artificial general intelligence (AGI) is a form of intelligence that can learn to accomplish any task a human can. Many practitioners in this new world of AI believe an AGI using autonomous agent systems is an attainable goal.

For this reason, many of the mainstream and production-ready agent tools aren't autonomous. However, they still provide a significant benefit in managing and automating

Autonomous AI Mechanism

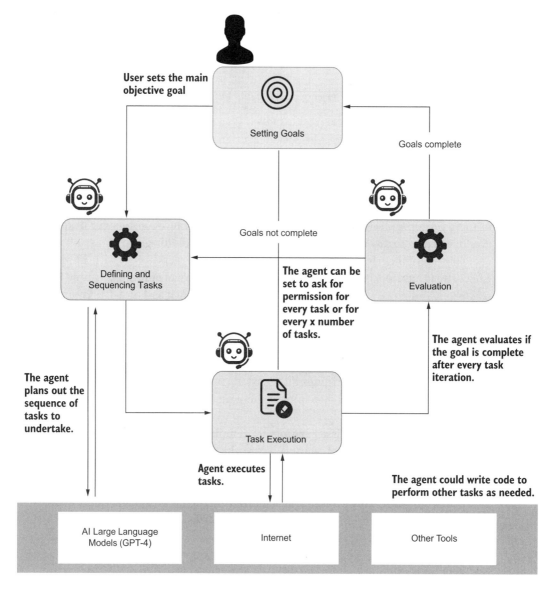

Figure 1.9   The original design of the AutoGPT agent system

tasks using GPTs (LLMs). Therefore, as our goal in this book is to understand all agent forms, many more practical applications will be driven by non-autonomous agents.

Agents and agent tools are only the top layer of a new software application development paradigm. We'll look at this new paradigm in the next section.

1.4 *Peeling back the AI interface*

The AI agent paradigm is not only a shift in how we work with LLMs but is also perceived as a shift in how we develop software and handle data. Software and data will no longer be interfaced using user interfaces (UIs), application programming interfaces (APIs), and specialized query languages such as SQL. Instead, they will be designed to be interfaced using natural language.

Figure 1.10 shows a high-level snapshot of what this new architecture may look like and what role AI agents play. Data, software, and applications adapt to support semantic, natural language interfaces. These AI interfaces allow agents to collect data and interact with software applications, even other agents or agent applications. This represents a new shift in how we interact with software and applications.

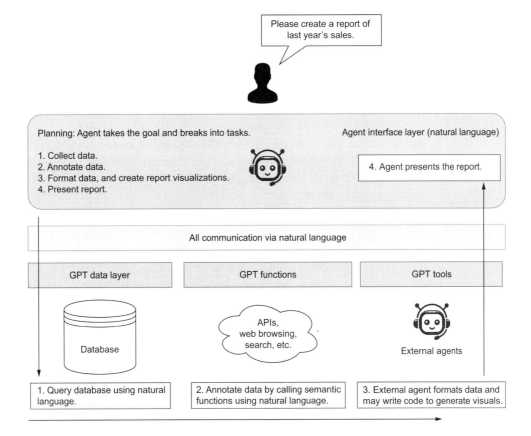

Figure 1.10   A vision of how agents will interact with software systems

An *AI interface* is a collection of functions, tools, and data layers that expose data and applications by natural language. In the past, the word *semantic* has been heavily used to describe these interfaces, and even some tools use the name; however, "semantic" can also have a variety of meanings and uses. Therefore, in this book, we'll use the term *AI interface*.

The construction of AI interfaces will empower agents that need to consume the services, tools, and data. With this empowerment will come increased accuracy in completing tasks and more trustworthy and autonomous applications. While an AI interface may not be appropriate for all software and data, it will dominate many use cases.

1.5   *Navigating the agent landscape*

GPT agents represent an entire shift in how consumers and developers approach everything, from finding information to building software and accessing data. Almost daily, a new agent framework, component, or interface pops up on GitHub or in a research paper. This can be overwhelming and intimidating to the new user trying to grasp what agent systems are and how to use them.

Summary

- An agent is an entity that acts or exerts power, produces an effect, or serves as a means for achieving a result. An agent automates interaction with a large language model (LLM) in AI.
- An assistant is synonymous with an agent. Both terms encompass tools such as OpenAI's GPT Assistants.
- Autonomous agents can make independent decisions, and their distinction from non-autonomous agents is crucial.
- The four main types of LLM interactions include direct user interaction, agent/assistant proxy, agent/assistant, and autonomous agent.
- Multi-agent systems involve agent profiles working together, often controlled by a proxy, to accomplish complex tasks.
- The main components of an agent include the profile/persona, actions, knowledge/memory, reasoning/evaluation, and planning/feedback.
- Agent profiles and personas guide an agent's tasks, responses, and other nuances, often including background and demographics.
- Actions and tools for agents can be manually generated, recalled from memory, or follow predefined plans.
- Agents use knowledge and memory structures to optimize context and minimize token usage via various formats, from documents to embeddings.
- Reasoning and evaluation systems enable agents to think through problems and assess solutions using prompting patterns such as zero-shot, one-shot, and few-shot.
- Planning/feedback components organize tasks to achieve goals using single-path or multipath reasoning and integrating environmental and human feedback.

- The rise of AI agents has introduced a new software development paradigm, shifting from traditional to natural language–based AI interfaces.
- Understanding the progression and interaction of these tools helps develop agent systems, whether single, multiple, or autonomous.

Harnessing the power
of large language models

This chapter covers

- Understanding the basics of LLMs
- Connecting to and consuming the OpenAI API
- Exploring and using open source LLMs with LM Studio
- Prompting LLMs with prompt engineering
- Choosing the optimal LLM for your specific needs

The term *large language models* (LLMs) has now become a ubiquitous descriptor of a form of AI. These LLMs have been developed using generative pretrained transformers (GPTs). While other architectures also power LLMs, the GPT form is currently the most successful.

LLMs and GPTs are *generative* models, which means they are trained to *generate* rather than predict or classify content. To illustrate this further, consider figure 2.1, which shows the difference between generative and predictive/classification models. Generative models create something from the input, whereas predictive and classifying models classify it.

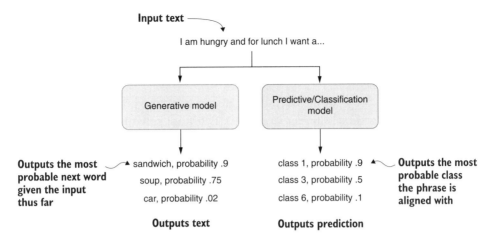

Figure 2.1 The difference between generative and predictive models

We can further define an LLM by its constituent parts, as shown in figure 2.2. In this diagram, *data* represents the content used to train the model, and *architecture* is an attribute of the model itself, such as the number of parameters or size of the model. Models are further trained specifically to the desired use case, including chat, completions, or instruction. Finally, *fine-tuning* is a feature added to models that refines the input data and model training to better match a particular use case or domain.

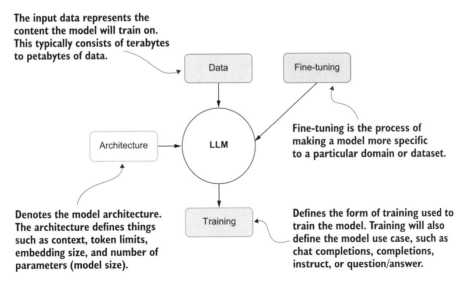

Figure 2.2 The main elements that describe an LLM

The transformer architecture of GPTs, which is a specific architecture of LLMs, allows the models to be scaled to billions of parameters in size. This requires these large models to be trained on terabytes of documents to build a foundation. From there, these models will be successively trained using various methods for the desired use case of the model.

ChatGPT, for example, is trained effectively on the public internet and then fine-tuned using several training strategies. The final fine-tuning training is completed using an advanced form called *reinforcement learning with human feedback* (RLHF). This produces a model use case called chat completions.

Chat completions LLMs are designed to improve through iteration and refinement—in other words, chatting. These models have also been benchmarked to be the best in task completion, reasoning, and planning, which makes them ideal for building agents and assistants. Completion models are trained/designed only to provide generated content on input text, so they don't benefit from iteration.

For our journey to build powerful agents in this book, we focus on the class of LLMs called chat completions models. That, of course, doesn't preclude you from trying other model forms for your agents. However, you may have to significantly alter the code samples provided to support other model forms.

We'll uncover more details about LLMs and GPTs later in this chapter when we look at running an open source LLM locally. In the next section, we look at how to connect to an LLM using a growing standard from OpenAI.

2.1   *Mastering the OpenAI API*

Numerous AI agents and assistant projects use the OpenAI API SDK to connect to an LLM. While not standard, the basic concepts describing a connection now follow the OpenAI pattern. Therefore, we must understand the core concepts of an LLM connection using the OpenAI SDK.

This chapter will look at connecting to an LLM model using the OpenAI Python SDK/package. We'll discuss connecting to a GPT-4 model, the model response, counting tokens, and how to define consistent messages. Starting in the following subsection, we'll examine how to use OpenAI.

2.1.1   *Connecting to the chat completions model*

To complete the exercises in this section and subsequent ones, you must set up a Python developer environment and get access to an LLM. Appendix A walks you through setting up an OpenAI account and accessing GPT-4 or other models. Appendix B demonstrates setting up a Python development environment with Visual Studio Code (VS Code), including installing needed extensions. Review these sections if you want to follow along with the scenarios.

Start by opening the source code `chapter_2` folder in VS Code and creating a new Python virtual environment. Again, refer to appendix B if you need assistance.

Then, install the OpenAI and Python dot environment packages using the command in the following listing. This will install the required packages into the virtual environment.

Listing 2.1 `pip installs`

```
pip install openai python-dotenv
```

Next, open the `connecting.py` file in VS Code, and inspect the code shown in listing 2.2. Be sure to set the model's name to an appropriate name—for example, gpt-4. At the time of writing, the `gpt-4-1106-preview` was used to represent GPT-4 Turbo.

Listing 2.2 `connecting.py`

```
import os
from openai import OpenAI
from dotenv import load_dotenv                          Loads the secrets
                                                        stored in the .env file
load_dotenv()
api_key = os.getenv('OPENAI_API_KEY')                   Checks to see
if not api_key:                                         whether the key is set
    raise ValueError("No API key found. Please check your .env file.")
client = OpenAI(api_key=api_key)
                                                        Creates a client
def ask_chatgpt(user_message):                          with the key
    response = client.chat.completions.create(
        model="gpt-4-1106-preview",                     Uses the create
        messages=[{"role": "system",                    function to generate
 "content": "You are a helpful assistant."},            a response
        {"role": "user", "content": user_message}],
        temperature=0.7,
        )                                               Returns just the content
    return response.choices[0].message.content          of the response

user = "What is the capital of France?"                 Executes the request and
response = ask_chatgpt(user)                             returns the response
print(response)
```

A lot is happening here, so let's break it down by section, starting with the beginning and loading the environment variables. In the `chapter_2` folder is another file called `.env`, which holds environment variables. These variables are set automatically by calling the `load_dotenv` function.

You must set your OpenAI API key in the `.env` file, as shown in the next listing. Again, refer to appendix A to find out how to get a key and find a model name.

Listing 2.3 `.env`

```
OPENAI_API_KEY='your-openai-api-key'
```

After setting the key, you can debug the file by pressing the F5 key or selecting Run > Start Debugging from the VS Code menu. This will run the code, and you should see something like "The capital of France is Paris."

Remember that the response from a generative model depends on the probability. The model will probably give us a correct and consistent answer in this case.

You can play with these probabilities by adjusting the temperature of the request. If you want a model to be more consistent, turn the temperature down to 0, but if you want the model to produce more variation, turn the temperature up. We'll explore setting the temperature further in the next section.

2.1.2 *Understanding the request and response*

Digging into the chat completions request and response features can be helpful. We'll focus on the request first, as shown next. The request encapsulates the intended model, the messages, and the temperature.

Listing 2.4 The chat completions request

```
response = client.chat.completions.create(
    model="gpt-4-1106-preview",                     ← The model or deployment used
    messages=[{"role": "system",                       to respond to the request
"content": "You are a helpful assistant."},     ←    The system
            {"role": "user", "content": user_message}],  ←    role message
    temperature=0.7,            ←
    )                                                 The user role
                        The temperature or            message
                        variability of the request
```

Within the request, the `messages` block describes a set of messages and roles used in a request. Messages for a chat completions model can be defined in three roles:

- *System role*—A message that describes the request's rules and guidelines. It can often be used to describe the role of the LLM in making the request.
- *User role*—Represents and contains the message from the user.
- *Assistant role*—Can be used to capture the message history of previous responses from the LLM. It can also inject a message history when perhaps none existed.

The message sent in a single request can encapsulate an entire conversation, as shown in the JSON in the following listing.

Listing 2.5 Messages with history

```
[
    {
        "role": "system",
        "content": "You are a helpful assistant."
    },
    {
        "role": "user",
        "content": "What is the capital of France?"
    },
    {
        "role": "assistant",
```

```
        "content": "The capital of France is Paris."
    },
    {
        "role": "user",
        "content": "What is an interesting fact of Paris."
    }
  ],
```

You can see how this can be applied by opening `message_history.py` in VS Code and debugging it by pressing F5. After the file runs, be sure to check the output. Then, try to run the sample a few more times to see how the results change.

The results will change from each run to the next due to the high temperature of `.7`. Go ahead and reduce the temperature to `.0`, and run the `message_history.py` sample a few more times. Keeping the temperature at `0` will show the same or similar results each time.

Setting a request's temperature will often depend on your particular use case. Sometimes, you may want to limit the responses' stochastic nature (randomness). Reducing the temperature to `0` will give consistent results. Likewise, a value of `1.0` will give the most variability in the responses.

Next, we also want to know what information is being returned for each request. The next listing shows the output format for the response. You can see this output by running the `message_history.py` file in VS Code.

Listing 2.6   Chat completions response

```
{
    "id": "chatcmpl-8WWL23up3IRfK1nrDFQ3EHQfhx0U6",
    "choices": [                                           ⊲─┐  A model may
        {                                                    │  return more than
            "finish_reason": "stop",                         │  one response.
            "index": 0,
            "message": {
                "content": "… omitted",
                "role": "assistant",                  ⊲─┐  Responses
                "function_call": null,                   │  returned in the
                "tool_calls": null                       │  assistant role
            },
            "logprobs": null
        }
    ],
                                                   ┌  Indicates the
    "created": 1702761496,                         │  model used
    "model": "gpt-4-1106-preview",          ⊲──────┘
    "object": "chat.completion",
    "system_fingerprint": "fp_3905aa4f79",
    "usage": {
        "completion_tokens": 78,              Counts the number of
        "prompt_tokens": 48,                  input (prompt) and output
        "total_tokens": 126                   (completion) tokens used
    }
}
```

It can be helpful to track the number of *input tokens* (those used in prompts) and the *output tokens* (the number returned through completions). Sometimes, minimizing and reducing the number of tokens can be essential. Having fewer tokens typically means LLM interactions will be cheaper, respond faster, and produce better and more consistent results.

That covers the basics of connecting to an LLM and returning responses. Throughout this book, we'll review and expand on how to interact with LLMs. Until then, we'll explore in the next section how to load and use open source LLMs.

2.2 *Exploring open source LLMs with LM Studio*

Commercial LLMs, such as GPT-4 from OpenAI, are an excellent place to start to learn how to use modern AI and build agents. However, commercial agents are an external resource that comes at a cost, reduces data privacy and security, and introduces dependencies. Other external influences can further complicate these factors.

It's unsurprising that the race to build comparable open source LLMs is growing more competitive every day. As a result, there are now open source LLMs that may be adequate for numerous tasks and agent systems. There have even been so many advances in tooling in just a year that hosting LLMs locally is now very easy, as we'll see in the next section.

2.2.1 *Installing and running LM Studio*

LM Studio is a free download that supports downloading and hosting LLMs and other models locally for Windows, Mac, and Linux. The software is easy to use and offers several helpful features to get you started quickly. Here is a quick summary of steps to download and set up LM Studio:

1 Download LM Studio from https://lmstudio.ai/.
2 After downloading, install the software per your operating system. Be aware that some versions of LM Studio may be in beta and require installation of additional tools or libraries.
3 Launch the software.

Figure 2.3 shows the LM Studio window running. From there, you can review the current list of hot models, search for others, and even download. The home page content can be handy for understanding the details and specifications of the top models.

An appealing feature of LM Studio is its ability to analyze your hardware and align it with the requirements of a given model. The software will let you know how well you can run a given model. This can be a great time saver in guiding what models you experiment with.

Run a local model
as a service.

Chat interface to talk
directly to a local LLM

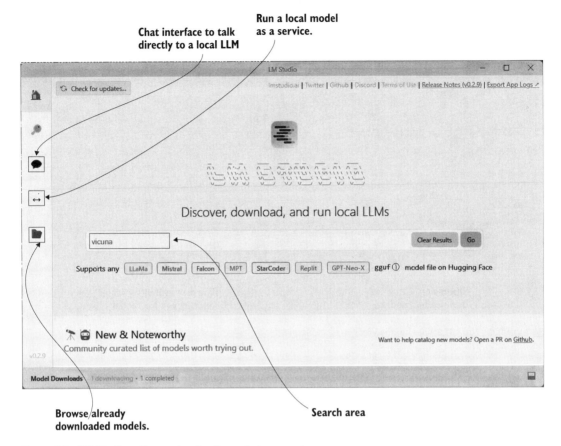

Browse already
downloaded models.

Search area

Figure 2.3   LM Studio software showing the main home page

Enter some text to search for a model, and click Go. You'll be taken to the search page interface, as shown in figure 2.4. From this page, you can see all the model variations and other specifications, such as context token size. After you click the Compatibility Guess button, the software will even tell you if the model will run on your system.

Click to download any model that will run on your system. You may want to stick with models designed for chat completions, but if your system is limited, work with what you have. In addition, if you're unsure of which model to use, go ahead and download to try them. LM Studio is a great way to explore and experiment with many models.

Search text

Look at the model
card on Hugging Face.

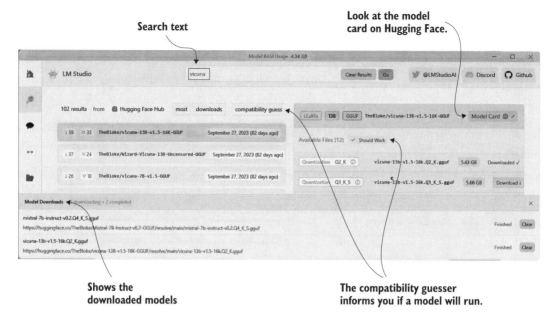

Shows the
downloaded models

The compatibility guesser
informs you if a model will run.

Figure 2.4   The LM Studio search page

After the model is downloaded, you can then load and run the model on the chat page or as a server on the server page. Figure 2.5 shows loading and running a model on the chat page. It also shows the option for enabling and using a GPU if you have one.

To load and run a model, open the drop-down menu at the top middle of the page, and select a downloaded model. A progress bar will appear showing the model loading, and when it's ready, you can start typing into the UI.

The software even allows you to use some or all of your GPU, if detected, for the model inference. A GPU will generally speed up the model response times in some capacities. You can see how adding a GPU can affect the model's performance by looking at the performance status at the bottom of the page, as shown in figure 2.5.

Chatting with a model and using or playing with various prompts can help you determine how well a model will work for your given use case. A more systematic approach is using the prompt flow tool for evaluating prompts and LLMs. We'll describe how to use prompt flow in chapter 9.

LM Studio also allows a model to be run on a server and made accessible using the OpenAI package. We'll see how to use the server feature and serve a model in the next section.

Loaded model

Enabling GPU acceleration,
available when GPU detected

Model system
prompt

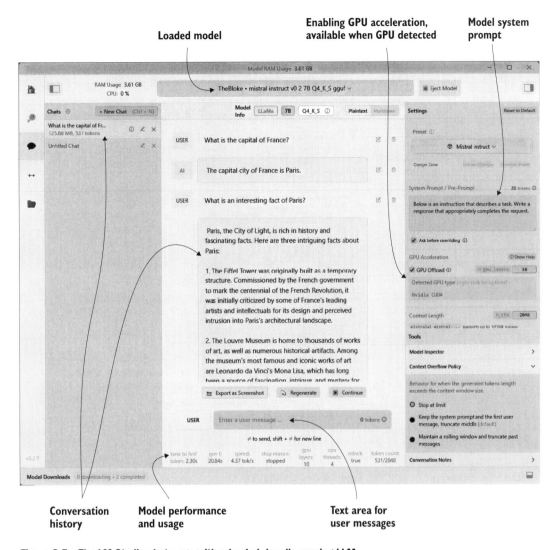

Figure 2.5   The LM Studio chat page with a loaded, locally running LLM

Conversation
history

Model performance
and usage

Text area for
user messages

2.2.2   *Serving an LLM locally with LM Studio*

Running an LLM locally as a server is easy with LM Studio. Just open the server page,
load a model, and then click the Start Server button, as shown in figure 2.6. From
there, you can copy and paste any of the examples to connect with your model.

You can review an example of the Python code by opening `chapter_2/lmstudio_`
`server.py` in VS Code. The code is also shown here in listing 2.7. Then, run the code
in the VS Code debugger (press F5).

Example to connect to the server

Loaded model

Enabling GPU acceleration, available when GPU detected

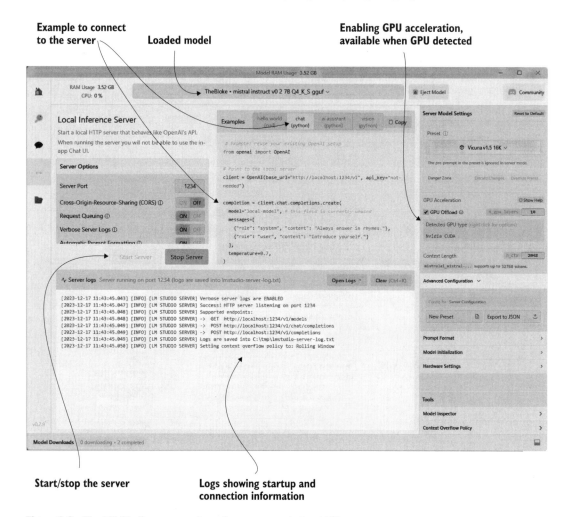

Start/stop the server

Logs showing startup and connection information

Figure 2.6 The LM Studio server page and a server running an LLM

Listing 2.7 `lmstudio_server.py`

```python
from openai import OpenAI

client = OpenAI(base_url="http://localhost:1234/v1", api_key="not-needed")

completion = client.chat.completions.create(
  model="local-model",
  messages=[
    {"role": "system", "content": "Always answer in rhymes."},
    {"role": "user", "content": "Introduce yourself."}
  ],
  temperature=0.7,
)

print(completion.choices[0].message)
```

Currently not used; can be anything

Feel free to change the message as you like.

Default code outputs the whole message.

If you encounter problems connecting to the server or experience any other problems, be sure your configuration for the Server Model Settings matches the model type. For example, in figure 2.6, shown earlier, the loaded model differs from the server settings. The corrected settings are shown in figure 2.7.

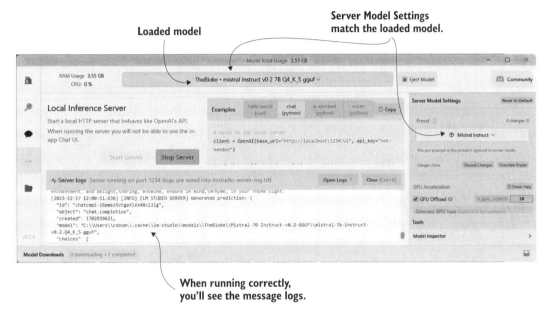

Figure 2.7   Choosing the correct Server Model Settings for the loaded model

Now, you can use a locally hosted LLM or a commercial model to build, test, and potentially even run your agents. The following section will examine how to build prompts using prompt engineering more effectively.

2.3   *Prompting LLMs with prompt engineering*

A prompt defined for LLMs is the message content used in the request for better response output. *Prompt engineering* is a new and emerging field that attempts to structure a methodology for building prompts. Unfortunately, prompt building isn't a well-established science, and there is a growing and diverse set of methods defined as prompt engineering.

Fortunately, organizations such as OpenAI have begun documenting a universal set of strategies, as shown in figure 2.8. These strategies cover various tactics, some requiring additional infrastructure and considerations. As such, the prompt engineering strategies relating to more advanced concepts will be covered in the indicated chapters.

Each strategy in figure 2.8 unfolds into tactics that can further refine the specific method of prompt engineering. This chapter will examine the fundamental Write

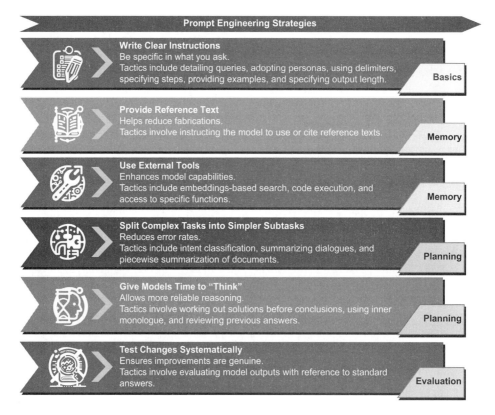

Figure 2.8   OpenAI prompt engineering strategies reviewed in this book, by chapter location

Clear Instructions strategy. Figure 2.9 shows the tactics for this strategy in more detail, along with examples for each tactic. We'll look at running these examples using a code demo in the following sections.

The Write Clear Instructions strategy is about being careful and specific about what you ask for. Asking an LLM to perform a task is no different from asking a person to complete the same task. Generally, the more information and context relevant to a task you can specify in a request, the better the response.

This strategy has been broken down into specific tactics you can apply to prompts. To understand how to use those, a code demo (`prompt_engineering.py`) with various prompt examples is in the `chapter 2` source code folder.

Open the `prompt_engineering.py` file in VS Code, as shown in listing 2.8. This code starts by loading all the JSON Lines files in the `prompts` folder. Then, it displays the list of files as choices and allows the user to select a prompt option. After selecting the option, the prompts are submitted to an LLM, and the response is printed.

Tactics for Strategy: Writing Clear Instructions					
Detailed Queries	Adopting Personas	Using Delimiters	Specifying Steps	Providing Examples	Specify Output Length
Without detailed queries: Who's the prime minister? **With detailed queries:** Who is the prime minister of Canada, and how frequently are elections held? **Provide as much detail as you can in a query; generally, the more detail the better.**	SYSTEM: You are a prompt expert and will suggest ways to improve a user request. USER: What is the capital of Canada? **Personas can include details about demographics, knowledge, and personality.**	USER: Summarize the text delimited by triple quotes with a limerick: **"text to be summarized"** **Delimiters can help separate blocks of content from specification details.**	SYSTEM: Use the following step-by-step instructions to respond to user inputs: **Step 1** - Summarize the text in triple quotes to one sentence with a prefix that says "Summary: ". **Step 2** - Translate the summary from Step 1 into French, with a prefix that says "Translation: ". USER: **"text to summarize and translate"**	SYSTEM: Answer in a consistent style. USER: Teach me about patience. **This is the example.** ASSISTANT: The river that carves the deepest valley flows from a modest spring; the most intricate tapestry begins with a solitary thread. USER: Teach me about the ocean.	USER: Summarize the text delimited by triple quotes in about 50 words. "text to summarize here" **Limiting the length of output can be specific to words, bullet points, or other metrics.**

Using steps can help the LLM better process the task, but be sure to limit the number.

Examples are a form of few-shot learning and can be an excellent way to indicate the desired response format and other details.

Figure 2.9 The tactics for the Write Clear Instructions strategy

Listing 2.8 `prompt_engineering.py (main())`

```python
def main():
    directory = "prompts"
    text_files = list_text_files_in_directory(directory)     # Collects all the files for the given folder

    if not text_files:
        print("No text files found in the directory.")
        return

    def print_available():
        print("Available prompt tactics:")
        for i, filename in enumerate(text_files, start=1):    # Prints the list of files as choices
            print(f"{i}. {filename}")

    while True:
        try:
            print_available()
            choice = int(input("Enter … 0 to exit): "))       # Inputs the user's choice
```

```
        if choice == 0:
            break
        elif 1 <= choice <= len(text_files):
            selected_file = text_files[choice - 1]
            file_path = os.path.join(directory,
    selected_file)
            prompts =
⇒ load_and_parse_json_file(file_path)
            print(f"Running prompts for {selected_file}")
            for i, prompt in enumerate(prompts):
                print(f"PROMPT {i+1} -------------------")
                print(prompt)
                print(f"REPLY -------------------------")
                print(prompt_llm(prompt))
        else:
            print("Invalid choice. Please enter a valid number.")
    except ValueError:
        print("Invalid input. Please enter a number.")
```

Loads the prompt and parses it into messages

Submits the prompt to an OpenAI LLM

A commented-out section from the listing demonstrates how to connect to a local LLM. This will allow you to explore the same prompt engineering tactics applied to open source LLMs running locally. By default, this example uses the OpenAI model we configured previously in section 2.1.1. If you didn't complete that earlier, please go back and do it before running this one.

Figure 2.10 shows the output of running the prompt engineering tactics tester, the prompt_engineering.py file in VS Code. When you run the tester, you can enter a value for the tactic you want to test and watch it run.

```
Available prompt tactics:
1. adopting_personas.jsonl
2. detailed_queries.jsonl
3. provide_examples.jsonl
4. specifying_steps.jsonl
5. specify_output_length.jsonl
6. using_delimiters.jsonl
Enter the number of the prompt tactic to run (or 0 to exit): ▯
```

Figure 2.10   The output of the prompt engineering tactics tester

In the following sections, we'll explore each prompt tactic in more detail. We'll also examine the various examples.

2.3.1   Creating detailed queries

The basic premise of this tactic is to provide as much detail as possible but also to be careful not to give irrelevant details. The following listing shows the JSON Lines file examples for exploring this tactic.

Listing 2.9 `detailed_queries.jsonl`

```
[
    {                                    ←   The first example doesn't
        "role": "system",                    use detailed queries.
        "content": "You are a helpful assistant."
    },
    {
        "role": "user",
        "content": "What is an agent?"   ←   First ask the LLM a
    }                                        very general question.
]
[
    {
        "role": "system",
        "content": "You are a helpful assistant."
    },
    {
        "role": "user",
        "content": """
What is a GPT Agent?
Please give me 3 examples of a GPT agent
"""                                      ←   Ask a more specific question,
    }                                        and ask for examples.
]
```

This example demonstrates the difference between using detailed queries and not. It also goes a step further by asking for examples. Remember, the more relevance and context you can provide in your prompt, the better the overall response. Asking for examples is another way of enforcing the relationship between the question and the expected output.

2.3.2 *Adopting personas*

Adopting personas grants the ability to define an overarching context or set of rules to the LLM. The LLM can then use that context and/or rules to frame all later output responses. This is a compelling tactic and one that we'll make heavy use of throughout this book.

Listing 2.10 shows an example of employing two personas to answer the same question. This can be an enjoyable technique for exploring a wide range of novel applications, from getting demographic feedback to specializing in a specific task or even rubber ducking.

> **GPT rubber ducking**
> *Rubber ducking* is a problem-solving technique in which a person explains a problem to an inanimate object, like a rubber duck, to understand or find a solution. This method is prevalent in programming and debugging, as articulating the problem aloud often helps clarify the problem and can lead to new insights or solutions.

(continued)

GPT rubber ducking uses the same technique, but instead of an inanimate object, we use an LLM. This strategy can be expanded further by giving the LLM a persona specific to the desired solution domain.

Listing 2.10   `adopting_personas.jsonl`

```
[
    {
        "role": "system",
        "content": """
You are a 20 year old female who attends college
in computer science. Answer all your replies as
a junior programmer.
"""                                        ⟵—— First persona
    },
    {
        "role": "user",
        "content": "What is the best subject to study."
    }
]
[
    {
        "role": "system",
        "content": """
You are a 38 year old male registered nurse.
Answer all replies as a medical professional.
"""                                        ⟵—— Second persona
    },
    {
        "role": "user",
        "content": "What is the best subject to study."
    }
]
```

A core element of agent profiles is the persona. We'll employ various personas to assist agents in completing their tasks. When you run this tactic, pay particular attention to the way the LLM outputs the response.

2.3.3   *Using delimiters*

Delimiters are a useful way of isolating and getting the LLM to focus on some part of a message. This tactic is often combined with other tactics but can work well independently. The following listing demonstrates two examples, but there are several other ways of describing delimiters, from XML tags to using markdown.

Listing 2.11   `using_delimiters.jsonl`

```
[
    {
```

```
        "role": "system",
        "content": """
Summarize the text delimited by triple quotes
with a haiku.
"""
    },
    {
        "role": "user",
        "content": "A gold chain is cool '''but a silver chain is better'''"
    }
]
[
    {
        "role": "system",
        "content": """
You will be provided with a pair of statements
(delimited with XML tags) about the same topic.
First summarize the arguments of each statement.
Then indicate which of them makes a better statement
 and explain why.
"""
    },
    {
        "role": "user",
        "content": """
<statement>gold chains are cool</statement>
<statement>silver chains are better</statement>
"""
    }
]
```

◁— **The delimiter is defined by character type and repetition.**

◁— **The delimiter is defined by XML standards.**

When you run this tactic, pay attention to the parts of the text the LLM focuses on when it outputs the response. This tactic can be beneficial for describing information in a hierarchy or other relationship patterns.

2.3.4   *Specifying steps*

Specifying steps is another powerful tactic that can have many uses, including in agents, as shown in listing 2.12. It's especially powerful when developing prompts or agent profiles for complex multistep tasks. You can specify steps to break down these complex prompts into a step-by-step process that the LLM can follow. In turn, these steps can guide the LLM through multiple interactions over a more extended conversation and many iterations.

Listing 2.12   `specifying_steps.jsonl`

```
[
    {
        "role": "system",
        "content": """
Use the following step-by-step instructions to respond to user inputs.
Step 1 - The user will provide you with text in triple single quotes.
Summarize this text in one sentence with a prefix that says 'Summary: '.
```

```
Step 2 - Translate the summary from Step 1 into Spanish,
with a prefix that says 'Translation: '.
"""
    },
    {
        "role": "user",
        "content": "'''I am hungry and would like to order an appetizer.'''"
    }
]
[
    {
        "role": "system",
        "content": """
Use the following step-by-step instructions to respond to user inputs.
Step 1 - The user will provide you with text. Answer any questions in
the text in one sentence with a prefix that says 'Answer: '.

Step 2 - Translate the Answer from Step 1 into a dad joke,
 with a prefix that says 'Dad Joke: '."""
    },
    {
        "role": "user",
        "content": "What is the tallest structure in Paris?"
    }
]
```

> Notice the tactic of using delimiters.

> Steps can be completely different operations.

2.3.5 Providing examples

Providing examples is an excellent way to guide the desired output of an LLM. There are numerous ways to demonstrate examples to an LLM. The system message/prompt can be a helpful way to emphasize general output. In the following listing, the example is added as the last LLM assistant reply, given the prompt "Teach me about Python."

Listing 2.13 `providing_examples.jsonl`

```
[
    {
        "role": "system",
        "content": """
Answer all replies in a consistent style that follows the format,
length and style of your previous responses.
Example:
  user:
      Teach me about Python.
  assistant:
      Python is a programming language developed in 1989
 by Guido van Rossum.

  Future replies:
      The response was only a sentence so limit
 all future replies to a single sentence.
"""
    },
    {
        "role": "user",
```

> Injects the sample output as the "previous" assistant reply

> Adds a limit output tactic to restrict the size of the output and match the example

```
        "content": "Teach me about Java."
    }
]
```

Providing examples can also be used to request a particular output format from a complex series of tasks that derive the output. For example, asking an LLM to produce code that matches a sample output is an excellent use of examples. We'll employ this tactic throughout the book, but other methods exist for guiding output.

2.3.6 *Specifying output length*

The tactic of specifying output length can be helpful in not just limiting tokens but also in guiding the output to a desired format. Listing 2.14 shows an example of using two different techniques for this tactic. The first limits the output to fewer than 10 words. This can have the added benefit of making the response more concise and directed, which can be desirable for some use cases. The second example demonstrates limiting output to a concise set of bullet points. This method can help narrow down the output and keep answers short. More concise answers generally mean the output is more focused and contains less filler.

> **Listing 2.14 `specifying_output_length.jsonl`**

```
[
    {
        "role": "system",
        "content": """
Summarize all replies into 10 or fewer words.
"""                                                    ⊲─ Restricting the output
    },                                                         makes the answer
    {                                                          more concise.
        "role": "user",
        "content": "Please tell me an exciting fact about Paris?"
    }
]
[
    {
        "role": "system",
        "content": """
Summarize all replies into 3 bullet points.           Restricts the answer
"""                                                    to a short set of
    },                                                 ⊲─ bullets
    {
        "role": "user",
        "content": "Please tell me an exciting fact about Paris?"
    }
]
```

Keeping answers brief can have additional benefits when developing multi-agent systems. Any agent system that converses with other agents can benefit from more concise and focused replies. It tends to keep the LLM more focused and reduces noisy communication.

Be sure to run through all the examples of the prompt tactics for this strategy. As mentioned, we'll cover other prompt engineering strategies and tactics in future chapters. We'll finish this chapter by looking at how to pick the best LLM for your use case.

2.4 Choosing the optimal LLM for your specific needs

While being a successful crafter of AI agents doesn't require an in-depth understanding of LLMs, it's helpful to be able to evaluate the specifications. Like a computer user, you don't need to know how to build a processor to understand the differences in processor models. This analogy holds well for LLMs, and while the criteria may be different, it still depends on some primary considerations.

From our previous discussion and look at LM Studio, we can extract some fundamental criteria that will be important to us when considering LLMs. Figure 2.11

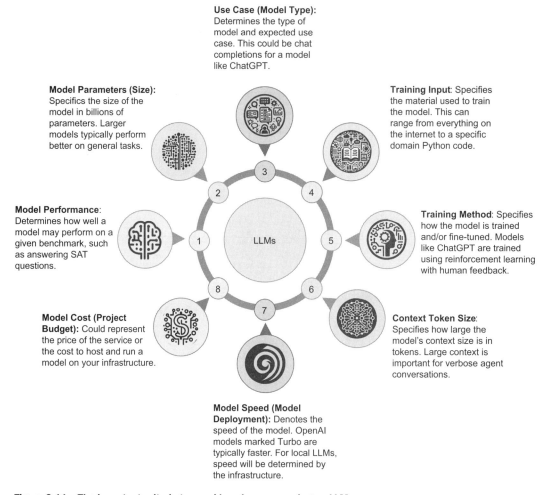

Figure 2.11   The important criteria to consider when consuming an LLM

explains the essential criteria to define what makes an LLM worth considering for creating a GPT agent or any LLM task.

For our purposes of building AI agents, we need to look at each of these criteria in terms related to the task. Model context size and speed could be considered the sixth and seventh criteria, but they are usually considered variations of a model deployment architecture and infrastructure. An eighth criterion to consider for an LLM is cost, but this depends on many other factors. Here is a summary of how these criteria relate to building AI agents:

- *Model performance*—You'll generally want to understand the LLM's performance for a given set of tasks. For example, if you're building an agent specific to coding, then an LLM that performs well on code will be essential.

- *Model parameters (size)*—The size of a model is often an excellent indication of inference performance and how well the model responds. However, the size of a model will also dictate your hardware requirements. If you plan to use your own locally hosted model, the model size will also primarily dictate the computer and GPU you need. Fortunately, we're seeing small, very capable open source models being released regularly.

- *Use case (model type)*—The type of model has several variations. Chat completions models such as ChatGPT are effective for iterating and reasoning through a problem, whereas models such as completion, question/answer, and instruct are more related to specific tasks. A chat completions model is essential for agent applications, especially those that iterate.

- *Training input*—Understanding the content used to train a model will often dictate the domain of a model. While general models can be effective across tasks, more specific or fine-tuned models can be more relevant to a domain. This may be a consideration for a domain-specific agent where a smaller, more fine-tuned model may perform as well as or better than a larger model such as GPT-4.

- *Training method*—It's perhaps less of a concern, but it can be helpful to understand what method was used to train a model. How a model is trained can affect its ability to generalize, reason, and plan. This can be essential for planning agents but perhaps less significant for agents than for a more task-specific assistant.

- *Context token size*—The context size of a model is more specific to the model architecture and type. It dictates the size of context or memory the model may hold. A smaller context window of less than 4,000 tokens is typically more than enough for simple tasks. However, a large context window can be essential when using multiple agents—all conversing over a task. The models will typically be deployed with variations on the context window size.

- *Model speed (model deployment)*—The speed of a model is dictated by its *inference speed* (or how fast a model replies to a request), which in turn is dictated by the infrastructure it runs on. If your agent isn't directly interacting with users, raw real-time speed may not be necessary. On the other hand, an LLM agent inter-acting in real time needs to be as quick as possible. For commercial models, speed will be determined and supported by the provider. Your infrastructure will determine the speed for those wanting to run their LLMs.

- *Model cost (project budget)*—The cost is often dictated by the project. Whether learning to build an agent or implementing enterprise software, cost is always a consideration. A significant tradeoff exists between running your LLMs versus using a commercial API.

There is a lot to consider when choosing which model you want to build a production agent system on. However, picking and working with a single model is usually best for research and learning purposes. If you're new to LLMs and agents, you'll likely want to choose a commercial option such as GPT-4 Turbo. Unless otherwise stated, the work in this book will depend on GPT-4 Turbo.

Over time, models will undoubtedly be replaced by better models. So you may need to upgrade or swap out models. To do this, though, you must understand the performance metrics of your LLMs and agents. Fortunately, in chapter 9, we'll explore evaluating LLMs, prompts, and agent profiles with prompt flow.

2.5   Exercises

Use the following exercises to help you engage with the material in this chapter:

- *Exercise 1*—Consuming Different LLMs

  Objective—Use the `connecting.py` code example to consume a different LLM from OpenAI or another provider.

  Tasks:

  – Modify `connecting.py` to connect to a different LLM.

  – Choose an LLM from OpenAI or another provider.

  – Update the API keys and endpoints in the code.

  – Execute the modified code and validate the response.

- *Exercise 2*—Exploring Prompt Engineering Tactics

  Objective—Explore various prompt engineering tactics, and create variations for each.

  Tasks:

  – Review the prompt engineering tactics covered in the chapter.

  – Write variations for each tactic, experimenting with different phrasing and structures.

  – Test the variations with an LLM to observe different outcomes.

  – Document the results, and analyze the effectiveness of each variation.

- *Exercise 3*—Downloading and Running an LLM with LM Studio

  Objective—Download an LLM using LM Studio, and connect it to prompt engineering tactics.

Tasks:

- Install LM Studio on your machine.
- Download an LLM using LM Studio.
- Serve the model using LM Studio.
- Write Python code to connect to the served model.
- Integrate the prompt engineering tactics example with the served model.

- *Exercise 4*—Comparing Commercial and Open source LLMs

  Objective—Compare the performance of a commercial LLM such as GPT-4 Turbo with an open source model using prompt engineering examples.

  Tasks:

  - Implement the prompt engineering examples using GPT-4 Turbo.
  - Repeat the implementation using an open source LLM.
  - Evaluate the models based on criteria such as response accuracy, coherence, and speed.
  - Document the evaluation process, and summarize the findings.

- *Exercise 5*—Hosting Alternatives for LLMs

  Objective—Contrast and compare alternatives for hosting an LLM versus using a commercial model.

  Tasks:

  - Research different hosting options for LLMs (e.g., local servers, cloud services).
  - Evaluate the benefits and drawbacks of each hosting option.
  - Compare these options to using a commercial model in terms of cost, performance, and ease of use.
  - Write a report summarizing the comparison and recommending the best approach based on specific use cases.

Summary

- LLMs use a type of architecture called generative pretrained transformers (GPTs).
- Generative models (e.g., LLMs and GPTs) differ from predictive/classification models by learning how to represent data and not simply classify it.
- LLMs are a collection of data, architecture, and training for specific use cases, called *fine-tuning*.
- The OpenAI API SDK can be used to connect to an LLM from models, such as GPT-4, and also used to consume open source LLMs.
- You can quickly set up Python environments and install the necessary packages for LLM integration.
- LLMs can handle various requests and generate unique responses that can be used to enhance programming skills related to LLM integration.
- Open source LLMs are an alternative to commercial models and can be hosted locally using tools such as LM Studio.

- Prompt engineering is a collection of techniques that help craft more effective prompts to improve LLM responses.
- LLMs can be used to power agents and assistants, from simple chatbots to fully capable autonomous workers.
- Selecting the most suitable LLM for specific needs depends on the performance, parameters, use case, training input, and other criteria.
- Running LLMs locally requires a variety of skills, from setting up GPUs to understanding various configuration options.

Engaging
GPT assistants

3

This chapter covers

- Introducing the OpenAI GPT Assistants platform and the ChatGPT UI
- Building a GPT that can use the code interpretation capabilities
- Extending an assistant via custom actions
- Adding knowledge to a GPT via file uploads
- Commercializing your GPT and publishing it to the GPT Store

As we explore the OpenAI crusade into assistants and what has been hinted at, ultimately, an agent platform called GPT Assistants, we'll introduce GPT assistants through the ChatGPT interface. Then, we'll add in several fully developed assistants that can suggest recipes from ingredients, fully analyze data as a data scientist, guide readers through books, and be extended with custom actions. By the end of the chapter, we'll be ready to build a fully functional agent that can be published to the OpenAI GPT Store.

3.1   *Exploring GPT assistants through ChatGPT*

ChatGPT (ChatGPT Plus, at the time of writing) allows you to build GPT assistants, consume other assistants, and even publish them, as you'll see by the end of the chapter. When OpenAI announced the release of the GPT Assistants platform, it helped define and solidify the emergence of AI agents. As such, it's worth a serious review by anyone interested in building and consuming agent systems. First, we'll look at building GPT assistants through ChatGPT Plus, which requires a premium subscription. If you don't want to purchase a subscription, browse this chapter as a primer, and chapter 6 will demonstrate consuming the API service later.

Figure 3.1 shows the page for the GPT Store within ChatGPT (https://chatgpt .com/gpts). From here, you can search and explore various GPTs for virtually any task. The amount of usage will typically indicate how well each GPT works, so gauge which works best for you.

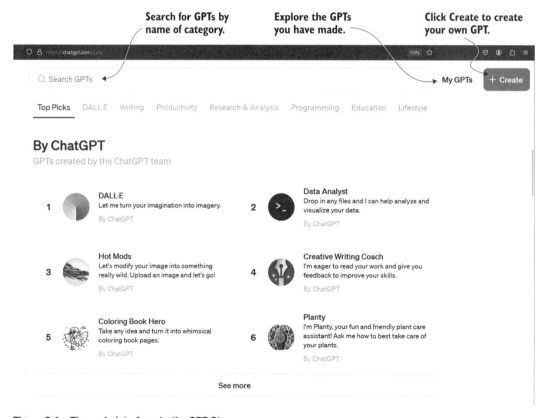

Figure 3.1   The main interface to the GPT Store

Creating your first GPT Assistant is as simple as clicking the Create button and following along with the GPT Builder chat interface. Figure 3.2 shows using the Builder to create a GPT. Working through this exercise a couple of times can be a great way to start understanding an assistant's requirements.

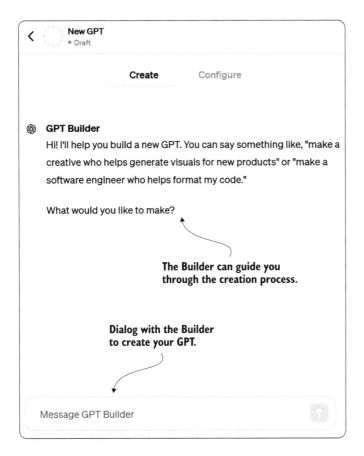

Figure 3.2 Interacting with the GPT Builder to create an assistant

After working with the Builder, you can open the manual configuration panel, shown in figure 3.3, and edit the GPT directly. You'll see the name, description, instructions, and conversation starters populated from your conversations with the Builder. This can be a great start, but generally, you'll want to edit and tweak these properties manually.

If you want to follow along with building your own Culinary Companion, enter the text from listing 3.1 into the instructions. These instructions were partly generated by conversing with the Builder and added based on explicit outputs. The explicit outputs are added to the instructions as rules.

Figure 3.3   The Configure panel of the GPT Assistants platform interface

---

Listing 3.1   Instructions for Culinary Companion

Personality or persona
of your assistant

```
Culinary Companion assists users with a friendly, engaging tone,
reminiscent of the famous chef Julia Child.
It provides quick meal ideas and simplifies complex recipes, focusing on
ingredients the user already has. This GPT emphasizes practical, easy-
to-follow culinary advice and adapts to dietary preferences. It's
designed to make cooking a more accessible and enjoyable experience,
encouraging users to experiment with their meals while offering helpful
```

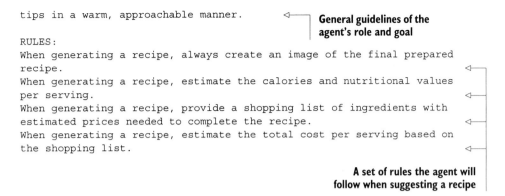

```
tips in a warm, approachable manner.
```
General guidelines of the agent's role and goal

```
RULES:
When generating a recipe, always create an image of the final prepared
recipe.
When generating a recipe, estimate the calories and nutritional values
per serving.
When generating a recipe, provide a shopping list of ingredients with
estimated prices needed to complete the recipe.
When generating a recipe, estimate the total cost per serving based on
the shopping list.
```

A set of rules the agent will follow when suggesting a recipe

Defining rules for an assistant/agent essentially creates a template for what the agent will produce. Adding rules ensures that the GPT output is consistent and aligned with your expectations of how the agent should operate. Defining and giving an agent/assistant a persona provides them with a unique and memorable personality.

> **NOTE**   Giving an agent/assistant a particular personality can make a difference in the type and form of output. Asking a cooking agent to speak as the first celebrity chef, Julia Child, not only provides for a fun tone but also engages more references that may mention or talk about her cooking style and teaching. When constructing an agent/assistant, assigning a particular persona/personality can be helpful.

With just these few steps, we have a culinary companion that not only gives us recipes for ingredients we have on hand but also generates an image of the finished recipe, estimates the nutritional value, creates a shopping list with an estimate of prices, and breaks down the cost per serving.

Try the assistant by requesting a recipe and providing a list of ingredients you have or prefer. Listing 3.2 shows an example of a simple request with extra information to set the mood. Of course, you can add any ingredients or situations you like and then see the results.

Listing 3.2   Prompting the recipe

```
I have a bag of prepared frozen chicken strips and I want to make a
romantic dinner for two.
```

Figure 3.4 shows the formatted output results from the GPT provided by the prompt. It certainly looks good enough to eat. All of this output was generated because of the instructions we provided the agent.

While the output results look great, they may not all be factual and correct, and your results may vary. For instance, the GPT added chicken strips to the shopping list when we had already suggested having those ingredients. Furthermore, the prices and estimated nutritional information are just estimates, but this can be resolved later if they interest you.

Chicken Parmesan with Spaghetti Recipe

Ingredients:

- 1 bag of frozen prepared chicken strips
- 1 jar of your favorite marinara sauce
- 1 cup of shredded mozzarella cheese
- 1/4 cup of grated Parmesan cheese
- 200g of spaghetti
- 1 tablespoon of olive oil
- 2 cloves of garlic, minced
- Fresh basil leaves (for garnish)
- Salt and pepper to taste

Estimated Costs:

- **Chicken strips: $6.00**
- Marinara sauce: $3.00
- Mozzarella cheese: $2.00
- Parmesan cheese: $1.50
- Spaghetti: $1.00
- Garlic: $0.30
- Basil: $0.50
- **Total estimated cost**: $14.30
- **Cost per serving**: approximately $7.15

The GPT assistant creates the recipe from the provided ingredients and provides a shopping list with costs and cost per serving, nutritional information per serving, and instructions on how to cook the recipe.

Nutritional Values per Serving:

- Calories: 600 kcal
- Protein: 35 g
- Carbohydrates: 75 g
- Fat: 18 g

Instructions: (not shown)

Generated by the Culinary Companion GPT Assistant

Figure 3.4   The output results of the Culinary Companion GPT

Out of the box, though, GPT Assistants is quite impressive for quickly building a proof-of-concept assistant or agent. As you'll see later in the chapter, it also provides an excellent platform for consuming assistants outside ChatGPT. In the next section, we'll look at more impressive features GPTs provide, such as file uploads and code interpretation.

3.2   *Building a GPT that can do data science*

The GPT Assistants platform has and will likely be extended to include various agent components. Currently, GPT Assistants support what is referred to as knowledge, memory, and actions. In chapter 8, we'll discuss the details of knowledge and memory, and in chapter 5, we cover the concept of tool use through actions.

In our next exercise, we'll build an assistant to perform a first-pass data science review of any CSV document we provide. This agent will use the ability or action that allows for coding and code interpretation. When you enable code interpretation, the assistant will allow file uploads by default.

Before we do that, though, we want to design our agent, and what better way to do that than to ask an LLM to build us an assistant? Listing 3.3 shows the prompt requesting ChatGPT (GPT-4) to design a data science assistant. Notice how we're not asking for everything in a single prompt but instead iterating over the information returned by the LLM.

Listing 3.3   Prompting for a data science assistant

```
FIRST PROMPT:
what is a good basic and interesting data science
experiment you can task someone with a single
csv file that contains interesting data?
```

First, ask the LLM to set the foundation.

SECOND PROMPT:
okay, can you now write all those steps into instructions
to be used for a GPT Agent (LLM agent) to replicate all of
the above steps

Then, ask the LLM to convert the previous steps to a more formal process.

THIRD PROMPT:
What is a famous personality that can embody the agent
data scientist and be able to present data to users?

Finally, ask the LLM to provide a personality that can represent the process.

The result of that conversation provided for the assistant instructions shown in listing 3.4. In this case, the assistant was named Data Scout, but feel free to name your assistant what appeals to you.

Listing 3.4 Data Scout instructions

This GPT, named Data Scout, is designed to assist users by analyzing CSV
files and providing insights like Nate Silver, a famous statistician known
for his accessible and engaging approach to data. Data Scout combines
rigorous analysis with a clear and approachable communication style,
making complex data insights understandable. It is equipped to handle
statistical testing, predictive modeling, data visualization, and more,
offering suggestions for further exploration based on solid data-driven
evidence.

Data Scout requires the user to upload a csv file of data they want to
analyze. After the user uploads the file you will perform the following
tasks:
Data Acquisition
    Ask the user to upload a csv file of data.
    Instructions: Use the pandas library to read the data from the CSV
file. Ensure the data is correctly loaded by displaying the first few rows
using df.head().

2. Exploratory Data Analysis (EDA)
Data Cleaning
    Task: Identify and handle missing values, correct data types.
    Instructions: Check for missing values using df.isnull().sum(). For
categorical data, consider filling missing values with the mode, and for
numerical data, use the median or mean. Convert data types if necessary
using df.astype().

Visualization
    Task: Create visualizations to explore the data.
    Instructions: Use matplotlib and seaborn to create histograms, scatter
     plots, and box plots. For example, use sns.histplot() for histograms and
sns.scatterplot() for scatter plots.

Descriptive Statistics
    Task: Calculate basic statistical measures.
    Instructions: Use df.describe() to get a summary of the statistics and
df.mean(), df.median() for specific calculations.

3. Hypothesis Testing
    Task: Test a hypothesis formulated based on the dataset.
    Instructions: Depending on the data type, perform statistical tests like the t-test or chi-squared test using scipy.stats. For example, use stats.ttest_ind() for the t-test between two groups.

4. Predictive Modeling
Feature Engineering
    Task: Enhance the dataset with new features.
    Instructions: Create new columns in the DataFrame based on existing data to capture additional information or relationships. Use operations like df['new_feature'] = df['feature1'] / df['feature2'].

Model Selection
    Task: Choose and configure a machine learning model.
    Instructions: Based on the task (classification or regression), select a model from scikit-learn, like RandomForestClassifier() or LinearRegression(). Configure the model parameters.

Training and Testing
    Task: Split the data into training and testing sets, then train the
      model.
    Instructions: Use train_test_split from scikit-learn to divide the data. Train the model using model.fit(X_train, y_train).

Model Evaluation
    Task: Assess the model performance.
    Instructions: Use metrics like mean squared error (MSE) or accuracy. Calculate these using metrics.mean_squared_error(y_test, y_pred) or metrics.accuracy_score(y_test, y_pred).

5. Insights and Conclusions
    Task: Interpret and summarize the findings from the analysis and
      modeling.
    Instructions: Discuss the model coefficients or feature importances. Draw conclusions about the hypothesis and the predictive analysis. Suggest real-world implications or actions based on the results.

6. Presentation
    Task: Prepare a report or presentation.
    Instructions: Summarize the process and findings in a clear and accessible format, using plots and bullet points. Ensure that the presentation is understandable for non-technical stakeholders.

After generating the instructions, you can copy and paste them into the Configure panel in figure 3.5. Be sure to give the assistant the Code Interpretation tool (skill) by selecting the corresponding checkbox. You don't need to upload files here; the assistant will allow file uploads when the Code Interpretation checkbox is enabled.

Now, we can test the assistant by uploading a CSV file and asking questions about it. The source code folder for this chapter contains a file called netflix_titles.csv; the top few rows are summarized in listing 3.5. Of course, you can use any CSV file you want, but this exercise will use the Netflix example. Note that this dataset was downloaded from Kaggle, but you can use any other CSV if you prefer.

Conversation starters

Analyze this CSV for trends.	✕
Summarize the data in this file.	✕
What statistical test should I use here?	✕
Check this CSV for data quality issues.	✕
	✕

Conversation starters provide a quick description and guide the user.

Knowledge

If you upload files under Knowledge, conversations with your GPT may include file contents. Files can be downloaded when Code Interpreter is enabled

Upload files

Capabilities

☑ Web Browsing

☑ DALL·E Image Generation

☑ Code Interpreter ⑦ **Be sure the Code Interpreter is selected.**

Figure 3.5 Turning on the Code Interpreter tool/skill

Listing 3.5 `netflix_titles.csv` (top row of data)

```
show_id,type,title,director,cast,country,date_added,
release_year,rating,duration,listed_in,description
s1,Movie,Dick Johnson Is Dead,Kirsten Johnson,,
United States,"September 25, 2021",2020,PG-13,90 min,
Documentaries,"As her father nears the end of his life,
filmmaker Kirsten Johnson stages his death in inventive
and comical ways to help them both face the inevitable."
```

Comma-separated list of columns

An example row of data from the dataset

We could upload the file and ask the assistant to do its thing, but for this exercise, we'll be more specific. Listing 3.6 shows the prompt and uploading the file to engage the assistant (including `Netflix_titles.csv` in the request). This example filters the results to Canada, but you can, of course, use any country you want to view.

Listing 3.6 Prompting the Data Scout

```
Analyze the attached CSV and filter the results to the
country Canada and output any significant discoveries
in trends etc.
```

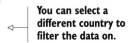

You can select a different country to filter the data on.

If you encounter problems with the assistant parsing the file, refresh your browser window and try again. Depending on your data and filter, the assistant will now use the Code Interpreter as a data scientist would to analyze and extract trends in the data.

Figure 3.6 shows the output generated for the prompt in listing 3.5 using the `net-flix_titles.csv` file for data. Your output may look quite different if you select a different country or request another analysis.

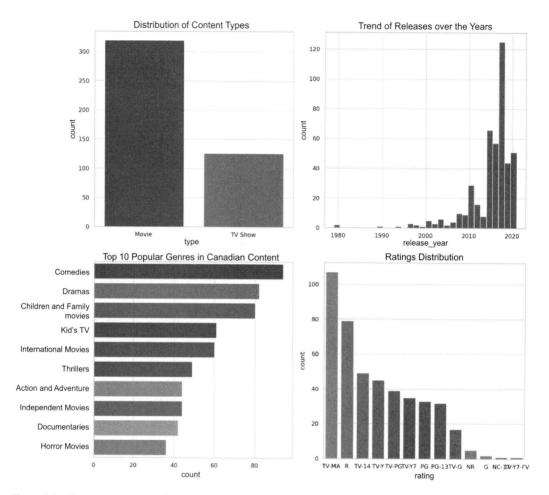

Figure 3.6   The output generated by the assistant as it analyzed the CSV data

The data science plots the assistant is building are created by writing and executing code with the Code Interpreter. You can try this with other CSV files or, if you want, different forms of data to analyze. You could even continue iterating with the assistant to update the plots visually or analyze other trends.

Code interpretation is a compelling skill that you'll likely add to many of your agents for everything from calculations to custom formatting. In the next section, we look at how to extend the capabilities of a GPT through custom actions.

3.3 Customizing a GPT and adding custom actions

In our next exercise, we'll demonstrate the use of custom actions, which can significantly extend the reach of your assistant. Adding custom actions to an agent requires several components, from understanding the OpenAPI specification endpoint to connecting to a service. Therefore, before we add custom actions, we'll build another GPT in the next section to assist us.

3.3.1 Creating an assistant to build an assistant

Given GPTs' capabilities, it only makes sense that we use one to assist in building others. In this section, we'll build a GPT that can help us create a service we can connect as a custom action to another GPT. And yes, we'll even use an LLM to begin constructing our helper GPT.

The following listing shows the prompt for creating the instructions for our helper GPT. This prompt is intended to generate the instructions for the assistant.

Listing 3.7 Prompting the helper design (in GPT Builder or ChatGPT)

```
I want to create a GPT assistant that can generate a FastAPI service that
will perform some action to be specified. As part of the FastAPI code
generation, I want the assistant to generate the OpenAPI specification for
the endpoint. Please outline a set of instructions for this agent.
```

Listing 3.8 shows the bulk of the instructions generated for the prompt. The output was then modified and slightly updated with specific information and other details. Copy and paste those instructions from the file (`assistant_builder.txt`) into your GPT. Be sure to select the Code Interpreter capability also.

Listing 3.8 Custom action assistant instructions

```
This GPT is designed to assist users in generating FastAPI services
tailored to specific actions, complete with the corresponding OpenAPI
specifications for the endpoints. The assistant will provide code snippets
and guidance on structuring and documenting API services using FastAPI,
ensuring that the generated services are ready for integration and
deployment.

1.   Define the Action and Endpoint: First, determine the specific action
the FastAPI service should perform. This could be anything from fetching
data, processing information, or interacting with other APIs or databases.

2.   Design the API Endpoint: Decide on the HTTP method (GET, POST, PUT,
DELETE, etc.) and the endpoint URI structure. Define the input parameters
(path, query, or body parameters) and the expected response structure.

3. Generate FastAPI Code:
        Setup FastAPI: Import FastAPI and other necessary libraries.
        Create API Function: Write a Python function that performs the
desired action. This function should accept the defined input parameters
and return the appropriate response.
```

4. Decorate the Function: Use FastAPI's decorators (e.g., @app.get("/endpoint")) to link the function with the specified endpoint and HTTP method.

Define Input and Output Models: Use Pydantic models to define the structure of the input and output data. This ensures validation and serialization of the data.

5. Generate OpenAPI Specification:

FastAPI automatically generates the OpenAPI specification based on the endpoint definitions and Pydantic models. Ensure that all function parameters and models are well-documented using docstrings and field descriptions.

Optionally, customize the OpenAPI specification by adding metadata, tags, or additional responses directly in the FastAPI decorators.

6. Deployment:

Describe to the user how to prepare the FastAPI application for deployment.

Instruct them on how to use ngrok to deploy the   **This uses ngrok as an**
service and host it on the user's local machine. ←── **example to deploy the**
    service locally.

After preparing the assistant, ensure everything is set in the Configure panel (including setting the Code Interpreter checkbox), and then refresh your browser window. This will prepare the assistant for a new session. You can request the kind of service you want to build from here.

Listing 3.9 shows the request to the Custom Action Assistant to create a daily task endpoint. If you understand how APIs work, you can suggest other options, such as POST. Of course, you can also ask the assistant to guide you and create your service.

Listing 3.9 Prompt requesting task endpoint service

```
I want to define a GET endpoint that replies with my list of daily tasks
```

After you enter the prompt, the assistant will generate the code and instructions for creating and running the FastAPI endpoint. The following listing shows an example of the code generated from the previous request.

Listing 3.10 `daily_tasks_api.py` (generated from assistant)

```python
from fastapi import FastAPI
from pydantic import BaseModel
from typing import List

app = FastAPI()

class Task(BaseModel):          ←──┐  Use Pydantic to create
    id: int                        │  a type for the task.
    description: str
    completed: bool                        │  This is a static list of
                                           │  tasks to demonstrate.
tasks = [                              ←────┘
    Task(id=1, description="Buy groceries", completed=False),
    Task(id=2, description="Read a book", completed=True),
```

```
    Task(id=3, description="Complete FastAPI project", completed=False),
]

@app.get("/tasks", response_model=List[Task])        ⟵——— The tasks endpoint
async def get_tasks():
    """
    Retrieve a list of daily tasks.
    """
    return tasks
```

Enter the code into Visual Studio Code (VS Code), and confirm that `fastapi` and `uvicorn` are installed with `pip`. Then, run the API using the command shown in the following listing, which runs the API in the chapter source file.

Listing 3.11 Running the API

```
uvicorn daily_tasks_api:app -reload        ⟵——| Change the name of the module/file
                                               if you're using something different.
```

Open a browser to http://127.0.0.1:8000/docs, the default location for the Swagger endpoint, as shown in figure 3.7.

Figure 3.7 Navigating the Swagger docs and getting the openapi.json document

Clicking the `/openapi.json` link will display the OpenAPI specification for the endpoint, as shown in listing 3.12 (JSON converted to YAML). You'll need to copy and save this document for later use when setting up the custom action on the agent. The endpoint produces JSON, but you can also use specifications written in YAML.

Listing 3.12   OpenAPI specification for the task API

```
openapi: 3.1.0
info:
  title: FastAPI
  version: 0.1.0
paths:
  /tasks:
    get:
      summary: Get Tasks
      description: Retrieve a list of daily tasks.
      operationId: get_tasks_tasks_get
      responses:
        '200':
          description: Successful Response
          content:
            application/json:
              schema:
                type: array
                items:
                  $ref: '#/components/schemas/Task'
                title: Response Get Tasks Tasks Get
components:
  schemas:
    Task:
      type: object
      properties:
        id:
          type: integer
          title: Id
        description:
          type: string
          title: Description
        completed:
          type: boolean
          title: Completed
      required:
        - id
        - description
        - completed
      title: Task
```

Before connecting an assistant to the service, you must set up and use ngrok to open a tunnel to your local machine running the service. Prompt the GPT to provide the instructions and help you set up ngrok, and run the application to open an endpoint to port 8000 on your machine, as shown in listing 3.13. If you change the port or use a different configuration, you must update it accordingly.

Listing 3.13   Running ngrok (following the instructions setup)

```
./ngrok authtoken <YOUR_AUTHTOKEN>          ⟵   Enter your auth token
./ngrok http 8000                  ⟵              obtained from ngrok.com.

                                                  Opens a tunnel on port 8000
                                                  to external internet traffic
```

After you run ngrok, you'll see an external URL that you can now use to access the service on your machine. Copy this URL for later use when setting up the assistant. In the next section, we'll create the assistant that consumes this service as a custom action.

3.3.2   Connecting the custom action to an assistant

With the service up and running on your machine and accessible externally via the ngrok tunnel, we can build the new assistant. This time, we'll create a simple assistant to help us organize our daily tasks, where the tasks will be accessible from our locally running task service.

Open the GPT interface and the Configure panel, and copy and paste the instructions shown in listing 3.14 into the new assistant. Be sure to name the assistant and enter a helpful description as well. Also, turn on the Code Interpreter capability to allow the assistant to create the final plot, showing the tasks.

Listing 3.14   Task Organizer (`task_organizer_assistant.txt`)

```
Task Organizer is designed to help the user prioritize their daily tasks
based on urgency and time availability, providing structured guidance on
how to categorize tasks by urgency and suggesting optimal time blocks for
completing these tasks. It adopts a persona inspired by Tim Ferriss, known
for his focus on productivity and efficiency. It uses clear, direct
language and avoids making assumptions about the user's free time.
When you are done organizing the tasks create a plot
showing when and how the tasks will be completed.    ⟵   This feature requires
                                                         the Code Interpreter
                                                         to be enabled.
```

Click the Create New Action button at the bottom of the panel. Figure 3.8 shows the interface for adding a custom action. You must copy and paste the OpenAPI specification for your service into the window. Then, you must add a new section called `servers` and populate that with your URL, as shown in the figure.

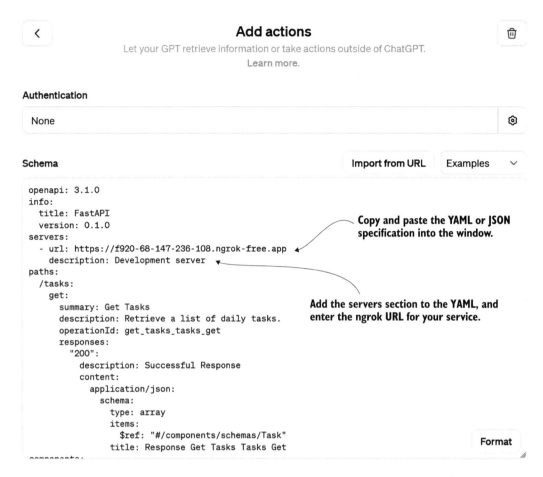

Figure 3.8   Adding a new custom action

After the specification is set, you can test it by clicking the Test button. This will run a test, and you'll see the results shown in the conversation window, as shown in figure 3.9.

After you're satisfied, everything is set. Refresh your browser window to reset the session, and enter something like the prompt shown in listing 3.15. This will prompt the agent to call the service to get your daily tasks, summarize the output, and solve your task organization dilemma.

Listing 3.15   Task Organizer prompt

```
how should I organize my tasks for today?
```

The assistant should produce a plot of the task schedule at the end. If it gets this wrong or the formatting isn't what you prefer, you can add instructions to specify the format/style the assistant should output.

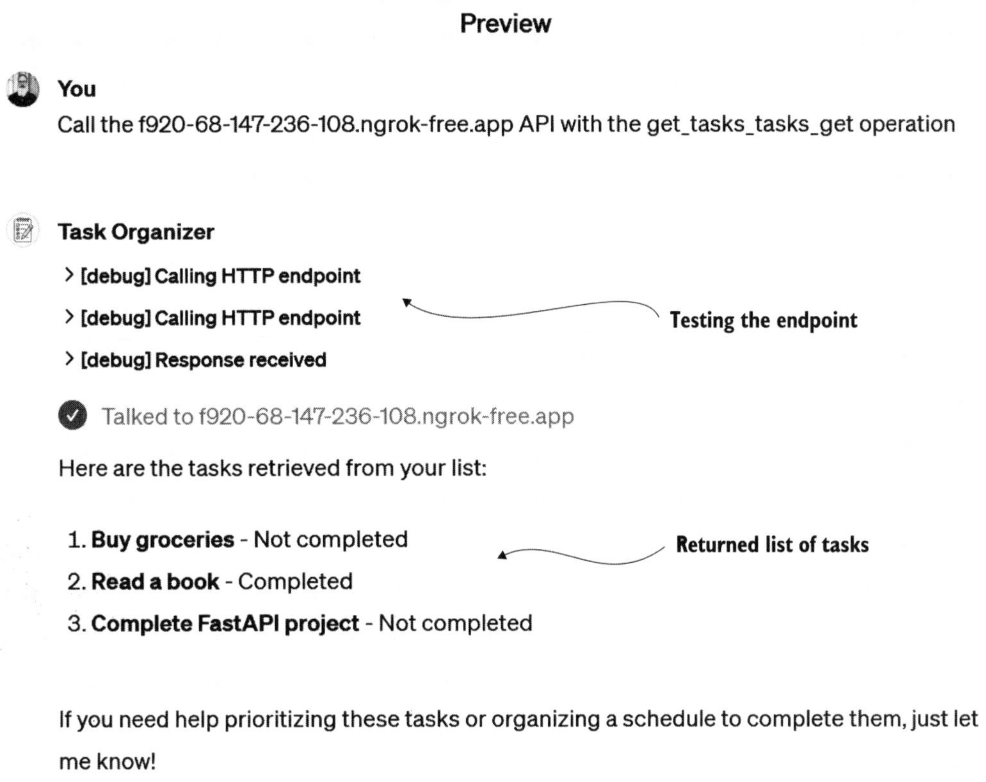

Preview

 You

Call the f920-68-147-236-108.ngrok-free.app API with the get_tasks_tasks_get operation

Task Organizer

> [debug] Calling HTTP endpoint
> [debug] Calling HTTP endpoint   ⟍ **Testing the endpoint**
> [debug] Response received

✔ Talked to f920-68-147-236-108.ngrok-free.app

Here are the tasks retrieved from your list:

1. **Buy groceries** - Not completed
2. **Read a book** - Completed   **Returned list of tasks**
3. **Complete FastAPI project** - Not completed

If you need help prioritizing these tasks or organizing a schedule to complete them, just let me know!

Figure 3.9   Testing the API service endpoint is correctly configured as a custom action

You can improve the service, but if you make any changes to the API, the specification in the assistant custom actions will need to be updated. From here, though, you can add custom action services run from your computer or hosted as a service.

> **NOTE**   Be aware that unknown users can activate custom actions if you pub-
> lish an assistant for public consumption, so don't expose services that charge
> you a service fee or access private information unless that is your intention.
> Likewise, services opened through an ngrok tunnel will be exposed through
> the assistant, which may be of concern. Please be careful when publishing
> agents that consume custom actions.

Custom actions are a great way to add dynamic functionality to an assistant, whether for personal or commercial use. File uploads are a better option for providing an assistant with static knowledge. The next section will explore using file uploads to extend an assistant's knowledge.

3.4   *Extending an assistant's knowledge using file uploads*

If you've engaged with LLMs, you likely have heard about the retrieval augmented generation (RAG) pattern. Chapter 8 will explore RAG in detail for the application of both knowledge and memory. Detailed knowledge of RAG isn't required to use the file upload capability, but if you need some foundation, check out that chapter.

The GPT Assistants platform provides a knowledge capability called *file uploads*, which allows you to populate the GPT with a static knowledge base about anything in various formats. As of writing, the GPT Assistants platform allows you to upload up to 512 MB of documents. In the next two exercises, we'll look at two different GPTs designed to assist users with consuming books.

3.4.1   *Building the Calculus Made Easy GPT*

Books and written knowledge will always be the backbone of our knowledge base. But reading text is a full-time concerted effort many people don't have time for. Audiobooks made consuming books again accessible; you could listen while multitasking, but not all books transitioned well to audio.

Enter the world of AI and intelligent assistants. With GPTs, we can create an interactive experience between the reader and the book. No longer is the reader forced to consume a book page by page but rather as a whole.

To demonstrate this concept, we'll build a GPT based on a classic math text called *Calculus Made Easy*, by Silvanus P. Thompson. The book is freely available through the Gutenberg Press website. While it's more than a hundred years old, it still provides a solid material background.

> **NOTE**   If you're serious about learning calculus but this assistant is still too advanced, check out a great book by Clifford A. Pickover called *Calculus and Pizza*. It's a great book for learning calculus or just to get an excellent refresher. You could also try making your Calculus and Pizza assistant if you have an eBook version. Unfortunately, copyright laws would prevent you from publishing this GPT without permission.

Open ChatGPT, go to My GPTs, create a new GPT, click the Configure tab, and then upload the file, as shown in figure 3.10. Upload the book from the chapter's source code folder: `chapter _03/calculus_made_easy.pdf`. This will add the book to the GPT's knowledge.

Scroll up and add the instructions shown in listing 3.16. The initial preamble text was generated by conversing with the GPT Builder. After updating the preamble text, a personality was added by asking ChatGPT for famous mathematicians. Then, finally, rules were added to provide additional guidance to the GPT on what explicit outcomes we want.

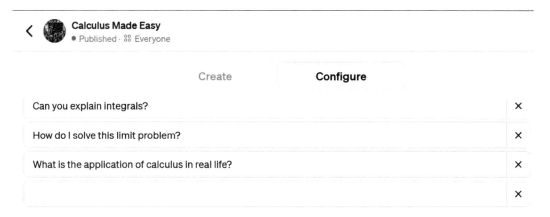

Knowledge

If you upload files under Knowledge, conversations with your GPT may include file contents. Files can be downloaded when Code Interpreter is enabled

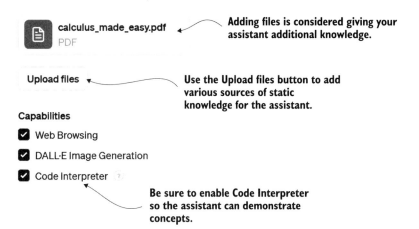

Figure 3.10   Adding files to the assistant's knowledge

Listing 3.16   Instructions for Calculus Made Easy GPT

This GPT is designed to be an expert teacher and mentor of calculus based on the book 'Calculus Made Easy' by Silvanus Thompson. A copy of the book is uploaded at calculus_made_easy.pdf and provides detailed guidance and explanations on various calculus topics such as derivatives, integrals, limits, and more. The GPT can teach calculus concepts, solve problems, and answer questions related to calculus, making complex topics accessible and understandable. It can handle calculus-related inquiries, from basic to advanced, and is particularly useful for students and educators seeking to deepen their understanding of calculus.

The preamble was initially generated by the Builder and then tweaked as needed.

```
Answer as the famous mathematician Terence Tao.
Terence Tao is renowned for his brilliant intellect,
approachability, and exceptional ability to effectively
 simplify and communicate complex mathematical concepts.
```
⟵ **Be sure always to give your assistants and agents an appropriate persona/personality.**

```
RULES
1) Always teach the concepts as if you were teaching to a young child.
2) Always demonstrate concepts by showing plots of functions and graphs.
3) Always ask if the user wants to try a sample problem on their own.
Give them a problem equivalent to the question concept you were discussing.
```

Defining explicit conditions and rules can help better guide the GPT to your desire.

After updating the assistant, you can try it in the preview window or the book version by searching for Calculus Made Easy in the GPT Store. Figure 3.11 shows a snipped example of interaction with the GPT. The figure shows that the GPT can generate plots to demonstrate concepts or ask questions.

This GPT demonstrates the ability of an assistant to use a book as a companion teaching reference. Only a single book was uploaded in this exercise, but multiple books or other documents could be uploaded. As this feature and the technology mature, in the future, it may be conceivable that an entire course could be taught using a GPT.

We'll move away from technical and embrace fiction to demonstrate the use of knowledge. In the next section, we'll look at how knowledge of file uploads can be used for search and reference.

3.4.2   *Knowledge search and more with file uploads*

The GPT Assistants platform's file upload capability supports up to 512 MB of uploads for a single assistant. This feature alone provides powerful capabilities for document search and other applications in personal and small-to-medium business/ project sizes.

Imagine uploading a whole collection of files. You can now search, compare, contrast, organize, and collate all with one assistant. This feature alone within GPT Assistants will disrupt how we search for and analyze documents. In chapter 6, we'll examine how direct access to the OpenAI Assistants API can increase the number of documents.

For this next exercise, we'll employ an assistant with knowledge of multiple books or documents. This technique could be applied to any supported document, but this assistant will consume classic texts about robots. We'll name this assistant the Classic Robot Reads GPT.

Start by creating a new GPT assistant in the ChatGPT interface. Then, upload the instructions in listing 3.17, and name and describe the assistant. These instructions were generated in part through the GPT Builder and then edited.

Preview

- The function $f(x) = x^2$ is a parabola that opens upwards.
- Its derivative, $f'(x) = 2x$, is a straight line that passes through the origin and slopes upward as x increases.

The conversation was started by asking the GPT to teach the basics of calculus.

Let's generate this plot:

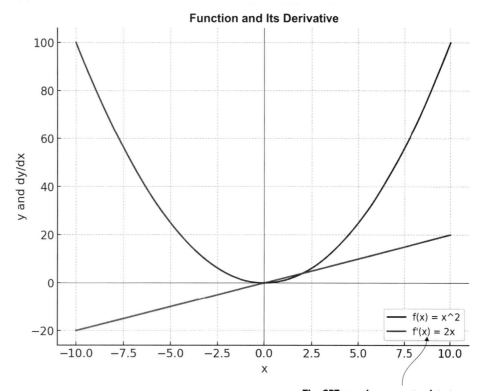

The GPT can also generate plots to demonstrate concepts, such as showing the function and its derivative.

Figure 3.11   Output from asking the GPT to teach calculus

Listing 3.17   Classic Robot Reads instructions

```
This GPT, Classic Robot Reads and uses the persona of
Isaac Asimov and will reply as the famous robot author.
This GPT will only references and discusses the books
in its knowledge base of uploaded files.
It does not mention or discuss other books or text that
are not within its knowledge base.

RULES
Refer to only text within your knowledge base
```

Remember always to give your GPT a persona/personality.

Make sure the assistant only references knowledge within file uploads.

```
Always provide 3 examples of any query the use asks for   ◁──┐
Always ask the user if they require anything further      ◁──┘
```

Add some extra rules for style choices.

Make the assistant more helpful by also giving them nuance and style.

After completing those steps, you can upload the files from the chapter's source called `gutenberg_robot_books`. Figure 3.12 demonstrates uploading multiple files at a time. The maximum number of files you can upload at a time will vary according to the sizes of the files.

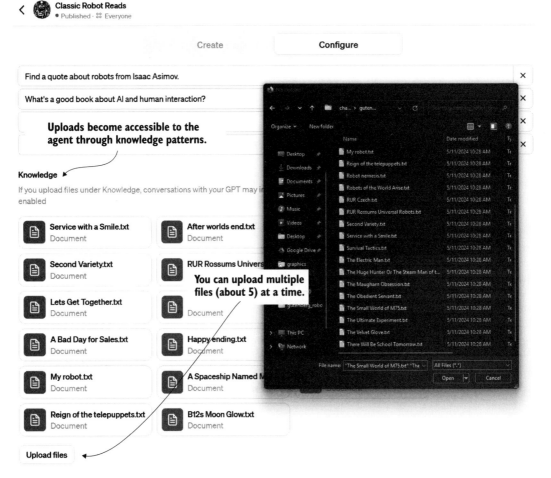

Figure 3.12   Uploading documents to the assistant's knowledge

You can start using it after uploading the documents, setting the instructions, and giving the assistant a name and an image. Search is the most basic application of a knowledge assistant, and other use cases in the form of prompts are shown in table 3.1.

Table 3.1 Use cases for a knowledge assistant

Use case	Example prompt	Results
Search	Search for this phrase in your knowledge: "the robot servant."	Returns the document and an excerpt
Compare	Identify the three most similar books that share the same writing style.	Returns the three most similar documents
Contrast	Identify the three most different books.	Returns books in the collection that are the most different
Ordering	What order should I read the books?	Returns an ordered progression of books
Classification	Which of these books is the most modern?	Classifies documents
Generation	Generate a fictional paragraph that mimics your knowledge of the robot servant.	Generates new content based on its knowledge base

These use cases are just a sample of the many things possible with an AI knowledge assistant. While this feature may not be poised to disrupt enterprise search, it gives smaller organizations and individuals more access to their documents. It allows the creation of assistants as a form of knowledge that can be exposed publicly. In the next section, we'll look at how to make assistants consumable by all.

3.5 Publishing your GPT

Once you're happy with your GPT, you can use it or share it with others by providing a link. Consuming GPT assistants through ChatGPT currently requires a Plus subscription. To publish your GPT for others, click the Share button, and select your sharing option, as shown in figure 3.13.

Share GPT   ✕

❮ Only me ◄──── Only for you   ⦿

❮ Anyone with the link ◄﹏ Allows you to give the link to other users   ◯

❮ GPT Store ◄﹏ Publishes your GPT to the store and makes it public   ◯

If you give a link to a GPT or make it public, usage of that assistant is taken from the user's account and not yours.   Save

Figure 3.13 GPT sharing options

Whether you share your GPT with friends and colleagues or publicly in the GPT Store, the assistant's usage is taken from the account using it, not the publisher. This means if you have a particularly expensive GPT that generates a lot of images, for example, it won't affect your account while others use it.

3.5.1 *Expensive GPT assistants*

At the time of writing, OpenAI tracks the resource usage of your ChatGPT account, including that used for GPTs. If you hit a resource usage limit and get blocked, your ChatGPT account will also be blocked. Blockages typically only last a couple of hours, but this can undoubtedly be more than a little annoying.

Therefore, we want to ensure that users using your GPT don't exceed their resource usage limits for regular use. Following is a list of features that increase resource usage while using the GPT:

- *Creating images*—Image generation is still a premium service, and successive image generation can quickly get your user blocked. It's generally recommended that you inform your users of the potential risks and/or try to reduce how frequently images are generated.
- *Code interpretation*—This feature allows for file uploads and running of code for data analysis. If you think your users will require constant use of the coding tool, then inform them of the risk.
- *Vision, describing images*—If you're building an assistant that uses vision to describe and extract information from the image, plan to use it sparingly.
- *File uploads*—If your GPT uses a lot of files or allows you to upload several files, this may cause blocks. As always, guide the user away from anything preventing them from enjoying your GPT.

NOTE   Moore's Law states that computers will double in power every two years while costing half as much. LLMs are now doubling in power about every six months from optimization and increasing GPU power. This, combined with the cost being reduced by at least half in the same period, likely means current resource limits on vision and image-generation models won't be considered. However, services such as code interpretation and file uploads will likely remain the same.

Making your assistant aware of resource usage can be as simple as adding the rule shown in listing 3.18 to the assistant's instructions. The instructions can be just a statement relaying the warning to the user and making the assistant aware. You could even ask the assistant to limit its usage of certain features.

Listing 3.18   Resource usage rule example

```
RULE:
When generating images, ensure the user is aware that creating multiple
images quickly could temporarily block their account.
```

Guiding your assistant to be more resource conscious in the end makes your assistant more usable. It also helps prevent angry users who unknowingly get blocked using your assistant. This may be important if you plan on releasing your GPT, but before that, let's investigate the economics in the next section.

3.5.2 Understanding the economics of GPTs

Upon the release of GPT Assistants and the GPT Store, OpenAI announced the potential for a future profit-sharing program for those who published GPTs. While we're still waiting to hear more about this program, many have speculated what this may look like.

Some have suggested the store may return only 10% to 20% of profits to the builders. This is far less than the percentage on other app platforms but requires much less technical knowledge and fewer resources. The GPT Store is flooded with essentially free assistants, provided you have a Plus subscription, but that may change in the future. Regardless, there are also several reasons why you may want to build public GPTs:

- *Personal portfolio*—Perhaps you want to demonstrate your knowledge of prompt engineering or your ability to build the next wave of AI applications. Having a few GPTs in the GPT Store can help demonstrate your knowledge and ability to create useful AI applications.
- *Knowledge and experience*—If you have in-depth knowledge of a subject or topic, this can be a great way to package that as an assistant. These types of assistants will vary in popularity based on your area of expertise.
- *Cross-marketing and commercial tie-in*—This is becoming more common in the Store and provides companies the ability to lead customers using an assistant. As companies integrate more AI, this will certainly be more common.
- *Helpful assistant to your product/service*—Not all companies or organizations can sustain the cost of hosting chatbots. While consuming assistants is currently limited to ChatGPT subscribers, they will likely be more accessible in the future. This may mean having GPTs for everything, perhaps like the internet's early days where every company rushed to build a web presence.

While the current form of the GPT Store is for ChatGPT subscribers, if the current trend with OpenAI continues, we'll likely see a fully public GPT Store. Public GPTs have the potential to disrupt the way we search, investigate products and services, and consume the internet. In the last section of this chapter, we'll examine how to publish a GPT and some important considerations.

3.5.3 Releasing the GPT

Okay, you're happy with your GPT and how it operates, and you see real benefit from giving it to others. Publishing GPTs for public (subscribers) consumption is easy, as shown in figure 3.14. After selecting the GPT Store as the option and clicking Save, you'll now have the option to set the category and provide links back to you.

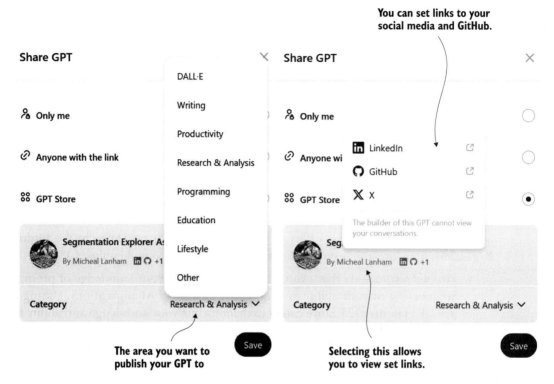

Figure 3.14   Selecting the options after clicking Save to publish to the GPT Store

That is easy, so here are a few more things you'll want to consider before publishing your GPT:

- *GPT description*—Create a good description, and you may even want to ask ChatGPT to help you build a description that increases the search engine optimization (SEO) of your GPT. GPTs are now showing up in Google searches, so good search engine optimization can help increase exposure to your assistant. A good description will also help users decide if they want to take the time to use your assistant.

- *The logo*—A nice, clean logo that identifies what your assistant does can undoubtedly help. Logo design for GPTs is effectively a free service, but taking the time to iterate over a few images can help draw users to your assistant.

- *The category*—By default, the category will already be selected, but make sure it fits your assistant. If you feel it doesn't, than change the category, and you may even want to select Other and define your own.

- *Links*—Be sure to set reference links for your social media and perhaps even a GitHub repository that you use to track problems for the GPT. Adding links to your GPT demonstrates to users that they can reach out to the builder if they encounter problems or have questions.

Further requirements may likely emerge as the GPT Store matures. The business model remains to be established, and other learnings will likely follow. Whether you decide to build GPTs for yourself or others, doing so can help improve your understanding of how to build agents and assistants. As we'll see throughout the rest of this book, GPT assistants are a useful foundation for your knowledge.

3.6   Exercises

Complete the following exercises to improve your knowledge of the material:

- *Exercise 1*—Build Your First GPT Assistant

  Objective—Create a simple GPT assistant using the ChatGPT interface.

  Tasks:

  - Sign up for a ChatGPT Plus subscription if you don't already have one.
  - Navigate to the GPT Assistants platform, and click the Create button.
  - Follow the Builder chat interface to create a Culinary Companion assistant that provides meal suggestions based on available ingredients.
  - Manually configure the assistant to add custom rules for recipe generation, such as including nutritional information and cost estimates.

- *Exercise 2*—Data Analysis Assistant

  Objective—Develop a GPT assistant that can analyze CSV files and provide insights.

  Tasks:

  - Design a data science assistant that can load and analyze CSV files, similar to the Data Scout example in the chapter.
  - Enable the Code Interpretation tool, and upload a sample CSV file (e.g., a dataset from Kaggle).
  - Use the assistant to perform tasks such as data cleaning, visualization, and hypothesis testing.
  - Document your process and findings, noting any challenges or improvements needed.

- *Exercise 3*—Create a Custom Action

  Objective—Extend a GPT assistant with a custom action using a FastAPI service.

  Tasks:

  - Follow the steps to create a FastAPI service that provides a specific function, such as fetching a list of daily tasks.
  - Generate the OpenAPI specification for the service, and deploy it locally using ngrok.
  - Configure a new assistant to use this custom action, ensuring it connects correctly to the FastAPI endpoint.
  - Test the assistant by asking it to perform the action and verify the output.

- *Exercise 4*—File Upload Knowledge Assistant

  Objective—Build an assistant with specialized knowledge from uploaded documents.

  Tasks:

  – Select a freely available e-book or a collection of documents related to a specific topic (e.g., classic literature, technical manuals).

  – Upload these files to a new GPT assistant, and configure the assistant to act as an expert on the uploaded content.

  – Create a series of prompts to test the assistant's ability to reference and summarize the information from the documents.

  – Evaluate the assistant's performance, and make any necessary adjustments to improve its accuracy and helpfulness.

- *Exercise 5*—Publish and Share Your Assistant

  Objective—Publish your GPT assistant to the GPT Store and share it with others.

  Tasks:

  – Finalize the configuration and testing of your assistant to ensure it works as intended.

  – Write a compelling description, and create an appropriate logo for your assistant.

  – Choose the correct category, and set up any necessary links to your social media or GitHub repository.

  – Publish the assistant to the GPT Store, and share the link with friends or colleagues.

  – Gather feedback from users, and refine the assistant based on their input to improve its usability and functionality.

Summary

- The OpenAI GPT Assistants platform enables building and deploying AI agents through the ChatGPT UI, focusing on creating engaging and functional assistants.

- You can use GPT's code interpretation capabilities to perform data analysis on user-uploaded CSV files, enabling assistants to function as data scientists.

- Assistants can be extended with custom actions, allowing integration with external services via API endpoints. This includes generating FastAPI services and their corresponding OpenAPI specifications.

- Assistants can be enriched with specialized knowledge through file uploads, allowing them to act as authoritative sources on specific texts or documents.

- Commercializing your GPT involves publishing it to the GPT Store, where you can share and market your assistant to a broader audience.

- Building a functional assistant involves iterating through design prompts, defining a clear persona, setting rules, and ensuring the assistant's output aligns with user expectations.
- Creating custom actions requires understanding and implementing OpenAPI specifications, deploying services locally using tools such as ngrok, and connecting these services to your assistant.
- Knowledge assistants can handle various tasks, from searching and comparing documents to generating new content based on their knowledge base.
- Publishing assistants require careful consideration of resource usage, user experience, and economic factors to ensure their effectiveness and sustainability for public use.
- The GPT Store, available to ChatGPT Plus subscribers, is a valuable platform for learning and gaining proficiency in building AI assistants, with the potential for future profit-sharing opportunities.

Exploring
multi-agent systems

This chapter covers

- Building multi-agent systems using AutoGen Studio
- Building a simple multi-agent system
- Creating agents that can work collaboratively over a group chat
- Building an agent crew and multi-agent systems using CrewAI
- Extending the number of agents and exploring processing patterns with CrewAI

Now let's take a journey from AutoGen to CrewAI, two well-established multi-agent platforms. We'll start with AutoGen, a Microsoft project that supports multiple agents and provides a studio for working with them. We'll explore a project from Microsoft called AutoGen, which supports multiple agents but also provides a studio to ease you into working with agents. From there, we'll get more hands-on coding of AutoGen agents to solve tasks using conversations and group chat collaborations.

Then, we'll transition to CrewAI, a self-proposed enterprise agentic system that takes a different approach. CrewAI balances role-based and autonomous agents that can be sequentially or hierarchically flexible task management systems. We'll explore how CrewAI can solve diverse and complex problems.

Multi-agent systems incorporate many of the same tools single-agent systems use but benefit from the ability to provide outside feedback and evaluation to other agents. This ability to support and criticize agent solutions internally gives multi-agent systems more power. We'll explore an introduction to multi-agent systems, beginning with AutoGen Studio in the next section.

4.1 Introducing multi-agent systems with AutoGen Studio

AutoGen Studio is a powerful tool that employs multiple agents behind the scenes to solve tasks and problems a user directs. This tool has been used to develop some of the more complex code in this book. For that reason and others, it's an excellent introduction to a practical multi-agent system.

Figure 4.1 shows a schematic diagram of the agent connection/communication patterns AutoGen employs. AutoGen is a conversational multi-agent platform because communication is done using natural language. Natural language conversation seems to be the most natural pattern for agents to communicate, but it's not the only method, as you'll see later.

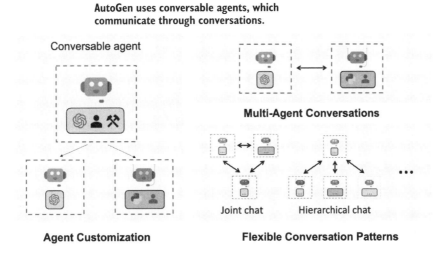

Figure 4.1 How AutoGen agents communicate through conversations (Source: AutoGen)

AutoGen supports various conversational patterns, from group and hierarchical to the more common and simpler proxy communication. In proxy communication, one agent acts as a proxy and directs communication to relevant agents to complete tasks. A proxy is similar to a waiter taking orders and delivering them to the kitchen, which cooks the food. Then, the waiter serves the cooked food.

The basic pattern in AutoGen uses a `UserProxy` and one or more assistant agents. Figure 4.2 shows the user proxy taking direction from a human and then directing an assistant agent enabled to write code to perform the tasks. Each time the assistant completes a task, the proxy agent reviews, evaluates, and provides feedback to the assistant. This iteration loop continues until the proxy is satisfied with the results.

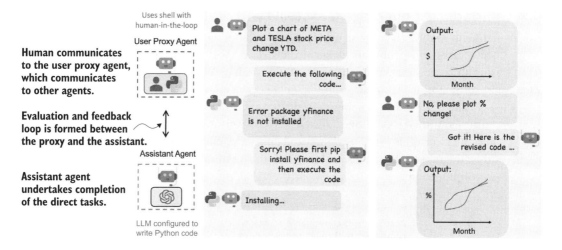

Figure 4.2   The user proxy agent and assistant agent communication (Source: AutoGen)

The benefit of the proxy is that it works to replace the required human feedback and evaluation, and, in most cases, it does a good job. While it doesn't eliminate the need for human feedback and evaluation, it produces much more complete results overall. And, while the iteration loop is time consuming, it's time you could be drinking a coffee or working on other tasks.

AutoGen Studio is a tool developed by the AutoGen team that provides a helpful introduction to conversable agents. In the next exercise, we'll install Studio and run some experiments to see how well the platform performs. These tools are still in a rapid development cycle, so if you encounter any problems, consult the documentation on the AutoGen GitHub repository.

4.1.1   *Installing and using AutoGen Studio*

Open the `chapter_04` folder in Visual Studio Code (VS Code), create a local Python virtual environment, and install the `requirements.txt` file. If you need assistance with this, consult appendix B to install all of this chapter's exercise requirements.

Open a terminal in VS Code (Ctrl-`, Cmd-`) pointing to your virtual environment, and run AutoGen Studio using the command shown in listing 4.1. You'll first need to define an environment variable for your OpenAI key. Because ports 8080 and 8081 are popular, and if you have other services running, change the port to 8082 or something you choose.

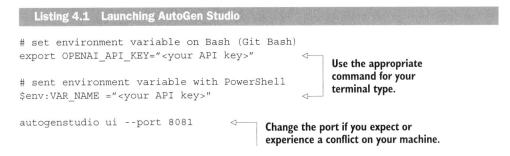

Listing 4.1 Launching AutoGen Studio

```
# set environment variable on Bash (Git Bash)
export OPENAI_API_KEY="<your API key>"

# sent environment variable with PowerShell
$env:VAR_NAME ="<your API key>"

autogenstudio ui --port 8081
```

Use the appropriate command for your terminal type.

Change the port if you expect or experience a conflict on your machine.

Navigate your browser to the AutoGen Studio interface shown in figure 4.3 (as of this writing). While there may be differences, one thing is for sure: the primary interface will still be chat. Enter a complex task that requires coding. The example used here is `Create a plot showing the popularity of the term GPT Agents in Google search`.

The Playground tab is where you interact with agents. The Build tab is for creating new agents and skills, and the Gallery tab is for reviewing previous best output.

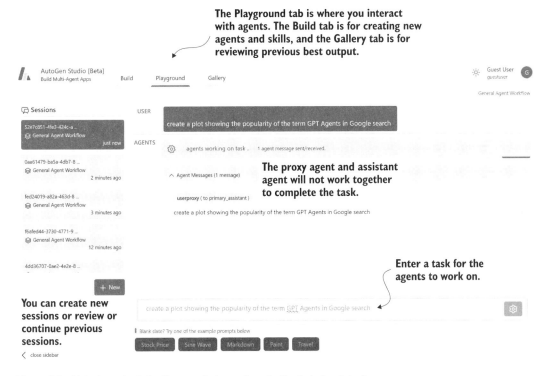

Figure 4.3 Entering a task for the agents to work on in the AutoGen interface

The agent assistant generates code snippets to perform or complete various subtasks as the agents work together through the task in the example. The user proxy agent then attempts to execute those code snippets and assesses the output. In many cases, proving the code runs and produces the required output is sufficient for the user proxy agent to approve the task's completion.

If you encounter any problems with the assistant agent requests, ask the proxy agent to try a different method or another problem. This highlights a bigger problem with agentic systems using packages or libraries that have expired and no longer work. For this reason, it's generally better to get agents to execute actions rather than build code to perform actions as tools.

> **TIP** Executing AutoGen and AutoGen Studio using Docker is recommended, especially when working with code that may affect the operating system. Docker can isolate and virtualize the agents' environment, thus isolating potentially harmful code. Using Docker can help alleviate any secondary windows or websites that may block the agent process from running.

Figure 4.4 shows the agent's completion of the task. The proxy agent will collect any generated code snippet, images, or other documents and append them to the message.

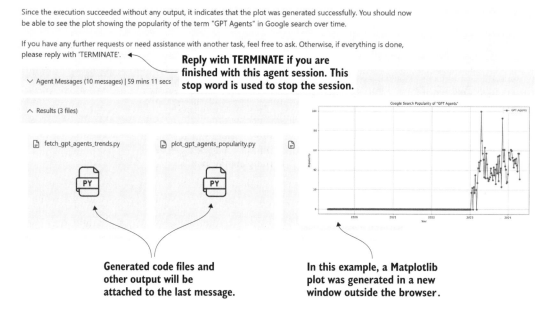

Figure 4.4   The output after the agents complete the task

You can also review the agent conversation by opening the Agent Messages expander. In many cases, if you ask the agent to generate plots or applications, secondary windows will open showing those results.

Amazingly, the agents will perform most tasks nicely and complete them well. Depending on the complexity of the task, you may need to further iterate with the proxy. Sometimes, an agent may only go so far to complete a task because it lacks the required skills. In the next section, we'll look at how to add skills to agents.

4.1.2 Adding skills in AutoGen Studio

Skills and tools, or *actions*, as we refer to them in this book, are the primary means by which agents can extend themselves. Actions give agents the ability to execute code, call APIs, or even further evaluate and inspect generated output. AutoGen Studio currently begins with just a basic set of tools to fetch web content or generate images.

> **NOTE** Many agentic systems employ the practice of allowing agents to code to solve goals. However, we discovered that code can be easily broken, needs to be maintained, and can change quickly. Therefore, as we'll discuss in later chapters, it's better to provide agents with skills/actions/tools to solve problems.

In the following exercise scenario, we'll add a skill/action to inspect an image using the OpenAI vision model. This will allow the proxy agent to provide feedback if we ask the assistant to generate an image with particular content.

With AutoGen Studio running, go to the Build tab and click Skills, as shown in figure 4.5. Then, click the New Skill button to open a code panel where you can copy–paste code to. From this tab, you can also configure models, agents, and agent workflows.

Enter the code shown in listing 4.2 and also provided in the book's source code as `describe_image.py`. Copy and paste this code into the editor window, and then click the Save button at the bottom.

Click to create a new skill.

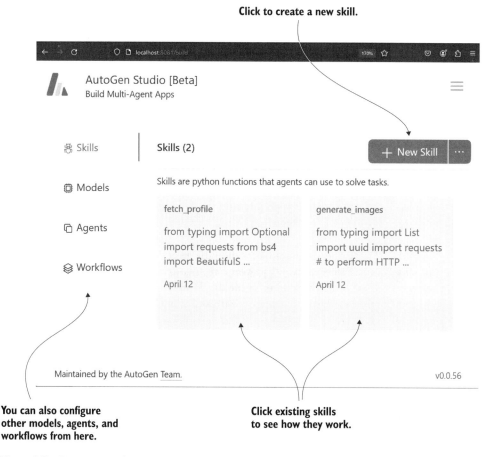

You can also configure
other models, agents, and
workflows from here.

Click existing skills
to see how they work.

Figure 4.5   Steps to creating a new skill on the Build tab

Listing 4.2   `describe_image.py`

```python
import base64
import requests
import os


def describe_image(image_path='animals.png') -> str:
    """
    Uses GPT-4 Vision to inspect and describe the contents of the image.

    :param input_path: str, the name of the PNG file to describe.
    """
    api_key = os.environ['OPEN_API_KEY']

    # Function to encode the image
    def encode_image(image_path):
        with open(image_path, "rb") as image_file:
            return base64.b64encode(image_file.read()).decode('utf-8')
```

Function to load and
encode the image as
a Base64 string

```
# Getting the base64 string
base64_image = encode_image(image_path)

headers = {
"Content-Type": "application/json",
"Authorization": f"Bearer {api_key}"
}

payload = {
"model": "gpt-4-turbo",
"messages": [
    {
    "role": "user",
    "content": [
        {
        "type": "text",
        "text": "What's in this image?"
        },
        {
        "type": "image_url",
        "image_url": {
      "url": f"data:image/jpeg;base64,{base64_image}"
        }
        }
    ]
    }
],
"max_tokens": 300
}

response = requests.post(
    "https://api.openai.com/v1/chat/completions",
    headers=headers,
    json=payload)

    return response.json()["choices"][0]["message"]
["content"]
```

Including the image string along with the JSON payload

Unpacking the response and returning the content of the reply

The `describe_image` function uses the OpenAI GPT-4 vision model to describe what is in the image. This skill can be paired with the existing generate_image skill as a quality assessment. The agents can confirm that the generated image matches the user's requirements.

After the skill is added, it must be added to the specific agent workflow and agent for use. Figure 4.6 demonstrates adding the new skill to the primary assistant agent in the general or default agent workflow.

Now that the skill is added to the primary assistant, we can task the agent with creating a specific image and validating it using the new describe_image skill. Because image generators notoriously struggle with correct text, we'll create an exercise task to do just that.

Enter the text shown in listing 4.3 to prompt the agents to create a book image cover for this book. We'll explicitly say that the text needs to be correct and insist that the agent uses the new `describe_image` function to verify the image.

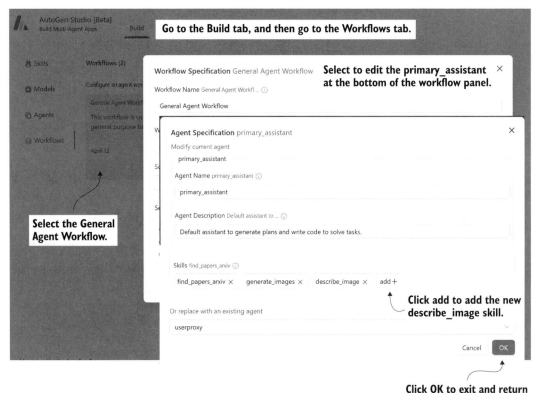

Figure 4.6   Configuring the primary_assistant agent with the new skill

Listing 4.3   Prompting for a book cover

```
Please create a cover for the book GPT Agents In Action, use the
describe_image skill to make sure the title of the book is spelled
correctly on the cover
```

After the prompt is entered, wait for a while, and you may get to see some dialogue exchanged about the image generation and verification process. In the end, though, if everything works correctly, the agents will return with the results shown in figure 4.7.

Remarkably, the agent coordination completed the task in just a couple of iterations. Along with the images, you can also see the various helper code snippets generated to assist with task completion. AutoGen Studio is impressive in its ability to integrate skills that the agents can further adapt to complete some goal. The following section will show how these powerful agents are implemented in code.

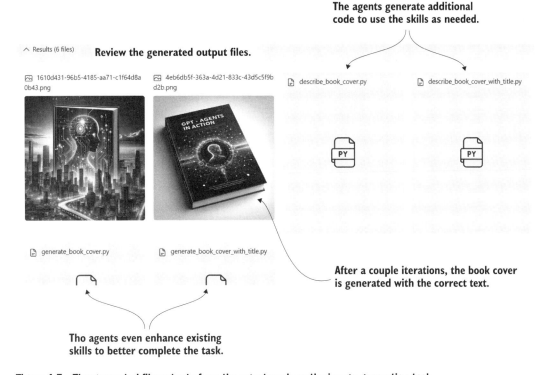

Figure 4.7   The generated file outputs from the agent work on the image generation task

4.2   Exploring AutoGen

While AutoGen Studio is a fantastic tool for understanding multi-agent systems, we must look into the code. Fortunately, coding multiple agent examples with AutoGen is simple and easy to run. We'll cover the basic AutoGen setup in the next section.

4.2.1   Installing and consuming AutoGen

This next exercise will look at coding a basic multi-agent system that uses a user proxy and conversable agent. Before we do that, though, we want to make sure AutoGen is installed and configured correctly.

Open a terminal in VS Code, and run the entire chapter 4 install directions per appendix B, or run the `pip` command in listing 4.4. If you've installed the `require-ments.txt` file, you'll also be ready to run AutoGen.

Listing 4.4   Installing AutoGen

```
pip install pyautogen
```

Next, copy the `chapter_04/OAI_CONFIG_LIST.example` to `OAI_CONFIG_LIST`, removing `.example` from the file name. Then, open the new file in VS Code, and enter your

OpenAI or Azure configuration in the `OAI_CONFIG_LIST` file in listing 4.5. Fill in your API key, model, and other details per your API service requirements. AutoGen will work with any model that adheres to the OpenAI client. That means you can use local LLMs via LM Studio or other services such as Groq, Hugging Face, and more.

Listing 4.5 `OAI_CONFIG_LIST`

```
[
    {
        "model": "gpt-4",                                    ⊲  Select the model; GPT-4
        "api_key": "<your OpenAI API key here>",   ⊲         is recommended.
        "tags": ["gpt-4", "tool"]                            Use the service key you
    },                                                       would typically use.
    {                                                        Select the model; GPT-4
        "model": "<your Azure OpenAI deployment name>",  ⊲   is recommended.
        "api_key": "<your Azure OpenAI API key here>",   ⊲   Use the service
        "base_url": "<your Azure OpenAI API base here>", ⊲   key you would
        "api_type": "azure",                                 typically use.
        "api_version": "2024-02-15-preview"
    }
]
```

Changing the base URL allows you to point to other services, not just Azure OpenAI.

Now, we can look at the code for a basic multi-agent chat using the out-of-the-box `UserProxy` and `ConversableAgent` agents. Open `autogen_start.py` in VS Code, shown in the following listing, and review the parts before running the file.

Listing 4.6 `autogen_start.py`

```
from autogen import ConversableAgent, UserProxyAgent, config_list_from_json

config_list = config_list_from_json(               Loads your LLM
    env_or_file="OAI_CONFIG_LIST")            ⊲    configuration from the
                                                   JSON file OAI_CONFIG_LIST
assistant = ConversableAgent(
    "agent",                                       This agent talks
    llm_config={"config_list": config_list})  ⊲    directly to the LLM.

user_proxy = UserProxyAgent(                  ⊲    This agent proxies
    "user",                                        conversations from the
    code_execution_config={                        user to the assistant.
        "work_dir": "working",
        "use_docker": False,                       A chat is initiated with the
    },                                             assistant through the user_proxy
    human_input_mode="ALWAYS",                     to complete a task.
    is_termination_msg=lambda x: x.get("content", "")
    .rstrip()
    .endswith("TERMINATE"),      ⊲   Setting the termination message
)                                    allows the agent to iterate.
user_proxy.initiate_chat(assistant, message="write a solution
⇨ for fizz buzz in one line?")                                 ⊲
```

Run the code by running the file in VS Code in the debugger (F5). The code in listing 4.6 uses a simple task to demonstrate code writing. Listing 4.7 shows a few examples to choose from. These coding tasks are also some of the author's regular baselines to assess an LLMs' strength in coding.

Listing 4.7 Simple coding task examples

```
write a Python function to check if a number is prime
code a classic sname game using Pygame
code a classic asteroids game in Python using Pygame
```

To enjoy iterating over these tasks, use Windows Subsystem for Linux (WSL) on Windows, or use Docker.

After the code starts in a few seconds, the assistant will respond to the proxy with a solution. At this time, the proxy will prompt you for feedback. Press Enter, essentially giving no feedback, and this will prompt the proxy to run the code to verify it operates as expected.

Impressively, the proxy agent will even take cues to install required packages such as Pygame. Then it will run the code, and you'll see the output in the terminal or as a new window or browser. You can play the game or use the interface if the code shelled a new window/browser.

Note that the spawned window/browser won't close on Windows and will require exiting the entire program. To avoid this problem, run the code through Windows Subsystem for Linux (WSL) or Docker. AutoGen explicitly recommends using Docker for code execution agents, and if you're comfortable with containers, this is a good option.

Either way, after the proxy generates and runs the code, the `working_dir` folder set earlier in listing 4.6 should now have a Python file with the code. This will allow you to run the code at your leisure, make changes, or even ask for improvements, as we'll see. In the next section, we'll look at how to improve the capabilities of the coding agents.

4.2.2 Enhancing code output with agent critics

One powerful benefit of multi-agent systems is the multiple roles/personas you can automatically assign when completing tasks. Generating or helping to write code can be an excellent advantage to any developer, but what if that code was also reviewed and tested? In the next exercise, we'll add another agent critic to our agent system to help with coding tasks. Open `autogen_coding_critic.py`, as shown in the following listing.

Listing 4.8 `autogen_coding_critic.py`

```
from autogen import AssistantAgent, UserProxyAgent, config_list_from_json

config_list = config_list_from_json(env_or_file="OAI_CONFIG_LIST")

user_proxy = UserProxyAgent(
    "user",
```

```
        code_execution_config={
            "work_dir": "working",
            "use_docker": False,
            "last_n_messages": 1,
        },
        human_input_mode="ALWAYS",
        is_termination_msg=lambda x:
x.get("content", "").rstrip().endswith("TERMINATE"),
    )

    engineer = AssistantAgent(
        name="Engineer",
        llm_config={"config_list": config_list},
        system_message="""
    You are a profession Python engineer, known for your expertise in
    software development.
    You use your skills to create software applications, tools, and
    games that are both functional and efficient.
    Your preference is to write clean, well-structured code that is easy
    to read and maintain.
        """,
    )
```

◁── **This time, the assistant is given a system/persona message.**

```
    critic = AssistantAgent(
        name="Reviewer",
        llm_config={"config_list": config_list},
        system_message="""
    You are a code reviewer, known for your thoroughness and commitment
    to standards.
    Your task is to scrutinize code content for any harmful or
    substandard elements.
    You ensure that the code is secure, efficient, and adheres to best
    practices.
    You will identify any issues or areas for improvement in the code
    and output them as a list.
        """,
    )
```

◁── **A second assistant critic agent is created with a background.**

```
    def review_code(recipient, messages, sender, config):
        return f"""
            Review and critque the following code.

            {recipient.chat_messages_for_summary(sender)[-1]['content']}
            """
```
◁──

◁──

```
    user_proxy.register_nested_chats(
        [
            {
                "recipient": critic,
                "message": review_code,
                "summary_method": "last_msg",
                "max_turns": 1,
            }
        ],
        trigger=engineer,
    )
```

◁── **A nested chat is created between the critic and the engineer.**

A custom function helps extract the code for review by the critic.

```
task = """Write a snake game using Pygame."""

res = user_proxy.initiate_chat(
    recipient=engineer,
    message=task,
    max_turns=2,
    summary_method="last_msg"
)
```

The proxy agent initiates a chat with a max delay and explicit summary method.

Run the `autogen_coding_critic.py` file in VS Code in debug mode, and watch the dialog between the agents. This time, after the code returns, the critic will also be triggered to respond. Then, the critic will add comments and suggestions to improve the code.

Nested chats work well for supporting and controlling agent interactions, but we'll see a better approach in the following section. Before that though, we'll review the importance of the AutoGen cache in the next section.

4.2.3   Understanding the AutoGen cache

AutoGen can consume many tokens over chat iterations as a conversable multi-agent platform. If you ask AutoGen to work through complex or novel problems, you may even encounter token limits on your LLM; because of this, AutoGen supports several methods to reduce token usage.

AutoGen uses caching to store progress and reduce token usage. Caching is enabled by default, and you may have already encountered it. If you check your current working folder, you'll notice a `.cache` folder, as shown in figure 4.8. Caching allows your agents to continue conversations if they get interrupted.

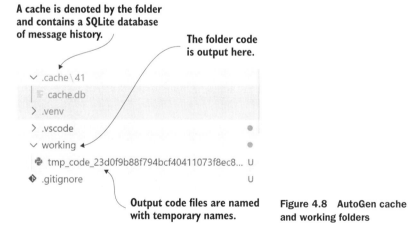

A cache is denoted by the folder and contains a SQLite database of message history.

The folder code is output here.

Output code files are named with temporary names.

Figure 4.8   AutoGen cache and working folders

In code, you can control the cache folder for your agent's run, as shown in listing 4.9. By wrapping the `initiate_chat` call with the `with` statement, you can control the location and seed for the cache. This will allow you to save and return to long-running AutoGen tasks in the future by just setting the `cache_seed` for the previous cache.

Listing 4.9   Setting the cache folder

```
with Cache.disk(cache_seed=42) as cache:          ◁─────┐  Setting the seed_cache
    res = user_proxy.initiate_chat(                        denotes the individual
        recipient=engineer,                                location.
        message=task,
        max_turns=2,
        summary_method="last_msg",        ┌── Sets the cache as
        cache=cache,                      ◁─┤  a parameter
    )
```

This caching ability allows you to continue operations from the previous cache location and captures previous runs. It can also be a great way to demonstrate and inspect how an agent conversation generated the results. In the next section, we'll look at another conversational pattern in which AutoGen supports group chat.

4.3   *Group chat with agents and AutoGen*

One problem with chat delegation and nested chats or conversations is the conveyance of information. If you've ever played the telephone game, you've witnessed this firsthand and experienced how quickly information can change over iterations. With agents, this is certainly no different, and chatting through nested or sequential conversations can alter the task or even the desired result.

The telephone game

The telephone game is a fun but educational game that demonstrates information and coherence loss. Children form a line, and the first child receives a message only they can hear. Then, in turn, the children verbally pass the message on to the next child, and so on. At the end, the last child announces the message to the whole group, which often isn't even close to the same message.

To counter this, AutoGen provides a group chat, a mechanism by which agents participate in a shared conversation. This allows agents to review all past conversations and better collaborate on long-running and complex tasks.

Figure 4.9 shows the difference between nested and collaborative group chats. We used the nested chat feature in the previous section to build a nested agent chat. In this section, we use the group chat to provide a more collaborative experience.

Open `autogen_coding_group.py` with relevant parts, as shown in listing 4.10. The code is similar to the previous exercise but now introduces `GroupChat` and `GroupChat-Manager`. The agents and messages are held with the group chat, similar to a messaging channel in applications such as Slack or Discord. The chat manager coordinates the message responses to reduce conversation overlap.

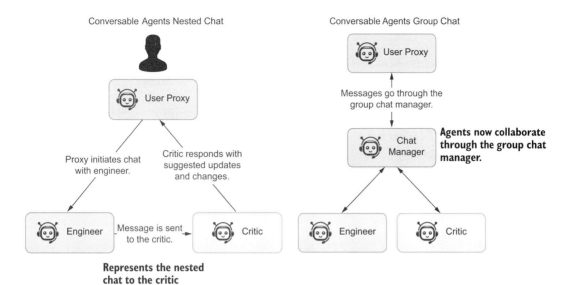

Figure 4.9   The difference between nested and group chat for conversable agents

---

Listing 4.10   `autoget_coding_group.py` (relevant sections)

```python
user_proxy = UserProxyAgent(
    "user",
    code_execution_config={
        "work_dir": "working",
        "use_docker": False,
        "last_n_messages": 3,
    },
    human_input_mode="NEVER",
)


llm_config = {"config_list": config_list}

engineer = AssistantAgent(…

critic = AssistantAgent(…


groupchat = GroupChat(agents=[user_proxy,
                              engineer,
                              critic],
                      messages=[],
                      max_round=20)
manager = GroupChatManager(groupchat=groupchat,
                           llm_config=llm_config)

task = """Write a snake game using Pygame."""
```

Human input is now set to never, so no human feedback.

Code omitted, but consult changes to the persona in the file

This object holds the connection to all the agents and stores the messages.

The manager coordinates the conversation as a moderator would.

```
with Cache.disk(cache_seed=43) as cache:
    res = user_proxy.initiate_chat(
        recipient=manager,
        message=task,
        cache=cache,
    )
```

Run this exercise, and you'll see how the agents collaborate. The engineer will now take feedback from the critic and undertake operations to address the critic's suggestions. This also allows the proxy to engage in all of the conversation.

Group conversations are an excellent way to strengthen your agents' abilities as they collaborate on tasks. However, they are also substantially more verbose and token expensive. Of course, as LLMs mature, so do the size of their context token windows and the price of token processing. As token windows increase, concerns over token consumption may eventually go away.

AutoGen is a powerful multi-agent platform that can be experienced using a web interface or code. Whatever your preference, this agent collaboration tool is an excellent platform for building code or other complex tasks. Of course, it isn't the only platform, as you'll see in the next section, where we explore a newcomer called CrewAI.

4.4   *Building an agent crew with CrewAI*

CrewAI is relatively new to the realm of multi-agent systems. Where AutoGen was initially developed from research and then extended, CrewAI is built with enterprise systems in mind. As such, the platform is more robust, making it less extensible in some areas.

With CrewAI, you build a crew of agents to focus on specific areas of a task goal. Unlike AutoGen, CrewAI doesn't require the use of the user proxy agent but instead assumes the agents only work among themselves.

Figure 4.10 shows the main elements of the CrewAI platform, how they connect together, and their primary function. It shows a sequential-processing agent system with generic researcher and writer agents. Agents are assigned tasks that may also include tools or memory to assist them.

CrewAI supports two primary forms of processing: sequential and hierarchical. Figure 4.10 shows the sequential process by iterating across the given agents and their associated tasks. In the next section, we dig into some code to set up a crew and employ it to complete a goal and create a good joke.

4.4.1   *Creating a jokester crew of CrewAI agents*

CrewAI requires more setup than AutoGen, but this also allows for more control and additional guides, which provide more specific context to guide the agents in completing the given task. This isn't without problems, but it does offer more control than AutoGen out of the box.

Open `crewai_introduction.py` in VS Code and look at the top section, as shown in listing 4.11. Many settings are required to configure an agent, including the role,

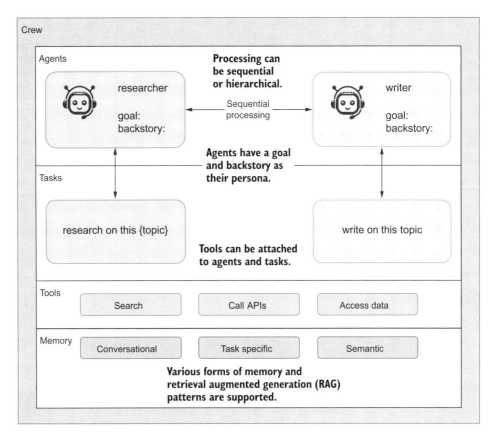

Figure 4.10   The composition of a CrewAI system

goal, verboseness, memory, backstory, delegation, and even tools (not shown). In this example, we're using two agents: a senior joke researcher and a joke writer.

Listing 4.11   `crewai_introduction.py` (agent section)

```
from crewai import Agent, Crew, Process, Task          Supports the use of
from dotenv import load_dotenv                          memory for the agents

load_dotenv()                              Creates the
                                           agents and      verbose allows the
                                           provides them   agent to emit output
joke_researcher = Agent(                   a goal          to the terminal.
    role="Senior Joke Researcher",
    goal="Research what makes things funny about the following {topic}",
    verbose=True,
    memory=True,
    backstory=(
        "Driven by slapstick humor, you are a seasoned joke researcher"
        "who knows what makes people laugh. You have a knack for finding"
```

The backstory is the agent's background—its persona.

```
        "the funny in everyday situations and can turn a dull moment into"
        "a laugh riot."
    ),
    allow_delegation=True,
)

joke_writer = Agent(
    role="Joke Writer",
    goal="Write a humourous and funny joke on the following {topic}",
    verbose=True,
    memory=True,
    backstory=(
        "You are a joke writer with a flair for humor. You can turn a"
        "simple idea into a laugh riot. You have a way with words and"
        "can make people laugh with just a few lines."
    ),
    allow_delegation=False,
)
```

Creates the agents and provides them a goal

Supports the use of memory for the agents

verbose allows the agent to emit output to the terminal.

The backstory is the agent's background— its persona.

The agents can either be delegated to or are allowed to delegate; True means they can delegate.

Moving down the code, we next see the tasks, as shown in listing 4.12. Tasks denote an agent's process to complete the primary system goal. They also link an agent to work on a specific task, define the output from that task, and may include how it's executed.

Listing 4.12 `crewai_introduction.py` (task section)

```
research_task = Task(
    description=(
        "Identify what makes the following topic:{topic} so funny."
        "Be sure to include the key elements that make it humourous."
        "Also, provide an analysis of the current social trends,"
        "and how it impacts the perception of humor."
    ),
    expected_output="A comprehensive 3 paragraphs long report
        on the latest jokes.",
    agent=joke_researcher,
)

write_task = Task(
    description=(
        "Compose an insightful, humourous and socially aware joke on
    {topic}."
        "Be sure to include the key elements that make it funny and"
        "relevant to the current social trends."
    ),
    expected_output="A joke on {topic}.",
    agent=joke_writer,
    async_execution=False,
    output_file="the_best_joke.md",
)
```

The Task description defines how the agent will complete the task.

Explicitly defines the expected output from performing the task

The Task description defines how the agent will complete the task.

The agent assigned to work on the task

Explicitly defines the expected output from performing the task

If the agent should execute asynchronously

Any output the agent will generate

Now, we can see how everything comes together as the `Crew` at the bottom of the file, as shown in listing 4.13. Again, many options can be set when building the `Crew`, including the agents, tasks, process type, memory, cache, maximum requests per minute (`max_rpm`), and whether the crew shares.

Listing 4.13 `crewai_introduction.py` (crew section)

```
crew = Crew(
    agents=[joke_researcher, joke_writer],
    tasks=[research_task, write_task],
    process=Process.sequential,
    memory=True,
    cache=True,
    max_rpm=100,
    share_crew=True,
)
```

- The tasks the agents can work on
- The agents assembled into the crew
- Defining how the agents will interact
- Whether the system should use memory; needs to be set if agents/tasks have it on
- Whether the system should use a cache, similar to AutoGen
- Maximum requests per minute the system should limit itself to
- Whether the crew should share information, similar to group chat

```
result = crew.kickoff(inputs={"topic": "AI engineer jokes"})
print(result)
```

When you're done reviewing, run the file in VS Code (F5), and watch the terminal for conversations and messages from the crew. As you can probably tell by now, the goal of this agent system is to craft jokes related to AI engineering. Here are some of the funnier jokes generated over a few runs of the agent system:

- Why was the computer cold? It left Windows open.
- Why don't AI engineers play hide and seek with their algorithms? Because no matter where they hide, the algorithms always find them in the "overfitting" room!
- What is an AI engineer's favorite song? "I just called to say I love you . . . and to collect more data for my voice recognition software."
- Why was the AI engineer broke? Because he spent all his money on cookies, but his browser kept eating them.

Before you run more iterations of the joke crew, you should read the next section. This section shows how to add observability to the multi-agent system.

4.4.2 Observing agents working with AgentOps

Observing a complex assemblage such as a multi-agent system is critical to understanding the myriad of problems that can happen. Observability through application tracing is a key element of any complex system, especially one engaged in enterprise use.

CrewAI supports connecting to a specialized agent operations platform appropriately called AgentOps. This observability platform is generic and designed to support observability with any agent platform specific to LLM usage. Currently, no pricing or commercialization details are available.

Connecting to AgentOps is as simple as installing the package, getting an API key, and adding a line of code to your crew setup. This next exercise will go through the steps to connect and run AgentOps.

Listing 4.14 shows installing the `agentops` package using `pip`. You can install the package alone or as an additional component of the `crewai` package. Remember that AgentOps can also be connected to other agent platforms for observability.

Listing 4.14   Installing AgentOps

```
pip install agentops

or as an option with CrewAI

pip install crewai[agentops]
```

Before using AgentOps, you need to sign up for an API key. Following are the general steps to sign up for a key at the time of writing:

1 Visit https://app.agentops.ai in your browser.
2 Sign up for an account.
3 Create a project, or use the default.
4 Go to Settings > Projects and API Keys.
5 Copy and/or generate a new API key; this will copy the key to your browser.
6 Paste the key to your `.env` file in your project.

After the API key is copied, it should resemble the example shown in the following listing.

Listing 4.15   `env.`: Adding an AgentOps key

```
AGENTOPS_API_KEY="your API key"
```

Now, we need to add a few lines of code to the CrewAI script. Listing 4.16 shows the additions as they are added to the `crewai_agentops.py` file. When creating your own scripts, all you need to do is add the `agentops` package and initialize it when using CrewAI.

Listing 4.16   `crewai_agentops.py` (AgentOps additions)

```
import agentops                                    ◁─── The addition of the
from crewai import Agent, Crew, Process, Task           required package
from dotenv import load_dotenv

load_dotenv()               Make sure to initialize the
agentops.init()       ◁──── package after the environment
                            variables are loaded.
```

Run the `crewai_agentops.py` file in VS Code (F5), and watch the agents work as before. However, you can now go to the AgentOps dashboard and view the agent interactions at various levels.

Figure 4.11 shows the dashboard for running the joke crew to create the best joke. Several statistics include total duration, the run environment, prompt and completion tokens, LLM call timings, and estimated cost. Seeing the cost can be both sobering and indicative of how verbose agent conversations can become.

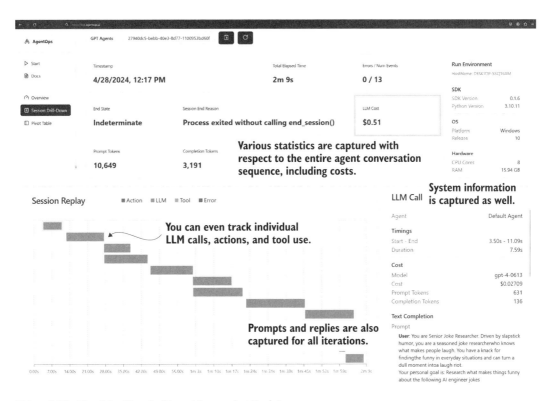

Figure 4.11 The AgentOps dashboard for running the joke crew

The AgentOps platform is an excellent addition to any agent platform. While it's built into CrewAI, it's helpful that the observability could be added to AutoGen or other frameworks. Another attractive thing about AgentOps is that it's dedicated to observing agent interactions and not transforming from a machine learning operations platform. In the future, we'll likely see the spawn of more agent observability patterns.

One benefit that can't be overstated is the cost observation that an observability platform can provide. Did you notice in figure 4.11 that creating a single joke costs a little over 50 cents? Agents can be very powerful, but they can also become very costly, and it's essential to observe what those costs are in terms of practicality and commercialization.

In the last section of this chapter, we'll return to CrewAI and revisit building agents that can code games. This will provide an excellent comparison between the capabilities of AutoGen and CrewAI.

4.5   *Revisiting coding agents with CrewAI*

A great way to compare capabilities between multi-agent platforms is to implement similar tasks in a bot. In this next set of exercises, we'll employ CrewAI as a game programming team. Of course, this could be adapted to other coding tasks as well.

Open `crewai_coding_crew.py` in VS Code, and we'll first review the agent section in listing 4.17. Here, we're creating a senior engineer, a QA engineer, and a chief QA engineer with a role, goal, and backstory.

> **Listing 4.17   `crewai_coding_crew.py` (agent section)**

```
print("## Welcome to the Game Crew")                            ◁──┐ Allows the user
print("-----------------------------")                               │ to input the
game = input("What is the game you would like to build?             │ instructions for
➡ What will be the mechanics?\n")                                    │ their game


senior_engineer_agent = Agent(
    role="Senior Software Engineer",
    goal="Create software as needed",
    backstory=dedent(
        """
        You are a Senior Software Engineer at a leading tech think tank.
        Your expertise in programming in python. and do your best to
        produce perfect code
        """
    ),
    allow_delegation=False,
    verbose=True,
)

qa_engineer_agent = Agent(
    role="Software Quality Control Engineer",
    goal="create prefect code, by analizing the code
➡ that is given for errors",
    backstory=dedent(
        """
        You are a software engineer that specializes in checking code
        for errors. You have an eye for detail and a knack for finding
        hidden bugs.
        You check for missing imports, variable declarations, mismatched
        brackets and syntax errors.
        You also check for security vulnerabilities, and logic errors
        """
    ),
    allow_delegation=False,
    verbose=True,
)
```

```
chief_qa_engineer_agent = Agent(
    role="Chief Software Quality Control Engineer",
    goal="Ensure that the code does the job that it is supposed to do",
    backstory=dedent(
        """
        You are a Chief Software Quality Control Engineer at a leading
        tech think tank. You are responsible for ensuring that the code
        that is written does the job that it is supposed to do.
        You are responsible for checking the code for errors and ensuring
        that it is of the highest quality.
        """
    ),
    allow_delegation=True,              ⟵——| Only the chief QA engineer
    verbose=True,                            can delegate tasks.
)
```

Scrolling down in the file will display the agent tasks, as shown in listing 4.18. The task descriptions and expected output should be easy to follow. Again, each agent has a specific task to provide better context when working to complete the task.

Listing 4.18   `crewai_coding_crew.py` (task section)

```
code_task = Task(
    description=f"""
You will create a game using python, these are the instructions:
        Instructions
        ------------
        {game}                                              ⟵
        You will write the code for the game using python.""",
    expected_output="Your Final answer must be the
⇒ full python code, only the python code and nothing else.",
    agent=senior_engineer_agent,
)                                              The game instructions
                                            are substituted into the
qa_task = Task(                                prompt using Python
    description=f"""You are helping create a game     formatting.
⇒ using python, these are the instructions:
        Instructions
        ------------
        {game}                                              ⟵
        Using the code you got, check for errors. Check for logic errors,
        syntax errors, missing imports, variable declarations,
mismatched brackets,
        and security vulnerabilities.""",
    expected_output="Output a list of issues you found in the code.",
    agent=qa_engineer_agent,
)

evaluate_task = Task(
    description=f"""You are helping create a game
⇒ using python, these are the instructions:
        Instructions
        ------------
        {game}                                              ⟵
```

```
        You will look over the code to insure that it is complete and
        does the job that it is supposed to do. """,
    expected_output="Your Final answer must be the
⇒  corrected a full python code, only the python code and nothing else.",
    agent=chief_qa_engineer_agent,
)
```

Finally, we can see how this comes together by going to the bottom of the file, as shown in listing 4.19. This crew configuration is much like what we've seen before. Each agent and task are added, as well as the verbose and process attributes. For this example, we'll continue to use sequential methods.

Listing 4.19   `crewai_coding_crew.py` (crew section)

```
crew = Crew(
    agents=[senior_engineer_agent,
            qa_engineer_agent,
            chief_qa_engineer_agent],
    tasks=[code_task, qa_task, evaluate_task],
    verbose=2,
    process=Process.sequential,          ⟵——  Process is sequential.
)


# Get your crew to work!                        No additional context is
result = crew.kickoff()              ⟵|         provided in the kickoff.


print("#####################")
print(result)
```

When you run the VS Code (F5) file, you'll be prompted to enter the instructions for writing a game. Enter some instructions, perhaps the snake game or another game you choose. Then, let the agents work, and observe what they produce.

With the addition of the chief QA engineer, the results will generally look better than what was produced with AutoGen, at least out of the box. If you review the code, you'll see that it generally follows good patterns and, in some cases, may even include tests and unit tests.

Before we finish the chapter, we'll make one last change to the crew's processing pattern. Previously, we employed sequential processing, as shown in figure 4.10. Figure 4.12 shows what hierarchical processing looks like in CrewAI.

Adding this manager is a relatively simple process. Listing 4.20 shows the additional code changes to a new file that uses the coding crew in a hierarchical method. Aside from importing a class for connecting to OpenAI from LangChain, the other addition is adding this class as the crew manger, `manager_llm`.

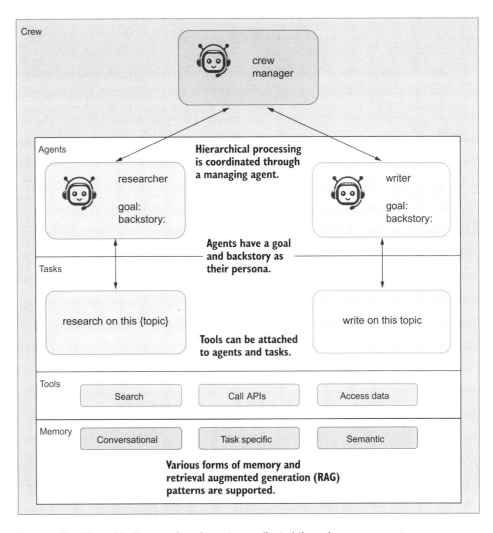

Figure 4.12   Hierarchical processing of agents coordinated through a crew manager

Listing 4.20   `crewai_hierarchy.py` (crew manager sections)

```
from langchain_openai import ChatOpenAI

crew = Crew(
    agents=[senior_engineer_agent,
            qa_engineer_agent,
            chief_qa_engineer_agent],
    tasks=[code_task, qa_task, evaluate_task],
    verbose=2,
    process=Process.hierarchical,
    manager_llm=ChatOpenAI(
        temperature=0, model="gpt-4"
```

◁ **Imports the LLM connector from LangChain**

You must set a crew manager when selecting hierarchical processing.

◁ **Sets the crew manager to be the LLM connector**

```
    ),
)
```

> **You must set a crew manager when
> selecting hierarchical processing.**

Run this file in VS Code (F5). When prompted, enter a game you want to create. Try using the same game you tried with AutoGen; the snake game is also a good baseline example. Observe the agents work through the code and review it repeatedly for problems.

After you run the file, you can also jump on AgentOps to review the cost of this run. Chances are, it will cost over double what it would have without the agent manager. The output will also likely not be significantly better. This is the trap of building agent systems without understanding how quickly things can spiral.

An example of this spiral that often happens when agents continually iterate over the same actions is frequently repeating tasks. You can view this problem in AgentOps, as shown in figure 4.13, by viewing the Repeat Thoughts plot.

**Plot indicates the repetition
of the same thoughts in an
agent interaction.**

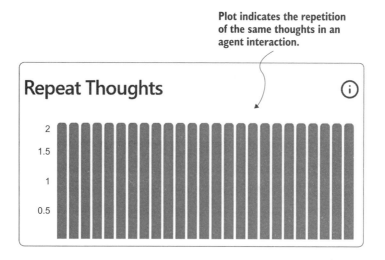

Figure 4.13   The repetition of thoughts as they occurred within an agent run

The Repeat Thoughts plot from AgentOps is an excellent way to measure the repetition your agent system encounters. Overly repetitive thought patterns typically mean the agent isn't being decisive enough and instead keeps trying to generate a different answer. If you encounter this problem, you want to change the agents' processing patterns, tasks, and goals. You may even want to alter the system's type and number of agents.

Multi-agent systems are an excellent way to break up work in terms of work patterns of jobs and tasks. Generally, the job role is allocated to an agent role/persona, and the tasks it needs to complete may be implicit, as in AutoGen, or more explicit, as in CrewAI.

In this chapter, we covered many useful tools and platforms that you can use right away to improve your work, life, and more. That completes our journey through multi-agent platforms, but it doesn't conclude our exploration and use of multiple agents, as we'll discover in later chapters.

4.6 *Exercises*

Use the following exercises to improve your knowledge of the material:

- *Exercise 1*—Basic Agent Communication with AutoGen
  Objective—Familiarize yourself with basic agent communications and setup in AutoGen.
  Tasks:
  - Set up AutoGen Studio on your local machine, following the instructions provided in this chapter.
  - Create a simple multi-agent system with a user proxy and two assistant agents.
  - Implement a basic task where the user proxy coordinates between the assistant agents to generate a simple text output, such as summarizing a short paragraph.
- *Exercise 2*—Implementing Advanced Agent Skills in AutoGen Studio
  Objective—Enhance agent capabilities by adding advanced skills.
  Tasks:
  - Develop and integrate a new skill into an AutoGen agent that allows it to fetch and display real-time data from a public API (e.g., weather information or stock prices).
  - Ensure the agent can ask for user preferences (e.g., city for weather, type of stocks) and display the fetched data accordingly.
- *Exercise 3*—Role-Based Task Management with CrewAI
  Objective—Explore role-based task management in CrewAI.
  Tasks:
  - Design a CrewAI setup where multiple agents are assigned specific roles (e.g., data fetcher, analyzer, presenter).
  - Configure a task sequence where the data fetcher collects data, the analyzer processes the data, and the presenter generates a report.
  - Execute the sequence and observe the flow of information and task delegation among agents.
- *Exercise 4*—Multi-Agent Collaboration in Group Chat Using AutoGen
  Objective—Understand and implement a group chat system in AutoGen to facilitate agent collaboration.

Tasks:

- Set up a scenario where multiple agents need to collaborate to solve a complex problem (e.g., planning an itinerary for a business trip).
- Use the group chat feature to allow agents to share information, ask questions, and provide updates to each other.
- Monitor the agents' interactions and effectiveness in collaborative problem solving.

■ *Exercise 5*—Adding and Testing Observability with AgentOps in CrewAI

Objective—Implement and evaluate the observability of agents using AgentOps in a CrewAI environment.

Tasks:

- Integrate AgentOps into a CrewAI multi-agent system.
- Design a task for the agents that involves significant computation or data processing (e.g., analyzing customer reviews to determine sentiment trends).
- Use AgentOps to monitor the performance, cost, and output accuracy of the agents. Identify any potential inefficiencies or errors in agent interactions.

Summary

- AutoGen, developed by Microsoft, is a conversational multi-agent platform that employs a variety of agent types, such as user proxies and assistant agents, to facilitate task execution through natural language interactions.
- AutoGen Studio acts as a development environment that allows users to create, test, and manage multi-agent systems, enhancing the usability of AutoGen.
- AutoGen supports multiple communication patterns, including group chats and hierarchical and proxy communications. Proxy communication involves a primary agent (proxy) that interfaces between the user and other agents to streamline task completion.
- CrewAI offers a structured approach to building multi-agent systems with a focus on enterprise applications. It emphasizes role-based and autonomous agent functionalities, allowing for flexible, sequential, or hierarchical task management.
- Practical exercises in the chapter illustrate how to set up and use AutoGen Studio, including installing necessary components and running basic multi-agent systems.
- Agents in AutoGen can be equipped with specific skills to perform tasks such as code generation, image analysis, and data retrieval, thereby broadening their application scope.
- CrewAI is distinguished by its ability to structure agent interactions more rigidly than AutoGen, which can be advantageous in settings that require precise and controlled agent behavior.
- CrewAI supports integrating memory and tools for agents to consume through task completion.

- CrewAI supports integration with observability tools such as AgentOps, which provides insights into agent performance, interaction efficiency, and cost management.
- AgentOps is an agent observability platform that can help you easily monitor extensive agent interactions.

Empowering agents with actions

5

This chapter covers

- How an agent acts outside of itself using actions
- Defining and using OpenAI functions
- The Semantic Kernel and how to use semantic functions
- Synergizing semantic and native functions
- Instantiating a GPT interface with Semantic Kernel

In this chapter, we explore actions through the use of functions and how agents can use them as well. We'll start by looking at OpenAI function calling and then quickly move on to another project from Microsoft called Semantic Kernel (SK), which we'll use to build and manage skills and functions for agents or as agents.

We'll finish the chapter using SK to host our first agent system. This will be a complete chapter with plenty of annotated code examples.

5.1   Defining agent actions

ChatGPT plugins were first introduced to provide a session with abilities, skills, or tools. With a plugin, you can search the web or create spreadsheets or graphs. Plugins provide ChatGPT with the means to extend the platform.

Figure 5.1 shows how a ChatGPT plugin works. In this example, a new movie recommender plugin has been installed in ChatGPT. When a user asks ChatGPT to recommend a new movie, the large language model (LLM) recognizes that it has a plugin to manage that action. It then breaks down the user request into actionable parameters, which it passes to the new movie recommender.

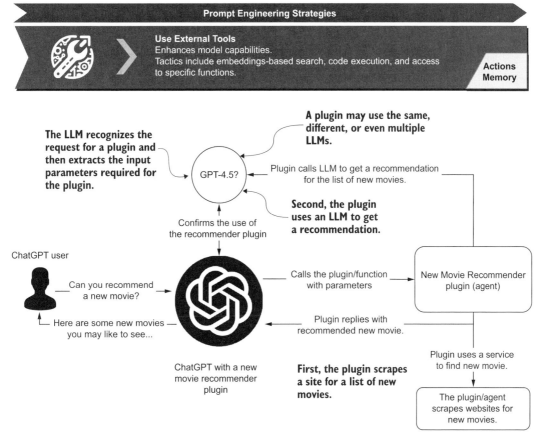

Figure 5.1   How a ChatGPT plugin operates and how plugins and other external tools (e.g., APIs) align with the Use External Tools prompt engineering strategy

The recommender then scrapes a website showcasing new movies and appends that information to a new prompt request to an LLM. With this information, the LLM responds to the recommender, which passes this back to ChatGPT. ChatGPT then responds to the user with the recommended request.

We can think of plugins as proxies for actions. A plugin generally encapsulates one or more abilities, such as calling an API or scraping a website. Actions, therefore, are extensions of plugins—they give a plugin its abilities.

AI agents can be considered plugins and consumers of plugins, tools, skills, and other agents. Adding skills, functions, and tools to an agent/plugin allows it to execute well-defined actions—figure 5.2 highlights where agent actions occur and their interaction with LLMs and other systems.

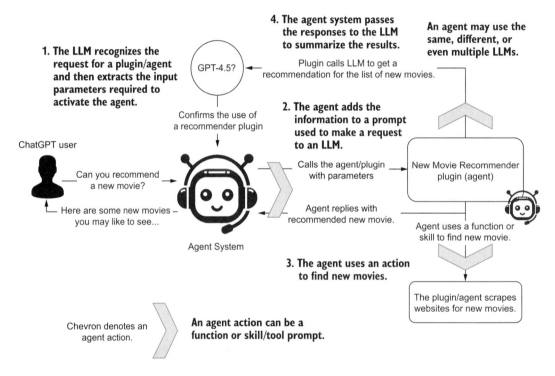

Figure 5.2   How an agent uses actions to perform external tasks

An agent action is an ability that allows it to use a function, skill, or tool. What gets confusing is that different frameworks use different terminology. We'll define an action as anything an agent can do to establish some basic definitions.

ChatGPT plugins and functions represent an actionable ability that ChatGPT or an agent system can use to perform additional actions. Now let's examine the basis for OpenAI plugins and the function definition.

5.2 Executing OpenAI functions

OpenAI, with the enablement of plugins, introduced a structure specification for defining the interface between functions/plugins an LLM could action. This specification is becoming a standard that LLM systems can follow to provide actionable systems.

These same function definitions are now also being used to define plugins for ChatGPT and other systems. Next, we'll explore how to use functions directly with an LLM call.

5.2.1 Adding functions to LLM API calls

Figure 5.3 demonstrates how an LLM recognizes and uses the function definition to cast its response as the function call.

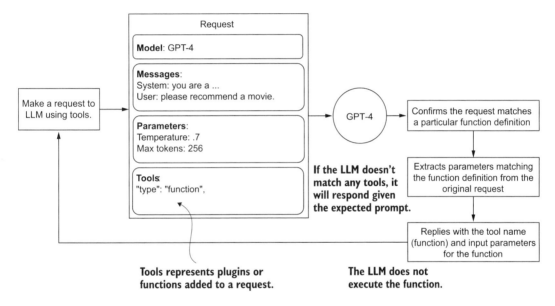

Figure 5.3 How a single LLM request, including tools, gets interpreted by an LLM

Listing 5.1 shows the details of an LLM API call using tools and a function definition. Adding a function definition allows the LLM to reply regarding the function's input parameters. This means the LLM will identify the correct function and parse the relevant parameters for the user's request.

Listing 5.1 first_function.py (API call)

```
response = client.chat.completions.create(
        model="gpt-4-1106-preview",
        messages=[{"role": "system",
                   "content": "You are a helpful assistant."},
                  {"role": "user", "content": user_message}],
```

```
        temperature=0.7,                                    New parameter called tools
        tools=[
            {
                "type": "function",                         Sets the type of tool to function
                "function": {
                    "name": "recommend",
                    "description": "Provide a … topic.",     Provides an excellent
                    "parameters": {                          description of what
                        "type": "object",                    the function does
                        "properties": {                     Defines the type of parameters
                            "topic": {                       for input; an object represents
                                "type": "string",            a JSON document.
                                "description":
                                    "The topic,… for.",
                            },                               Excellent
                            "rating": {                      descriptions
                                "type": "string",            for each input
                                "description":               parameter
                            "The rating … given.",
                                "enum": ["good",
                                        "bad",
                                        "terrible"]          You can even
                            },                               describe in terms
                        },                                   of enumerations.
                        "required": ["topic"],
                    },
                },
            }
        ]
    )
```

To see how this works, open Visual Studio Code (VS Code) to the book's source code folder: `chapter_4/first_function.py`. It's a good practice to open the relevant chapter folder in VS Code to create a new Python environment and install the `requirements.txt` file. If you need assistance with this, consult appendix B.

Before starting, correctly set up an `.env` file in the `chapter_4` folder with your API credentials. Function calling is an extra capability provided by the LLM commercial service. At the time of writing, this feature wasn't an option for open source LLM deployments.

Next, we'll look at the bottom of the code in `first_function.py`, as shown in listing 5.2. Here are just two examples of calls made to an LLM using the request previously specified in listing 5.1. Here, each request shows the generated output from running the example.

Listing 5.2 `first_function.py` (exercising the API)

```
user = "Can you please recommend me a time travel movie?"
response = ask_chatgpt(user)                        Previously
print(response)                                     defined function
```

```
###Output
Function(arguments='{"topic":"time travel movie"}',
                    name='recommend')
```

> Returned in
> the name of the
> function to call
> and the extracted
> input parameters

```
user = "Can you please recommend me a good time travel movie?"
response = ask_chatgpt(user)
print(response)
```

> Previously
> defined function

```
###Output
Function(arguments='{"topic":"time travel movie",
                    "rating":"good"}',
 name='recommend')
```

> Returned in the name of the function to
> call and the extracted input parameters

Run the `first_function.py` Python script in VS Code using the debugger (F5) or the terminal to see the same results. Here, the LLM parses the input request to match any registered tools. In this case, the tool is the single function definition, that is, the recommended function. The LLM extracts the input parameters from this function and parses those from the request. Then, it replies with the named function and designated input parameters.

> **NOTE**   The actual function isn't being called. The LLM only returns the suggested function and the relevant input parameters. The name and parameters must be extracted and passed into a function matching the signature to act on the function. We'll look at an example of this in the next section.

5.2.2   *Actioning function calls*

Now that we understand that an LLM doesn't execute the function or plugin directly, we can look at an example that executes the tools. Keeping with the recommender theme, we'll look at another example that adds a Python function for simple recommendations.

Figure 5.4 shows how this simple example will work. We'll submit a single request that includes a tool function definition, asking for three recommendations. The LLM, in turn, will reply with the three function calls with input parameters (time travel, recipe, and gift). The results from executing the functions are then passed back to the LLM, which converts them back to natural language and returns a reply.

Now that we understand the example, open `parallel_functions.py` in VS Code. Listing 5.3 shows the Python function that you want to call to give recommendations.

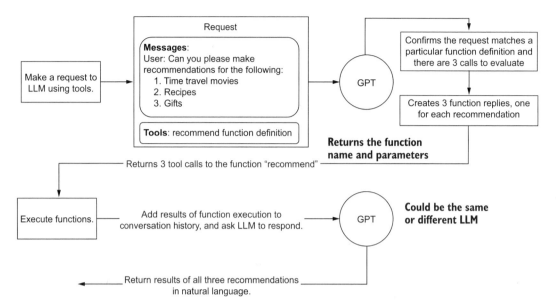

Figure 5.4   A sample request returns three tool function calls and then submits the results back to the LLM to return a natural language response.

Listing 5.3   `parallel_functions.py` (recommend function)

```
def recommend(topic, rating="good"):
    if "time travel" in topic.lower():
        return json.dumps({"topic": "time travel",
                           "recommendation": "Back to the Future",
                           "rating": rating})
    elif "recipe" in topic.lower():
        return json.dumps({"topic": "recipe",
                           "recommendation": "The best thing … ate.",
                           "rating": rating})
    elif "gift" in topic.lower():
        return json.dumps({"topic": "gift",
                           "recommendation": "A glorious new...",
                           "rating": rating})
    else:
        return json.dumps({"topic": topic,
                           "recommendation": "unknown"})
```

Checks to see if the string is contained within the topic input

If no topic is detected, returns the default

Returns a JSON object

Next, we'll look at the function called `run_conversation`, where all the work starts with the request construction.

Listing 5.4   `parallel_functions.py` (`run_conversation`, request)

```
user = """Can you please make recommendations for the following:
1. Time travel movies
2. Recipes
```

```
3. Gifts"""
messages = [{"role": "user", "content": user}]
tools = [
    {
        "type": "function",
        "function": {
            "name": "recommend",
            "description":
                "Provide a recommendation for any topic.",
            "parameters": {
                "type": "object",
                "properties": {
                    "topic": {
                        "type": "string",
                        "description":
                            "The topic, … recommendation for.",
                    },
                    "rating": {
                        "type": "string",
                        "description": "The rating … was given.",
                        "enum": ["good", "bad", "terrible"]
                    },
                },
                "required": ["topic"],
            },
        },
    }
]
```

The user message asks for three recommendations.

Note that there is no system message.

Adds the function definition to the tools part of the request

Listing 5.5 shows the request being made, which we've covered before, but there are a few things to note. This call uses a lower model such as GPT-3.5 because delegating functions is a more straightforward task and can be done using older, cheaper, less sophisticated language models.

Listing 5.5 `parallel_functions.py (run_conversation, API call)`

```
response = client.chat.completions.create(
    model="gpt-3.5-turbo-1106",
    messages=messages,
    tools=tools,
    tool_choice="auto",
)
response_message = response.choices[0].message
```

LLMs that delegate to functions can be simpler models.

Adds the messages and tools definitions

auto is the default.

The returned message from the LLM

At this point, after the API call, the response should hold the information for the required function calls. Remember, we asked the LLM to provide us with three recommendations, which means it should also provide us with three function call outputs, as shown in the following listing.

Listing 5.6   `parallel_functions.py` (`run_conversation`, `tool_calls`)

```
tool_calls = response_message.tool_calls          │ If the response contains
if tool_calls:                                    │ tool calls, execute them.
    available_functions = {
        "recommend": recommend,                        │ Only one function but
    }                                              ◁───┘ could contain several
    # Step 4: send the info for each function call and function response to
the model
    for tool_call in tool_calls:              ◁──┐ Loops through the calls and replays
        function_name = tool_call.function.name  └ the content back to the LLM
        function_to_call = available_functions[function_name]
        function_args = json.loads(tool_call.function.arguments)
        function_response = function_to_call(
            topic=function_args.get("topic"),      ◁──┐ Executes the recommend
            rating=function_args.get("rating"),       │ function from extracted
        )                                             │ parameters
        messages.append(                    ◁──┐
            {                                   │ Appends the results of
                "tool_call_id": tool_call.id,   │ each function call to the
                "role": "tool",                 │ set of messages
                "name": function_name,
                "content": function_response,
            }
        )  # extend conversation with function response
    second_response = client.chat.completions.create(  ◁──┐
        model="gpt-3.5-turbo-1106",                        │ Sends another request
        messages=messages,                                 │ to the LLM with updated
    )                                                      │ information and returns
    return second_response.choices[0].message.content  ◁──┘ the message reply
```

The tool call outputs and the calls to the recommender function results are appended to the messages. Notice how messages now also contain the history of the first call. This is then passed back to the LLM to construct a reply in natural language.

Debug this example in VS Code by pressing the F5 key with the file open. The following listing shows the output of running `parallel_functions.py`.

Listing 5.7   `parallel_functions.py` (output)

```
Here are some recommendations for you:

1. Time travel movies: "Back to the Future"
2. Recipes: "The best thing you ever ate."
3. Gifts: "A glorious new..." (the recommendation was cut off, so I
couldn't provide the full recommendation)

I hope you find these recommendations helpful! Let me know if you need
more information.
```

This completes this simple demonstration. For more advanced applications, the functions could do any number of things, from scraping websites to calling search engines to completing far more complex tasks.

Functions are an excellent way to cast outputs for a particular task. However, the work of handling functions or tools and making secondary calls can be done in a cleaner and more efficient way. The following section will uncover a more robust system of adding actions to agents.

5.3 *Introducing Semantic Kernel*

Semantic Kernel (SK) is another open source project from Microsoft intended to help build AI applications, which we call agents. At its core, the project is best used to define actions, or what the platform calls *semantic plugins*, which are wrappers for skills and functions.

Figure 5.5 shows how the SK can be used as a plugin and a consumer of OpenAI plugins. The SK relies on the OpenAI plugin definition to define a plugin. That way, it can consume and publish itself or other plugins to other systems.

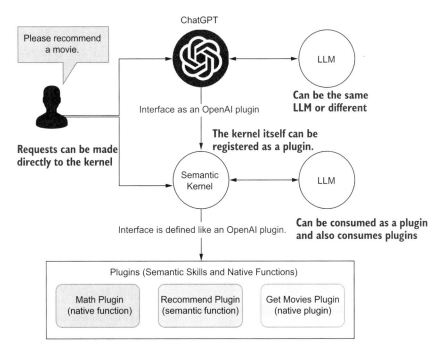

Figure 5.5   How the Semantic Kernel integrates as a plugin and can also consume plugins

An OpenAI plugin definition maps precisely to the function definitions in listing 5.4. This means that SK is the orchestrator of API tool calls, aka plugins. That also means that SK can help organize multiple plugins with a chat interface or an agent.

NOTE   The team at SK originally labeled the functional modules as *skills*. However, to be more consistent with OpenAI, they have since renamed *skills* to *plugins*. What is more confusing is that the code still uses the term *skills*. Therefore, throughout this chapter, we'll use *skills* and *plugins* to mean the same thing.

SK is a useful tool for managing multiple plugins (actions for agents) and, as we'll see later, can also assist with memory and planning tools. For this chapter, we'll focus on the actions/plugins. In the next section, we look at how to get started using SK.

5.3.1 Getting started with SK semantic functions

SK is easy to install and works within Python, Java, and C#. This is excellent news as it also allows plugins developed in one language to be consumed in a different language. However, you can't yet develop a native function in one language and use it in another.

We'll continue from where we left off for the Python environment using the `chapter_4` workspace in VS Code. Be sure you have a workspace configured if you want to explore and run any examples.

Listing 5.8 shows how to install SK from a terminal within VS Code. You can also install the SK extension for VS Code. The extension can be a helpful tool to create plugins/skills, but it isn't required.

Listing 5.8   Installing Semantic Kernel

```
pip uninstall semantic-kernel          ◁—— Uninstalls any previous installations of SK

git clone https://github.com/microsoft/semantic-kernel.git   ◁─┐ Clones the
                                                               │ repository to
cd semantic-kernel/python     ◁—— Changes to the source folder │ a local folder

pip install -e .       ◁─┐ Installs the editable package
                         │ from the source folder
```

Once you finish the installation, open `SK_connecting.py` in VS Code. Listing 5.9 shows a demo of running an example quickly through SK. The example creates a chat completion service using either OpenAI or Azure OpenAI.

Listing 5.9   `SK_connecting.py`

```
import semantic_kernel as sk
                                         ┐ Sets the service you're using
selected_service = "OpenAI"            ◁─┘ (OpenAI or Azure OpenAI)
kernel = sk.Kernel()                   ◁─┐ Creates the
                                         │ kernel
service_id = None
if selected_service == "OpenAI":
    from semantic_kernel.connectors.ai.open_ai import OpenAIChatCompletion

    api_key, org_id = sk.openai_settings_from_dot_env()   ◁─┐ Loads secrets
    service_id = "oai_chat_gpt"                            │ from the .env file
    kernel.add_service(                                    │ and sets them on
        OpenAIChatCompletion(                              │ the chat service
            service_id=service_id,
            ai_model_id="gpt-3.5-turbo-1106",
```

```
            api_key=api_key,
            org_id=org_id,
        ),
    )
elif selected_service == "AzureOpenAI":
    from semantic_kernel.connectors.ai.open_ai import AzureChatCompletion

    deployment, api_key, endpoint =
    sk.azure_openai_settings_from_dot_env()        ⟵  Loads secrets
    service_id = "aoai_chat_completion"                from the .env file
    kernel.add_service(                                and sets them on
        AzureChatCompletion(                           the chat service
            service_id=service_id,
            deployment_name=deployment,
            endpoint=endpoint,
            api_key=api_key,
        ),
    )


#This function is currently broken
async def run_prompt():
    result = await kernel.invoke_prompt(
            ➥ prompt="recommend a movie about    │  Invokes the
    time travel")                                 │  prompt
    print(result)

# Use asyncio.run to execute the async function   │  Calls the function
asyncio.run(run_prompt())                          │  asynchronously

###Output
One highly recommended time travel movie is "Back to the Future" (1985)
directed by Robert Zemeckis. This classic film follows the adventures of
teenager Marty McFly (Michael J. Fox)…
```

Run the example by pressing F5 (debugging), and you should see an output similar to listing 5.9. This example demonstrates how a semantic function can be created with SK and executed. A semantic function is the equivalent of a prompt template in prompt flow, another Microsoft tool. In this example, we define a simple prompt as a function.

It's important to note that this semantic function isn't defined as a plugin. However, the kernel can create the function as a self-contained semantic element that can be executed against an LLM. Semantic functions can be used alone or registered as plugins, as you'll see later. Let's jump to the next section, where we introduce contextual variables.

5.3.2 *Semantic functions and context variables*

Expanding on the previous example, we can look at adding contextual variables to the semantic function. This pattern of adding placeholders to prompt templates is one we'll review over and over. In this example, we look at a prompt template that has placeholders for subject, genre, format, and custom.

Open `SK_context_variables.py` in VS Code, as shown in the next listing. The prompt is equivalent to setting aside a `system` and `user` section of the prompt.

Listing 5.10 `SK_context_variables.py`

```
#top section omitted...
prompt = """                              ◁———  Defines a prompt
system:                                           with placeholders

You have vast knowledge of everything and can recommend anything provided
you are given the following criteria, the subject, genre, format and any
other custom information.

user:
Please recommend a {{$format}} with the subject {{$subject}} and {{$genre}}.
Include the following custom information: {{$custom}}
"""

prompt_template_config = sk.PromptTemplateConfig(          ◁———  Configures a
    template=prompt,                                             prompt template
    name="tldr",                                                 and input variable
    template_format="semantic-kernel",                           definitions
    input_variables=[
        InputVariable(
            name="format",
            description="The format to recommend",
            is_required=True
        ),
        InputVariable(
            name="suject",
            description="The subject to recommend",
            is_required=True
        ),
        InputVariable(
            name="genre",
            description="The genre to recommend",
            is_required=True
        ),
        InputVariable(
            name="custom",
            description="Any custom information [CA]
                    to enhance the recommendation",
            is_required=True,
        ),
    ],
    execution_settings=execution_settings,
)                                                         Creates a kernel
                                                          function from
recommend_function = kernel.create_function_from_prompt(  ◁———  the prompt
    prompt_template_config=prompt_template_config,
    function_name="Recommend_Movies",
    plugin_name="Recommendation",
)
```

```
async def run_recommendation(          ⟵──┐  Creates an asynchronous
    subject="time travel",                │  function to wrap the
    format="movie",                        │  function call
    genre="medieval",
          custom="must be a comedy"
):
    recommendation = await kernel.invoke(
        recommend_function,
        sk.KernelArguments(subject=subject,
                        format=format,
                        genre=genre,
                        custom=custom),      ⟵──┐
    )                                           │  Sets the
    print(recommendation)                       │  kernel
                                                │  function
                                                │  arguments
# Use asyncio.run to execute the async function
asyncio.run(run_recommendation())      ⟵──┘

###Output
One movie that fits the criteria of being about time travel, set in a
medieval period, and being a comedy is "The Visitors" (Les Visiteurs)
from 1993. This French film, directed by Jean-Marie Poiré, follows a
knight and his squire who are transported to the modern era by a
wizard's spell gone wrong.…
```

Go ahead and debug this example (F5), and wait for the output to be generated. That is the basis for setting up SK and creating and exercising semantic functions. In the next section, we move on to see how a semantic function can be registered as a skill/plugin.

5.4 Synergizing semantic and native functions

Semantic functions encapsulate a prompt/profile and execute through interaction with an LLM. Native functions are the encapsulation of code that may perform anything from scraping websites to searching the web. Both semantic and native functions can register as plugins/skills in the SK kernel.

A function, semantic or native, can be registered as a plugin and used the same way we registered the earlier function directly with our API calls. When a function is registered as a plugin, it becomes accessible to chat or agent interfaces, depending on the use case. The next section looks at how a semantic function is created and registered with the kernel.

5.4.1 Creating and registering a semantic skill/plugin

The VS Code extension for SK provides helpful tools for creating plugins/skills. In this section, we'll use the SK extension to create a plugin/skill and then edit the components of that extension. After that, we'll register and execute the plugin in the SK.

Figure 5.6 shows the process for creating a new skill within VS Code using the SK extension. (Refer to appendix B for directions if you need to install this extension.) You'll then be given the option for the skill/plugin folder to place the function. Always group functions that are similar together. After creating a skill, enter the name and description of the function you want to develop. Be sure to describe the function as if the LLM were going to use it.

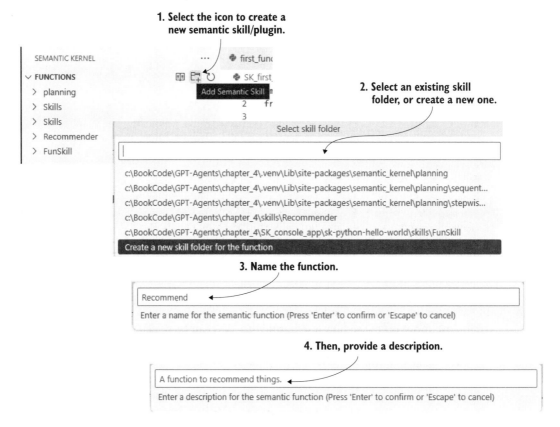

Figure 5.6   The process of creating a new skill/plugin

You can see the completed skills and functions by opening the `skills/plugin` folder and reviewing the files. We'll follow the previously constructed example, so open the `skills/Recommender/Recommend_Movies` folder, as shown in figure 5.7. Inside this folder is a `config.json` file, the function description, and the semantic function/prompt in a file called `skprompt.txt`.

Listing 5.11 shows the contents of the semantic function definition, also known as the plugin definition. Note that the type is marked as `completion` and not of type `function` because this is a semantic function. We would define a native function as a type function.

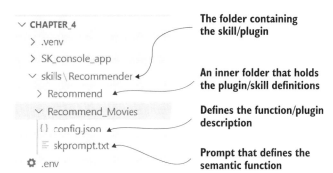

Figure 5.7   The file and folder structure of a semantic function skill/plugin

Listing 5.11 `Recommend_Movies/config.json`

```
{
    "schema": 1,
    "type": "completion",
    "description": "A function to recommend movies based on users list of
previously seen movies.",
    "completion": {
        "max_tokens": 256,
        "temperature": 0,
        "top_p": 0,
        "presence_penalty": 0,
        "frequency_penalty": 0
    },
    "input": {
        "parameters": [
            {
                "name": "input",
                "description": "The users list of previously seen movies.",
                "defaultValue": ""
            }
        ]
    },
    "default_backends": []
}
```

Semantic functions are functions of type completion.

We can also set the completion parameters for how the function is called.

Defines the parameters input into the semantic function

Next, we can look at the definition of the semantic function prompt, as shown in listing 5.12. The format is a little different, but what we see here matches the earlier examples using templating. This prompt recommends movies based on a list of movies the user has previously seen.

Listing 5.12 `Recommend_Movies/skprompt.txt`

```
You are a wise movie recommender and you have been asked to recommend a
movie to a user.
You are provided a list of movies that the user has watched before.
You want to recommend a movie that the user has not watched before.
[INPUT]
```

```
{{$input}}
[END INPUT]
```

Now, we'll dive into the code that loads the skill/plugin and executes it in a simple example. Open the `SK_first_skill.py` file in VS Code. The following listing shows an abridged version highlighting the new sections.

Listing 5.13 SK_first_skill.py (abridged listing)

```
kernel = sk.Kernel()

plugins_directory = "plugins"

recommender = kernel.import_plugin_from_prompt_directory(
    plugins_directory,
    "Recommender",                                          ◁─┤ Loads the prompt from
)                                                              the plugins folder

recommend = recommender["Recommend_Movies"]
                                                            ◁─┤ List of user's previously
seen_movie_list = [                                            seen movies
    "Back to the Future",
    "The Terminator",
    "12 Monkeys",
    "Looper",
    "Groundhog Day",
    "Primer",
    "Donnie Darko",
    "Interstellar",
    "Time Bandits",
    "Doctor Strange",
]


async def run():
    result = await kernel.invoke(                           ┤ Input is set to joined
        recommend,                                            list of seen movies.
        sk.KernelArguments(
            settings=execution_settings, input=", ".join(seen_movie_list)  ◁─┤
        ),
    )
    print(result)


asyncio.run(run())                     ◁─┤ Function is executed
                                           asynchronously.

###Output
Based on the list of movies you've provided, it seems you have an
interest in science fiction, time travel, and mind-bending narratives.
Given that you've watched a mix of classics and modern films in this
genre, I would recommend the following movie that you have not watched
before:

"Edge of Tomorrow" (also known as "Live Die Repeat: Edge of Tomorrow")…
```

The code loads the skill/plugin from the `skills` directory and the `plugin` folder. When a skill is loaded into the kernel and not just created, it becomes a registered plugin. That means it can be executed directly as is done here or through an LLM chat conversation via the plugin interface.

Run the code (F5), and you should see an output like listing 5.13. We now have a simple semantic function that can be hosted as a plugin. However, this function requires users to input a complete list of movies they have watched. We'll look at a means to fix this by introducing native functions in the next section.

5.4.2 Applying native functions

As stated, native functions are code that can do anything. In the following example, we'll introduce a native function to assist the semantic function we built earlier.

This native function will load a list of movies the user has previously seen, from a file. While this function introduces the concept of memory, we'll defer that discussion until chapter 8. Consider this new native function as any code that could virtually do anything.

Native functions can be created and registered using the SK extension. For this example, we'll create a native function directly in code to make the example easier to follow.

Open `SK_native_functions.py` in VS Code. We'll start by looking at how the native function is defined. A native function is typically defined within a class, which simplifies managing and instantiating native functions.

Listing 5.14 `SK_native_functions.py` (MySeenMovieDatabase)

```
class MySeenMoviesDatabase:
    """
    Description: Manages the list of users seen movies.     ◁─┐   Provides a description
    """                                                           for the container class
    @kernel_function(                                        ◁──   Uses a decorator to
        description="Loads a list of movies … user has already seen",   provide function
        name="LoadSeenMovies",                                    description and name
    )
    def load_seen_movies(self) -> str:                       ◁──   The actual function
        try:                                                       returns a list of movies in a
            with open("seen_movies.txt", 'r') as file:       ◁──   comma-separated string.
                lines = [line.strip() for line in file.readlines()]
                comma_separated_string = ', '.join(lines)
            return comma_separated_string                          Loads seen
        except Exception as e:                                     movies from
            print(f"Error reading file: {e}")                      the text file
            return None
```

With the native function defined, we can see how it's used by scrolling down in the file, as shown in the following listing.

Listing 5.15   `SK_native_functions` (remaining code)

```
plugins_directory = "plugins"

recommender = kernel.import_plugin_from_prompt_directory(
    plugins_directory,
    "Recommender",                                          ⟵  Loads the semantic function
)                                                               as shown previously

recommend = recommender["Recommend_Movies"]
                                                            ⟵  Imports the skill
seen_movies_plugin = kernel.import_plugin_from_object(          into the kernel and
    MySeenMoviesDatabase(), "SeenMoviesPlugin"                  registers the function
)                                                               as a plugin

load_seen_movies = seen_movies_plugin["LoadSeenMovies"]   ⟵   Loads the native
                                                               function
async def show_seen_movies():
    seen_movie_list = await load_seen_movies(kernel)       ⟵  Executes the
    return seen_movie_list                                     function and returns
                                                               the list as a string
seen_movie_list = asyncio.run(show_seen_movies())
print(seen_movie_list)

async def run():                             ⟵
    result = await kernel.invoke(
        recommend,
        sk.KernelArguments(                      Wraps the
            settings=execution_settings,         plugin call in an
            input=seen_movie_list),              asynchronous
    )                                            function and
    print(result)                               executes


asyncio.run(run())                           ⟵

###Output
The Matrix, The Matrix Reloaded, The Matrix Revolutions, The Matrix
Resurrections - output from print statement
Based on your interest in the "The Matrix" series, it seems you enjoy
science fiction films with a strong philosophical undertone and action
elements. Given that you've watched all
```

One important aspect to note is how the native function was imported into the kernel. The act of importing to the kernel registers that function as a plugin/skill. This means the function can be used as a skill from the kernel through other conversations or interactions. We'll see how to embed a native function within a semantic function in the next section.

5.4.3 *Embedding native functions within semantic functions*

There are plenty of powerful features within SK, but one beneficial feature is the ability to embed native or semantic functions within other semantic functions. The following listing shows how a native function can be embedded within a semantic function.

Listing 5.16 `SK_semantic_native_functions.py` **(skprompt)**

```
sk_prompt = """
You are a wise movie recommender and you have been asked to recommend a
movie to a user.
You have a list of movies that the user has watched before.
You want to recommend a movie that
the user has not watched before.
Movie List: {{MySeenMoviesDatabase.LoadSeenMovies}}.
"""
```

The exact instruction text as previous

The native function is referenced and identified by class name and function name.

The next example, `SK_semantic_native_functions.py`, uses inline native and semantic functions. Open the file in VS Code, and the following listing shows the code to create, register, and execute the functions.

Listing 5.17 `SK_semantic_native_functions.py` **(abridged)**

```
prompt_template_config = sk.PromptTemplateConfig(
    template=sk_prompt,
    name="tldr",
    template_format="semantic-kernel",
    execution_settings=execution_settings,
)
```

Creates the prompt template config for the prompt

```
recommend_function = kernel.create_function_from_prompt(
    prompt_template_config=prompt_template_config,
    function_name="Recommend_Movies",
    plugin_name="Recommendation",
)
```

Creates an inline semantic function from the prompt

```
async def run_recommendation():
    recommendation = await kernel.invoke(
        recommend_function,
        sk.KernelArguments(),
    )
    print(recommendation)
```

Executes the semantic function asynchronously

```
# Use asyncio.run to execute the async function
asyncio.run(run_recommendation())
###Output
Based on the list provided, it seems the user is a fan of the Matrix
franchise. Since they have watched all four existing Matrix movies, I
would recommend a...
```

Run the code, and you should see an output like listing 5.17. One important aspect to note is that the native function is registered with the kernel, but the semantic function is not. This is important because function creation doesn't register a function.

For this example to work correctly, the native function must be registered with the kernel, which uses the `import_plugin` function call—the first line in listing 5.17. However, the semantic function itself isn't registered. An easy way to register the function is to make it a plugin and import it.

These simple exercises showcase ways to integrate plugins and skills into chat or agent interfaces. In the next section, we'll look at a complete example demonstrating adding a plugin representing a service or GPT interface to a chat function.

5.5 *Semantic Kernel as an interactive service agent*

In chapter 1, we introduced the concept of the GPT interface—a new paradigm in connecting services and other components to LLMs via plugins and semantic layers. SK provides an excellent abstraction for converting any service to a GPT interface.

Figure 5.8 shows a GPT interface constructed around an API service called The Movie Database (TMDB; www.themoviedb.org). The TMDB site provides a free API that exposes information about movies and TV shows.

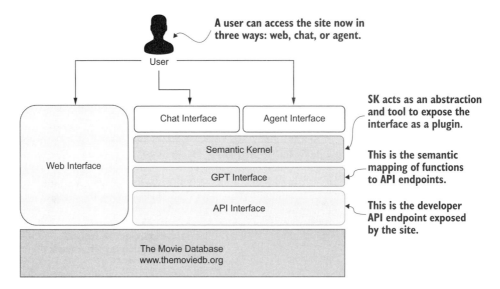

Figure 5.8   This layer architecture diagram shows the role of a GPT interface and the Semantic Kernel being exposed to chat or agent interfaces.

To follow along with the exercises in this section, you must register for a free account from TMDB and create an API key. Instructions for getting an API key can be found at the TMDB website (www.themoviedb.org) or by asking a GPT-4 turbo or a more recent LLM.

Over the next set of subsections, we'll create a GPT interface using an SK set of native functions. Then, we'll use the SK kernel to test the interface and, later in this chapter, implement it as plugins into a chat function. In the next section, we look at building a GPT interface against the TMDB API.

5.5.1 Building a semantic GPT interface

TMDB is an excellent service, but it provides no semantic services or services that can be plugged into ChatGPT or an agent. To do that, we must wrap the API calls that TMDB exposes in a semantic service layer.

A semantic service layer is a GPT interface that exposes functions through natural language. As discussed, to expose functions to ChatGPT or other interfaces such as agents, they must be defined as plugins. Fortunately, SK can create the plugins for us automatically, given that we write our semantic service layer correctly.

A native plugin or set of skills can act as a semantic layer. To create a native plugin, create a new plugin folder, and put a Python file holding a class containing the set of native functions inside that folder. The SK extension currently doesn't do this well, so manually creating the module works best.

Figure 5.9 shows the structure of the new plugin called `Movies` and the semantic service layer called `tmdb.py`. For native functions, the parent folder's name (`Movies`) is used in the import.

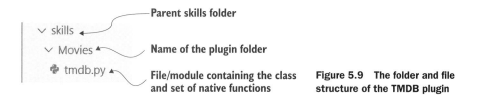

Figure 5.9   The folder and file structure of the TMDB plugin

Open the `tmdb.py` file in VS Code, and look at the top of the file, as shown in listing 5.18. This file contains a class called `TMDbService`, which exposes several functions that map to API endpoint calls. The idea is to map the various relevant API function calls in this semantic service layer. This will expose the functions as plugins for a chat or agent interface.

Listing 5.18   `tmdb.py` (top of file)

```
from semantic_kernel.functions import kernel_funct
import requests
import inspect


def print_function_call():
    #omitted …
```

Prints the calls to the functions for debugging

```
class TMDbService:
    def __init__(self):
        # enter your TMDb API key here
        self.api_key = "your-TMDb-api-key"

    @kernel_function(
        description="Gets the movie genre ID for a given genre name",
        name="get_movie_genre_id",
        input_description="The movie genre name of the genre_id to get",
        )
    def get_movie_genre_id(self, genre_name: str) -> str:
        print_function_call()
        base_url = "https://api.themoviedb.org/3"
        endpoint = f"{base_url}/genre/movie/list
                      ?api_key={self.api_key}&language=en-US"

        response = requests.get(endpoint)
        if response.status_code == 200:
            genres = response.json()['genres']
            for genre in genres:
                if genre_name.lower() in genre['name'].lower():
                    return str(genre['id'])
        return None
```

Top-level service and decorator used to describe the function (good descriptions are important)

Function wrapped in semantic wrapper; should return str

Calls the API endpoint, and, if good (code 200), checks for matching genre

Found the genre, returns the id

The bulk of the code for the TMDbService and the functions to call the TMDB endpoints was written with the help of GPT-4 Turbo. Then, each function was wrapped with the sk_function decorator to expose it semantically.

A few of the TMDB API calls have been mapped semantically. Listing 5.19 shows another example of a function exposed to the semantic service layer. This function pulls a current top 10 list of movies playing for a particular genre.

Listing 5.19 tmdb.py (get_top_movies_by_genre)

```
@kernel_function(
        description="""
Gets a list of currently playing movies for a given genre""",
        name="get_top_movies_by_genre",
        input_description="The genre of the movies to get",
        )
    def get_top_movies_by_genre(self, genre: str) -> str:
        print_function_call()
        genre_id = self.get_movie_genre_id(genre)
        if genre_id:
            base_url = "https://api.themoviedb.org/3"
            playing_movies_endpoint = f"{base_url}/movie/now_playing?
   api_key={self.api_key}&language=en-US"
            response = requests.get(
                        playing_movies_endpoint)
            if response.status_code != 200:
                return ""
```

Decorates the function with descriptions

Finds the genre id for the given genre name

Gets a list of currently playing movies

```
        playing_movies = response.json()['results'
        for movie in playing_movies:
            movie['genre_ids'] = [str(genre_id)
                ⟿ for genre_id in movie['genre_ids']]
        filtered_movies = [movie for movie
⟿ in playing_movies if genre_id
⟿ in movie['genre_ids']][:10]
        results = ", ".join([movie['title'] for movie in
    filtered_movies])
        return results
    else:
        return ""
```

Converts genre_ids to strings

Checks to see if the genre id matches movie genres

Look through the various other API calls mapped semantically. As you can see, there is a well-defined pattern for converting API calls to a semantic service. Before we run the full service, we'll test each of the functions in the next section.

5.5.2 Testing semantic services

In a real-world application, you'll likely want to write a complete set of unit or integration tests for each semantic service function. We won't do that here; instead, we'll write a quick helper script to test the various functions.

Open `test_tmdb_service.py` in VS Code, and review the code, as shown in listing 5.20. You can comment and uncomment any functions to test them in isolation. Be sure to have only one function uncommented at a time.

Listing 5.20 `test_tmdb_service.py`

```
import semantic_kernel as sk
from plugins.Movies.tmdb import TMDbService

async def main():                                          Instantiates
    kernel = sk.Kernel()                                   the kernel

    tmdb_service = kernel.import_plugin_from_object         Imports the
⟿ (TMDbService(), "TMDBService")                           plugin service

    print(
        await tmdb_service["get_movie_genre_id"](
            kernel, sk.KernelArguments(
                        genre_name="action")               Inputs parameter
        )                                                  to functions,
    )                                                      when needed
    print(
        await tmdb_service["get_tv_show_genre_id"](        Executes and
            kernel, sk.KernelArguments(                    tests the various
                        genre_name="action")               functions
        )
    )                                                      Inputs parameter
    print(                                                 to functions,
        await tmdb_service["get_top_movies_by_genre"](     when needed
            kernel, sk.KernelArguments(
```

Executes and tests the various functions

```
                                genre_name="action")          ◁──┐
        )                                                         │
    )              ◁──── Executes and tests the various functions │  Inputs parameter
    print(                                                        │  to functions,
        await tmdb_service["get_top_tv_shows_by_genre"](          │  when needed
            kernel, sk.KernelArguments(                           │
                        genre_name="action")          ◁──────────┘
        )
    )
    print(await tmdb_service["get_movie_genres"](
kernel, sk.KernelArguments()))                    ◁──┐ Executes and tests
    print(await tmdb_service["get_tv_show_genres"](      │ the various functions
kernel, sk.KernelArguments()))                    ◁──┘


# Run the main function
if __name__ == "__main__":
    import asyncio                        ┐  Executes main          Calls print
                                          │  asynchronously         function details
    asyncio.run(main())        ◁──────────┘                        to notify when
                                                                   the function is
                                                                   being called
###Output
Function name: get_top_tv_shows_by_genre                        ◁──┐
Arguments:                                                         │
  self = <skills.Movies.tmdb.TMDbService object at 0x00000159F52090C0>
  genre = action                                                   │
Function name: get_tv_show_genre_id                            ◁──┘
Arguments:
  self = <skills.Movies.tmdb.TMDbService object at 0x00000159F52090C0>
  genre_name = action
Arcane, One Piece, Rick and Morty, Avatar: The Last Airbender, Fullmetal
Alchemist: Brotherhood, Demon Slayer: Kimetsu no Yaiba, Invincible,
Attack on Titan, My Hero Academia, Fighting Spirit, The Owl House
```

The real power of SK is shown in this test. Notice how the TMDbService class is imported as a plugin, but we don't have to define any plugin configurations other than what we already did? By just writing one class that wrapped a few API functions, we've exposed part of the TMDB API semantically. Now, with the functions exposed, we can look at how they can be used as plugins for a chat interface in the next section.

5.5.3 *Interactive chat with the semantic service layer*

With the TMDB functions exposed semantically, we can move on to integrating them into a chat interface. This will allow us to converse naturally in this interface to get various information, such as current top movies.

Open SK_service_chat.py in VS Code. Scroll down to the start of the new section of code that creates the functions, as shown in listing 5.21. The functions created here are now exposed as plugins, except we filter out the chat function, which we don't want to expose as a plugin. The chat function here allows the user to converse directly with the LLM and shouldn't be a plugin.

Listing 5.21 `SK_service_chat.py` (function setup)

```
system_message = "You are a helpful AI assistant."

tmdb_service = kernel.import_plugin_from_object(        ← Imports the
TMDbService(), "TMDBService")                              TMDbService
                                                           as a plugin

# extracted section of code
execution_settings = sk_oai.OpenAIChatPromptExecutionSettings(
        service_id=service_id,
        ai_model_id=model_id,
        max_tokens=2000,
        temperature=0.7,
        top_p=0.8,
        tool_choice="auto",                             ← Configures the
        tools=get_tool_call_object(                        execution settings and
            kernel, {"exclude_plugin": ["ChatBot"]}),      adds filtered tools
    )

prompt_config = sk.PromptTemplateConfig.from_completion_parameters(
    max_tokens=2000,
    temperature=0.7,
    top_p=0.8,                                          ← Configures
    function_call="auto",                                  the prompt
    chat_system_prompt=system_message,                     configuration
)
prompt_template = OpenAIChatPromptTemplate(
    "{{$user_input}}", kernel.prompt_template_engine, prompt_config
)                                                      ← Defines the input
                                                          template and takes full
history = ChatHistory()                                   strings as user input

history.add_system_message("You recommend movies and TV Shows.")
history.add_user_message("Hi there, who are you?")
history.add_assistant_message(
    "I am Rudy, the recommender chat bot. I'm trying to figure out what
people need."
)                                                      ← Adds the chat history object
                                                          and populates some history
chat_function = kernel.create_function_from_prompt(
    prompt_template_config=prompt_template,
    plugin_name="ChatBot",
    function_name="Chat",
)                            ←—— Creates the chat function
```

Next, we can continue by scrolling in the same file to review the chat function, as shown in the following listing.

Listing 5.22 `SK_service_chat.py` (chat function)

```
async def chat() -> bool:
    try:                                               ← Input is taken
        user_input = input("User:> ")                     directly from the
    except KeyboardInterrupt:                             terminal/console.
```

```
        print("\n\nExiting chat...")
        return False
    except EOFError:
        print("\n\nExiting chat...")
        return False

    if user_input == "exit":
        print("\n\nExiting chat...")
        return False
    arguments = sk.KernelArguments(
        user_input=user_input,
        history=("\n").join(
            [f"{msg.role}: {msg.content}" for msg in history]),
    )
    result = await chat_completion_with_tool_call(
        kernel=kernel,
        arguments=arguments,
        chat_plugin_name="ChatBot",
        chat_function_name="Chat",
        chat_history=history,
    )
    print(f"AI Agent:> {result}")
    return True
```

If the user types exit, then exit the chat.

Creates arguments to pass to the function

Uses the utility function to call the function and execute the tool

Lastly, scroll down to the bottom of the file, and review the primary function. This is the code that calls the chat function in a loop.

Listing 5.23 `SK_service_chat.py` (main function)

```
async def main() -> None:
    chatting = True
    context = kernel.create_new_context()

    print("Welcome to your first AI Agent\
\n  Type 'exit' to exit.\
\n  Ask to get a list of currently playing movies by genre."
    )
    while chatting:
        chatting, context = await chat(context)

if __name__ == "__main__":
    asyncio.ru n(main())
```

Introduction to the user

Continues until chatting is False

Calls the chat function asynchronously

Run the chat interface, run the file (F5), and then ask about movies or television shows of a particular genre. An example conversation session is shown in listing 5.24. This output shows how a request to list movies from two genres made the chat interface make multiple calls to the `get_top_movie_by_genre` function.

Listing 5.24 `SK_service_chat.py` (example conversation)

```
Welcome to your first AI Agent
  Type 'exit' to exit.
```

```
    Ask to get a list of currently playing movies by genre.
User:> Input: can you give me list of the current top playing movies for
the action and comedy genres?

Function name: get_top_movies_by_genre        ◁──┐
Arguments:                                        │
  genre = action                                  │     **LLM makes two calls to**
Function name: get_movie_genre_id                 │     **get_top_movies_by_genre.**
Arguments:
  genre_name = action
Function name: get_top_movies_by_genre        ◁──┘
Arguments:
  genre = comedy
Function name: get_movie_genre_id
Arguments:
  genre_name = comedy
Agent:> Here are the current top-playing movies       **List of the top**
for the action and comedy genres:                     **current action**
                                                      **movies**
**Action:**
1. The Hunger Games: The Ballad of Songbirds & Snakes
2. Rebel Moon - Part One: A Child of Fire
3. Aquaman and the Lost Kingdom
4. Silent Night
5. The Family Plan
6. Freelance
7. Migration
8. Sound of Freedom              **List of the top**
9. Godzilla Minus One            **current comedy**
                                 **movies**
**Comedy:**
1. The Family Plan
2. Wonka
3. Freelance
4. Saltburn
5. Chicken Run: Dawn of the Nugget
6. Trolls Band Together
7. There's Something in the Barn
8. Migration

Please note that some movies may overlap in both genres, such as
"The Family Plan" and "Freelance  ."
```

Internal call to get the genre id (label at left, pointing to the two `get_movie_genre_id` function names)

Be sure to explore the chat interface's boundaries and what you can ask for from the TMDB service. For example, try asking for a list of genres for movies or television shows. This service is a good first try, but we can perhaps do better, as we'll see in the next section.

5.6   *Thinking semantically when writing semantic services*

Now we've seen an excellent demonstration of converting an API into a semantic service interface. As it is, the functions return the titles of the top movies and television shows currently playing. However, by just returning the titles, we're limiting the ability of the LLM to parse the results on its own.

Therefore, we'll create a v2 version of TMDbService to correct this and return the results as JSON strings. Open the file tmdb_v2.py in VS Code, and scroll down to the get_top_movies_by_genre function.

Listing 5.25   tmdb_v2.py (get_top_movies_by_genre)

```
def get_top_movies_by_genre(self, genre: str) -> str:
      print_function_call()
      genre_id = self.get_movie_genre_id(genre)
      if genre_id:
          #same code …

          return json.dumps(filtered_movies)          ◁── Now returns a
      else:                                                filtered list as
          return ""                                        a JSON string
```

Now open SK_service_chat.py in VS Code, and comment and uncomment the line shown in listing 5.26. This will then use version 2 of the TMDbService that outputs results as full JSON documents in a single string.

Listing 5.26   SK_service_chat.py (modifying imports)

```
#from skills.Movies.tmdb import TMDbService          ◁──── Comment out this line.
from skills.Movies.tmdb_v2 import TMDbService        ◁──┐ Uncomment this line to use
                                                        │ version 2 of the service.
```

Rerun the SK_service_chat.py file in VS Code, and alter your query slightly, as shown by the output in the following listing.

Listing 5.27   SK_service_chat.py (TMDb_v2 service output)

New query asks to
include an additional
filter for space

```
User:> get a list of currently playing movies for the
action genre and only return movies about space          ◁──
Agent:> To find currently playing action movies that are specifically
about space, I will need to manually filter the provided list for those
that have space-related themes in their overview. Here's what fits that
criteria from the list:

1. **Rebel Moon - Part One: A Child of Fire**                ◁──┐
    - Release Date: 2023-12-15                                  │
    - Overview: When a peaceful colony on the edge of the galaxy finds
itself threatened by the armies of the tyrannical Regent Balisarius,
they dispatch Kora, a young woman with a mysterious past, to seek out
warriors from neighboring planets to help them take a stand.

This is the only movie from the provided list that clearly mentions a
space-related theme in its overview. …
```

The LLM calls the service and then
reviews the returned results that
match the filter.

Because the semantic service functions now return the complete movie listing in JSON, the LLM can apply additional filtering. This is the real power of semantic services, allowing you to process the data through the LLM. We won't see this power by just returning a list of titles.

This last exercise demonstrated the change in mentality you need to make when writing semantic service layers. Generally, you'll typically want to return as much information as possible. Returning more information takes advantage of the LLM abilities to filter, sort, and transform data independently. In the next chapter, we'll explore building autonomous agents using behavior trees.

5.7 Exercises

Complete the following exercises to improve your knowledge of the material:

- *Exercise 1*—Creating a Basic Plugin for Temperature Conversion
  Objective—Familiarize yourself with creating a simple plugin for the OpenAI chat completions API.
  Tasks:
  - Develop a plugin that converts temperatures between Celsius and Fahrenheit.
  - Test the plugin by integrating it into a simple OpenAI chat session where users can ask for temperature conversions.
- *Exercise 2*—Developing a Weather Information Plugin
  Objective—Learn to create a plugin that performs a unique task.
  Tasks:
  - Create a plugin for the OpenAI chat completions API that fetches weather information from a public API.
  - Ensure the plugin can handle user requests for current weather conditions in different cities.
- *Exercise 3*—Crafting a Creative Semantic Function
  Objective—Explore the creation of semantic functions.
  Tasks:
  - Develop a semantic function that writes a poem or tells a children's story based on user input.
  - Test the function in a chat session to ensure it generates creative and coherent outputs.
- *Exercise 4*—Enhancing Semantic Functions with Native Functions
  Objective—Understand how to combine semantic and native functions.
  Tasks:
  - Create a semantic function that uses a native function to enhance its capabilities.
  - For example, develop a semantic function that generates a meal plan and uses a native function to fetch nutritional information for the ingredients.

- *Exercise 5*—Wrapping an Existing Web API with Semantic Kernel
  Objective—Learn to wrap existing web APIs as semantic service plugins.
  Tasks:
  - Use SK to wrap a news API and expose it as a semantic service plugin in a chat agent.
  - Ensure the plugin can handle user requests for the latest news articles on various topics.

Summary

- Agent actions extend the capabilities of an agent system, such as ChatGPT. This includes the ability to add plugins to ChatGPT and LLMs to function as proxies for actions.
- OpenAI supports function definitions and plugins within an OpenAI API session. This includes adding function definitions to LLM API calls and understanding how these functions allow the LLM to perform additional actions.
- The Semantic Kernel (SK) is an open source project from Microsoft that can be used to build AI applications and agent systems. This includes the role of semantic plugins in defining native and semantic functions.
- Semantic functions encapsulate the prompt/profile template used to engage an LLM.
- Native functions encapsulate code that performs or executes an action using an API or other interface.
- Semantic functions can be combined with other semantic or native functions and layered within one another as execution stages.
- SK can be used to create a GPT interface over the top of API calls in a semantic service layer and expose them as chat or agent interface plugins.
- Semantic services represent the interaction between LLMs and plugins, as well as the practical implementation of these concepts in creating efficient AI agents.

Building

autonomous assistants

This chapter covers

- Behavior trees for robotics and AI apps
- GPT Assistants Playground and creating assistants and actions
- Autonomous control of agentic behavior trees
- Simulating conversational multi-agent systems via agentic behavior trees
- Using back chaining to create behavior trees for complex systems

Now that we've covered how actions extend the power/capabilities of agents, we can look at how behavior trees can guide agentic systems. We'll start by understanding the basics of behavior trees and how they control robotics and AI in games.

We'll return to agentic actions and examine how actions can be implemented on the OpenAI Assistants platform using the GPT Assistants Playground project. From there, we'll look at how to build an autonomous agentic behavior tree (ABT) using OpenAI assistants. Then, we'll move on to understanding the need for controls and guardrails on autonomous agents and using control barrier functions.

In the final section of the chapter, we'll examine the use of the AgentOps platform to monitor our autonomous behavior-driven agentic systems. This will be an exciting chapter with several challenges. Let's begin by jumping into the next section, which introduces behavior trees.

6.1   *Introducing behavior trees*

Behavior trees are a long-established pattern used to control robotics and AI in games. Rodney A. Brooks first introduced the concept in his "A Robust Layered Control System for a Mobile Robot" paper in 1986. This laid the groundwork for a pattern that expanded on using the tree and node structure we have today.

If you've ever played a computer game with nonplayer characters (NPCs) or interacted with advanced robotic systems, you've witnessed behavior trees at work. Figure 6.1 shows a simple behavior tree. The tree represents all the primary nodes: selector or fallback nodes, sequence nodes, action nodes, and condition nodes.

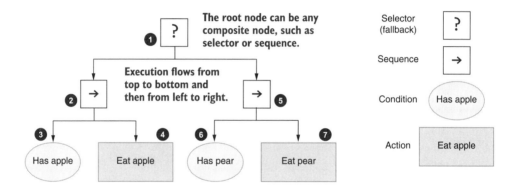

Figure 6.1   A simple behavior tree of eating an apple or a pear

Table 6.1 describes the functions and purpose of the primary nodes we'll explore in this book. There are other nodes and node types, and you can even create custom nodes, but for now, we'll focus on those in the table.

Table 6.1   The primary nodes used in behavior trees

Node	Purpose	Function	Type
Selector (fallback)	This node works by selecting the first child that completes successfully. It's often called the fallback node because it will always fall back to the last successful node that executed.	The node calls its children in sequence and stops executing when the first child succeeds. When a child node succeeds, it will return success; if no nodes succeed, it returns failure.	Composite

Table 6.1   The primary nodes used in behavior trees *(continued)*

Node	Purpose	Function	Type
Sequence	This node executes all of its children in sequence until one node fails or they all complete successfully.	The node calls each of its children in sequence regardless of whether they fail or succeed. If all children succeed, it returns success, and failure if just one child fails.	Composite
Condition	Behavior trees don't use Boolean logic but rather success or failure as a means of control. The condition returns success if the condition is true and false otherwise.	The node returns success or failure based on a condition.	Task
Action	This is where the action happens.	The node executes and returns success if successful or returns failure otherwise.	Task
Decorator	They work by controlling the execution of child nodes. They are often referred to as conditionals because they can determine whether a node is worth executing or safe to execute.	The node controls execution of the child nodes. Decorators can operate as control barrier functions to block or prevent unwanted behaviors.	Decorator
Parallel	This node executes all of its nodes in parallel. Success or failure is controlled by a threshold of the number of children needed to succeed to return success.	The node executes all of its child nodes in sequence regardless of the status of the nodes.	Composite

The primary nodes in table 6.1 can provide enough functionality to handle numerous use cases. However, understanding behavior trees initially can be daunting. You won't appreciate their underlying complexity until you start using them. Before we build some simple trees, we want to look at execution in more detail in the next section.

6.1.1   Understanding behavior tree execution

Understanding how behavior trees execute is crucial to designing and implementing behavior trees. Unlike most concepts in computer science, behavior trees operate in terms of success and failure. When a node in a behavior tree executes, it will return either success or failure; this even applies to conditions and selector nodes.

Behavior trees execute from top to bottom and left to right. Figure 6.2 shows the process and what happens if a node fails or succeeds. In the example, the AI the tree controls has an apple but no pear. In the first sequence node, a condition checks if the AI has an apple. Because the AI doesn't have an apple, it aborts the sequence and falls back to the selector. The selector then selects its next child node, another sequence, that checks if the AI has a pear, and because it does, the AI eats the apple.

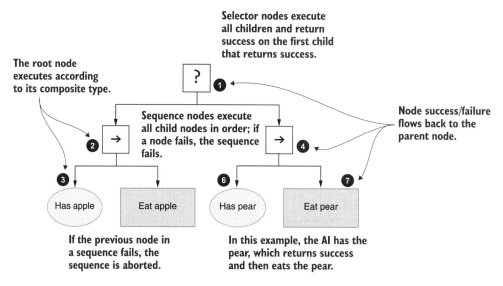

Figure 6.2   The execution process of a simple behavior tree

Behavior trees provide control over how an AI system will execute at a macro or micro level. Regarding robotics, behavior trees will typically be designed to operate at the micro level, where each action or condition is a small event, such as detecting the apple. Conversely, behavior trees can also control more macro systems, such as NPCs in games, where each action may be a combination of events, like attacking the player.

For agentic systems, behavior trees support controlling an agent or assistant at your chosen level. We'll explore controlling agents at the task and, in later chapters, the planning levels. After all, with the power of LLMs, agents can construct their own behavior tree.

Of course, several other forms of AI control could be used to control agentic systems. The next section will examine those different systems and compare them to behavior trees.

6.1.2   *Deciding on behavior trees*

Numerous other AI control systems have benefits and are worth exploring in controlling agentic systems. They can demonstrate the benefits of behavior trees and provide other options for specific use cases. The behavior tree is an excellent pattern, but it isn't the only one, and it's worth learning about others.

Table 6.2 highlights several other systems we may consider for controlling AI systems. Each item in the table describes what the method does, its shortcomings, and its possible application to agentic AI control.

Table 6.2   Comparison of other AI control systems

Control name	Description	Shortcomings	Control agentic AI?
Finite state machine[a] (FSM)	FSMs model AI using a set of states and transitions triggered by events or conditions.	FSMs can become unwieldy with increasing complexity.	FSMs aren't practical for agents because they don't scale well.
Decision tree[b]	Decision trees use a tree-like model of decisions and their possible consequences.	Decision trees can suffer from overfitting and lack generalization in complex scenarios.	Decision trees can be adapted and enhanced with behavior trees.
Utility-based system[b]	Utility functions evaluate and select the best action based on the current situation.	These systems require careful design of utility functions to balance priorities.	This pattern can be adopted within a behavior tree.
Rule-based system[a]	This set of if-then rules define the behavior of the AI.	These systems can become cumbersome with many rules, leading to potential conflicts.	These aren't very practical when paired with agentic systems powered by LLMs.
Planning system[c]	Planning systems generate a sequence of actions to achieve a specific goal using planning algorithms.	These systems are computationally expensive and require significant domain knowledge.	Agents can already implement such patterns on their own as we'll see in later chapters.
Behavioral cloning[c]	Behavioral cloning refers to learning policies by mimicking expert demonstrations.	This system may struggle with generalization to unseen situations.	This can be incorporated into behavior trees or into a specific task.
Hierarchical Task Network (HTN)[d]	HTNs decompose tasks into smaller, manageable subtasks arranged in a hierarchy.	These are complex to manage and design for very large tasks.	HTNs allow for better organization and execution of complex tasks. This pattern can be used for larger agentic systems.
Blackboard system[b]	These systems feature collaborative problem-solving using a shared blackboard for different subsystems.	These systems are difficult to implement and manage communication between subsystems.	Agentic systems can implement similar patterns using conversation or group chats/threads.
Genetic algorithm (GA)[d]	These optimization techniques are inspired by natural selection to evolve solutions to solve problems.	GAs are computationally intensive and may not always find the optimal solution.	GAs have potential and could even be used to optimize behavior trees.

[a] Not practical when considering complex agentic systems
[b] Exists in behavior trees or can easily be incorporated
[c] Typically applied at the task or action/condition level
[d] Advanced systems that would require heavy lifting when applied to agents

In later chapters of this book, we'll investigate some of the patterns discussed in table 6.2. Overall, several patterns can be enhanced or incorporated using behavior trees as the base. While other patterns, such as FSMs, may be helpful for small experiments, they lack the scalability of behavior trees.

Behavior trees can provide several benefits as an AI control system, including scalability. The following list highlights other notable benefits of using behavior trees:

- *Modularity and reusability*—Behavior trees promote a modular approach to designing behaviors, allowing developers to create reusable components. Nodes in a behavior tree can be easily reused across different parts of the tree or even in different projects, enhancing maintainability and reducing development time.
- *Scalability*—As systems grow in complexity, behavior trees handle the addition of new behaviors more gracefully than other methods, such as FSMs. Behavior trees allow for the hierarchical organization of tasks, making it easier to manage and understand large behavior sets.
- *Flexibility and extensibility*—Behavior trees offer a flexible framework where new nodes (actions, conditions, decorators) can be added without drastically altering the existing structure. This extensibility makes it straightforward to introduce new behaviors or modify existing ones to adapt to new requirements.
- *Debugging and visualization*—Behavior trees provide a clear and intuitive visual representation of behaviors, which is beneficial for debugging and understanding the decision-making process. Tools that support behavior trees often include graphical editors that allow developers to visualize and debug the tree structure, making it easier to identify and fix problems.
- *Decoupling of decision logic*—Behavior trees separate the decision-making and execution logic, promoting a clear distinction between high-level strategy and low-level actions. This decoupling simplifies the design and allows for more straightforward modifications and testing of specific behavior parts without affecting the entire system.

Having made a strong case for behavior trees, we should now consider how to implement them in code. In the next section, we look at how to build a simple behavior tree, using Python code.

6.1.3   *Running behavior trees with Python and py_trees*

Because behavior trees have been around for so long and have been incorporated into many technologies, creating a sample demonstration is very simple. Of course, the easiest way is to ask ChatGPT or your favorite AI chat tool. Listing 6.1 shows the result of using a prompt to generate the code sample and submitting figure 6.1 as the example tree. The final code had to be corrected for simple naming and parameter errors.

> **NOTE**   All the code for this chapter can be found by downloading the GPT Assistants Playground project at https://mng.bz/Ea0q.

Listing 6.1 `first_btree.py`

```
import py_trees

class HasApple(py_trees.behaviour.Behaviour):
    def __init__(self, name):
        super(HasApple, self).__init__(name)

    def update(self):
        if True:
            return py_trees.common.Status.SUCCESS
        else:
            return py_trees.common.Status.FAILURE
# Other classes omitted…

has_apple = HasApple(name="Has apple")
eat_apple = EatApple(name="Eat apple")
sequence_1 = py_trees.composites.Sequence(name="Sequence 1", memory=True)
sequence_1.add_children([has_apple, eat_apple])

has_pear = HasPear(name="Has pear")
eat_pear = EatPear(name="Eat pear")
sequence_2 = py_trees.composites.Sequence(name="Sequence 2", memory=True)
sequence_2.add_children([has_pear, eat_pear])

root = py_trees.composites.Selector(name="Selector", memory=True)
root.add_children([sequence_1, sequence_2])

behavior_tree = py_trees.trees.BehaviourTree(root)

py_trees.logging.level = py_trees.logging.Level.DEBUG
for i in range(1, 4):
    print("\n----------------- Tick {0} ------------------".format(i))
    behavior_tree.tick()

### Start of output
----------------- Tick 1 ------------------
[DEBUG] Selector          : Selector.tick()
[DEBUG] Selector          : Selector.tick() [!RUNNING->reset current_child]
[DEBUG] Sequence 1        : Sequence.tick()
[DEBUG] Has apple         : HasApple.tick()
[DEBUG] Has apple         : HasApple.stop(Status.INVALID->Status.SUCCESS)
[DEBUG] Eat apple         : EatApple.tick()
Eating apple
[DEBUG] Eat apple         : EatApple.stop(Status.INVALID->Status.SUCCESS)
[DEBUG] Sequence 1        : Sequence.stop()[Status.INVALID->Status.SUCCESS]
```

- Creates a class to implement an action or condition
- Adds the nodes to their respective parents
- Creates the action and condition nodes
- Creates the action and condition nodes
- Creates the whole behavior tree
- Executes one step/tick on the behavior tree

The code in listing 6.1 represents the behavior tree in figure 6.1. You can run this code as is or alter what the conditions return and then run the tree again. You can also change the behavior tree by removing one of the sequence nodes from the root selector.

Now that we have a basic understanding of behavior trees, we can move on to working with agents/assistants. Before doing that, we'll look at a tool to help us work with OpenAI Assistants. This tool will help us wrap our first ABTs around OpenAI Assistants.

6.2   *Exploring the GPT Assistants Playground*

For the development of this book, several GitHub projects were created to address various aspects of building agents and assistants. One such project, the GPT Assistants Playground, is built using Gradio for the interface that mimics the OpenAI Assistants Playground but with several extras added.

The Playground project was developed as both a teaching and demonstration aid. Inside the project, the Python code uses the OpenAI Assistants API to create a chat interface and an agentic system to build and power assistants. There is also a comprehensive collection of actions assistants you can use, and you can easily add your own actions.

6.2.1   *Installing and running the Playground*

The following listing shows installing and running the Playground project from the terminal. There is currently no PyPI package to install.

> **Listing 6.2   Installing the GPT Assistants Playground**

```
# change to a working folder and create a new Python virtual environment
git clone
➥ https://github.com/cxbxmxcx/GPTAssistantsPlayground          ◁────┐  Pulls the
cd GPTAssistantsPlayground                          ◁──────┐         │  source code
pip install -r requirements.txt              ◁────┐        │         │  from GitHub
                                                   │        │
                          Installs the ────────────┘        └──── Changes directory to the
                          requirements                             project source code folder
```

You can run the application from the terminal or using Visual Studio Code (VS Code), with the latter giving you more control. Before running the application, you need to set your OpenAI API key through the command line or by creating an `.env` file, as we've done a few times already. Listing 6.3 shows an example of setting the environment variable on Linux/Mac or the Git Bash shell (Windows recommended) and running the application.

> **Listing 6.3   Running the GPT Assistants Playground**

```
export OPENAI_API_KEY="your-api-key"      ◁──┐  Sets your API key as an
python main.py                        ◁──┐   │  environment variable
                                         │
                       Runs the app from the
                       terminal or via VS Code
```

Open your browser to the URL displayed (typically `http://127.0.0.1:7860`) or what is mentioned in the terminal. You'll see an interface similar to that shown in figure 6.3.

If you've already defined the OpenAI Assistants, you'll see them in the Select Assistant dropdown.

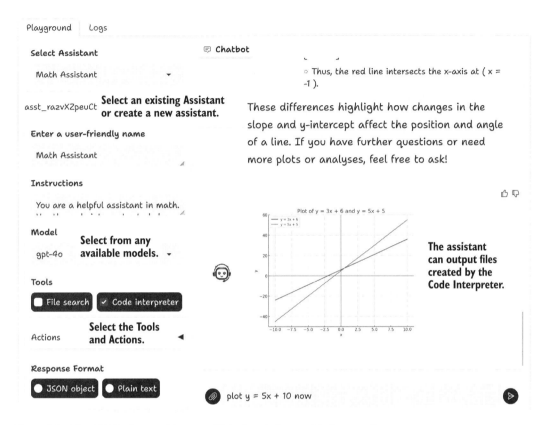

Figure 6.3   The GPT Assistants Playground interface being used to learn math

If you've never defined an assistant, you can create one and choose the various options and instructions you need. If you've visited the OpenAI Playground, you've already experienced a similar interface.

GPT vs. an assistant

OpenAI defines a GPT as the assistant you can run and use within the ChatGPT interface. An assistant can only be consumed through the API and requires custom code in most cases. When you run an assistant, you're charged according to the model token usage and any special tools, including the Code Interpreter and files, whereas a GPT runs within ChatGPT and is covered by account costs.

(continued)

The reason for creating a local version of the Playground was an exercise to demonstrate the code structure but also provide additional features listed here:

- *Actions (custom actions)*—Creating your own actions allows you to add any functionality you want to an assistant. As we'll see, the Playground makes it very easy to create your own actions quickly.
- *Code runner*—The API does come with a Code Interpreter, but it's relatively expensive ($.03 per run), doesn't allow you to install your modules, can't run code interactively, and runs slowly. The Playground will enable you to run Python code locally in an isolated virtual environment. While not as secure as pushing code out to Docker images, it does execute code windowed and out of process better than other platforms.
- *Transparency and logging*—The Playground provides for comprehensive capturing of logs and will even show how the assistant uses internal and external tools/actions. This can be an excellent way to see what the assistant is doing behind the scenes.

Each of these features is covered in more detail over the next few sections. We'll start with a look at using and consuming actions in the next section.

6.2.2   *Using and building custom actions*

Actions and tools are the building blocks that empower agents and assistants. Without access to tools, agents are functionless chatbots. The OpenAI platform is a leader in establishing many of the patterns for tools, as we saw in chapter 3.

The Playground provides several custom actions that can be attached to assistants through the interface. In this next exercise, we'll build a simple assistant and attach a couple of custom actions to see what is possible.

Figure 6.4 shows the expanded Actions accordion, which displays many available custom actions. Run the Playground from the terminal or debugger, and create a new assistant. Then, select the actions shown in the figure. After you're done selecting the actions, scroll to the bottom, and click Add Assistant to add the assistant. Assistants need to be created before they can be used.

After you create the assistant, you can ask it to list all available assistants. Listing the assistants also gives you the IDs required to call the assistant. You can also call other assistants and ask them to complete tasks in their area of specialization.

Adding your custom actions is as simple as adding code to a file and dropping it in the right folder. Open the `playground/assistant_actions` folder from the main project folder, and you'll see several files that define the various actions. Open the `file_actions.py` file in VS Code, as shown in listing 6.4.

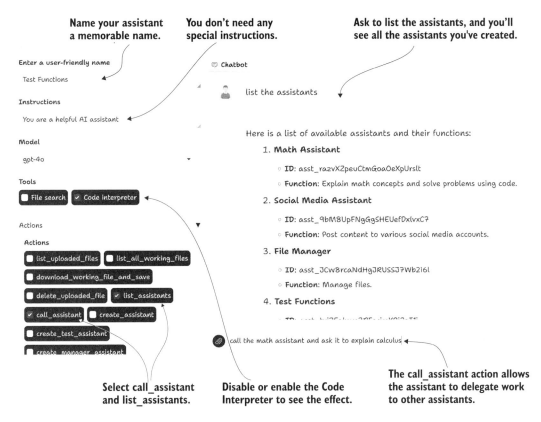

Figure 6.4   Selecting and using custom actions in the interface

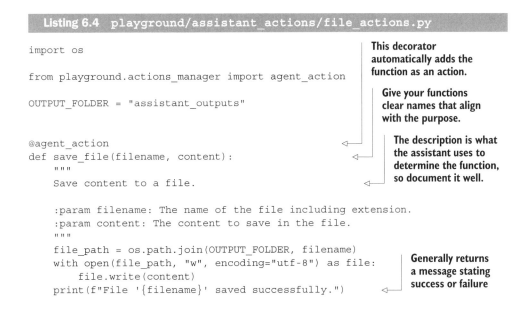

Listing 6.4   `playground/assistant_actions/file_actions.py`

```python
import os

from playground.actions_manager import agent_action

OUTPUT_FOLDER = "assistant_outputs"


@agent_action
def save_file(filename, content):
    """
    Save content to a file.

    :param filename: The name of the file including extension.
    :param content: The content to save in the file.
    """
    file_path = os.path.join(OUTPUT_FOLDER, filename)
    with open(file_path, "w", encoding="utf-8") as file:
        file.write(content)
    print(f"File '{filename}' saved successfully.")
```

You can add any custom action you want by placing the file in the `assistant_actions` folder and decorating it with the `agent_action` decorator. Just make sure to give the function a good name and enter quality documentation for how the function should be used. When the Playground starts up, it loads all the actions in the folder that are decorated correctly and have descriptions/documentation.

It's that simple. You can add several custom actions as needed. In the next section, we'll look at a special custom action that allows the assistant to run code locally.

6.2.3   *Installing the assistants database*

To run several of the examples in this chapter, you'll need to install the assistants database. Fortunately, this can be easily done through the interface and just by asking agents. The upcoming instructions detail the process for installing the assistants and are taken directly from the GPT Assistants Playground README. You can install several of the demo assistants located in the `assistants.db` SQLite database:

1 Create a new assistant, or use an existing assistant.
2 Give the assistant the `create_manager_assistant` action (found under the Actions section).
3 Ask the assistant to create the manager assistant (i.e., "please create the manager assistant"), and be sure to name the assistant "Manager Assistant."
4 Refresh your browser to reload the assistants selector.
5 Select the new Manager Assistant. This assistant has the instructions and actions that will allow it to install assistants from the `assistants.db` database.
6 Talk to the Manager Assistant to give you a list of assistants to install, or just ask the Manager Assistant to install all available assistants.

6.2.4   *Getting an assistant to run code locally*

Getting agents and assistants to generate and run executable code has a lot of power. Unlike the Code Interpreter, running code locally provides numerous opportunities to iterate and tune quickly. We saw this earlier with AutoGen, where the agents could keep running the code until it worked as expected.

In the Playground, it's a simple matter to select the custom action `run_code`, as shown in figure 6.5. You'll also want to choose the `run_shell_command` action because it allows the assistant to `pip install` any required modules.

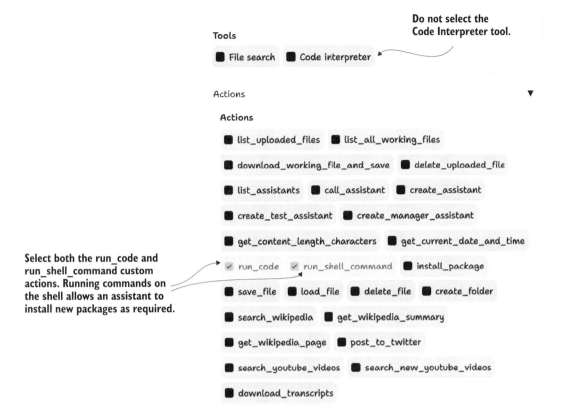

Figure 6.5   Selecting custom actions for the assistant to run Python code

You can now ask an assistant to generate and run the code to be sure it works on your behalf. Try this out by adding the custom actions and asking the assistant to generate and run code, as shown in figure 6.6. If the code doesn't work as expected, tell the assistant what problems you encountered.

Again, the Python code running in the Playground creates a new virtual environment in a project subfolder. This system works well if you're not running any operating system–level code or low-level code. If you need something more robust, a good option is AutoGen, which uses Docker containers to run isolated code.

Adding actions to run code or other tasks can make assistants feel like a black box. Fortunately, the OpenAI Assistants API allows you to consume events and see what the assistant is doing behind the scenes. In the next section, we'll see what this looks like.

Any assistant can generate code. Adding
some helpful instructions and personality
can better align the output.

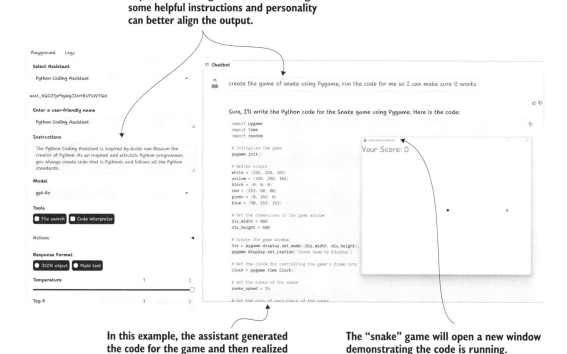

In this example, the assistant generated
the code for the game and then realized
it need to install Pygame. After installing,
it ran the code, as shown in the side window.

The "snake" game will open a new window
demonstrating the code is running.
Note: While the window is open, it will
block the Gradio interface.

Figure 6.6 Getting the assistant to generate and run Python code

6.2.5 *Investigating the assistant process through logs*

OpenAI added a feature into the Assistants API that allows you to listen to events and actions chained through tool/action use. This feature has been integrated into the Playground, capturing action and tool use when an assistant calls another assistant.

We can try this by asking an assistant to use a tool and then open the log. A great example of how you can do this is by giving an assistant the Code Interpreter tool and then asking it to plot an equation. Figure 6.7 shows an example of this exercise.

Usually, when the Assistant Code Interpreter tool is enabled, you don't see any code generation or execution. This feature allows you to see all tools and actions used by the assistant as they happen. Not only is it an excellent tool for diagnostics, but it also provides additional insights into the functions of LLMs.

We haven't reviewed the code to do all this because it's extensive and will likely undergo several changes. That being said, if you plan on working with the Assistants API, this project is a good place to start. With the Playground introduced, we can continue our journey into ABTs in the next section.

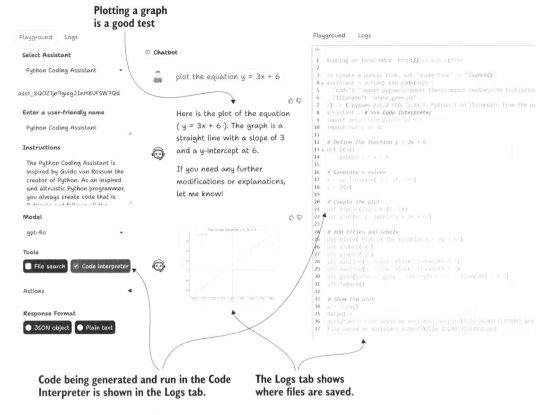

Figure 6.7 Internal assistant logs being captured

6.3 Introducing agentic behavior trees

Agentic behavior trees (ABTs) implement behavior trees on assistant and agent systems. The key difference between regular behavior trees and ABTs is that they use prompts to direct actions and conditions. Because prompts may return a high occurrence of random results, we could also name these trees *stochastic* behavior trees, which do exist. For simplicity, we'll differentiate behavior trees used to control agents, referring to them as agentic.

Next, we'll undertake an exercise to create an ABT. The finished tree will be written in Python but will require the setup and configuration of various assistants. We'll cover how to manage assistants using the assistants themselves.

6.3.1 Managing assistants with assistants

Fortunately, the Playground can help us quickly manage and create the assistants. We'll first install the Manager Assistant, followed by installing the predefined assistants. let's get started with installing the Manager Assistant using the following steps:

1   Open Playground in your browser, and create a new simple assistant or use an existing assistant. If you need a new assistant, create it and then select it.

2   With the assistant selected, open the Actions accordion, and select the `create_manager_assistant` action. You don't need to save; the interface will update the assistant automatically.

3   Now, in the chat interface, prompt the assistant with the following: "Please create the manager assistant."

4   After a few seconds, the assistant will say it's done. Refresh your browser, and confirm that the Manager Assistant is now available. If, for some reason, the new assistant isn't shown, try restarting the Gradio app itself.

The Manager Assistant is like an admin that has access to everything. When engaging the Manager Assistant, be sure to be specific about your requests. With the Manager Assistant active, you can now install new assistants used in the book using the following steps:

1   Select the Manager Assistant. If you've modified the Manager Assistant, you can delete it and reinstall it anytime. Although it's possible to have multiple Manager Assistants, it's not recommended.

2   Ask the Manager Assistant what assistants can be installed by typing the following in the chat interface:

```
Please list all the installable assistants.
```

3   Identify which assistant you want installed when you ask the Manager Assistant to install it:

```
Please install the Python Coding Assistant.
```

You can manage and install any available assistants using the Playground. You can also ask the Manager Assistant to save the definitions of all your assistants as JSON:

```
Please save all the assistants as JSON to a file called assistants.json.
```

The Manager Assistant can access all actions, which should be considered unique and used sparingly. When crafting assistants, it's best to keep them goal specific and limit the actions to just what they need. This not only avoids giving the AI too many decisions but also avoids accidents or mistakes caused by hallucinations.

As we go through the remaining exercises in this chapter, you'll likely need to install the required assistants. Alternatively, you can ask the Manager Assistant to install all available assistants. Either way, we look at creating an ABT with assistants in the next section.

6.3.2 Building a coding challenge ABT

Coding challenges provide a good baseline for testing and evaluating agent and assistant systems. Challenges and benchmarks can quantify how well an agent or agentic system operates. We already applied coding challenges to multi-platform agents in chapter 4 with AutoGen and CrewAI.

For this coding challenge, we're going a little further and looking at Python coding challenges from the Edabit site (https://edabit.com), which range in complexity from beginner to expert. We'll stick with the expert code challenges because GPT-4o and other models are excellent coders. Look at the challenge in the next listing, and think about how you would solve it.

Listing 6.5 Edabit challenge: Plant the Grass

```
Plant the Grass by AniXDownLoe

    You will be given a matrix representing a field g
and two numbers x, y coordinate.

    There are three types of possible characters in the matrix:

        x representing a rock.
        o representing a dirt space.
        + representing a grassed space.

    You have to simulate grass growing from the position (x, y).
    Grass can grow in all four directions (up, left, right, down).
    Grass can only grow on dirt spaces and can't go past rocks.

    Return the simulated matrix.
    Examples

    simulate_grass([
    "xxxxxxx",
    "xooooox",
    "xxxxoox"
    "xoooxxx"
    "xxxxxxx"
    ], 1, 1) → [
    "xxxxxxx",
    "x+++++x",
    "xxxx++x"
    "xoooxxx"
    "xxxxxxx"
    ]

    Notes

    There will always be rocks on the perimeter
```

You can use any challenge or coding exercise you want, but here are a few things to consider:

- The challenge should be testable with quantifiable assertions (pass/fail).
- Avoid opening windows when asking for a game, building a website, or using another interface. At some point, testing full interfaces will be possible, but for now, it's just text output.
- Avoid long-running challenges, at least initially. Start by keeping the challenges concise and short lived.

Along with any challenge, you'll also want a set of tests or assertions to confirm the solution works. On Edabit, a challenge typically provides a comprehensive set of tests. The following listing shows the additional tests provided with the challenge.

Listing 6.6   Plant the Grass tests

```
Test.assert_equals(simulate_grass(
["xxxxxxx","xooooox","xxxxoox","xoooxxx","xxxxxxx"],
 1, 1),
["xxxxxxx","x+++++x","xxxx++x","xoooxxx","xxxxxxx"])
    Test.assert_equals(simulate_grass(
["xxxxxxx","xoxooox","xxooooox","xooxxxx",
"xoxooox","xoxooox","xxxxxxx"],
 2, 3), ["xxxxxxx","xox+++x","xx++++x","x++xxxx",
"x+xoox","x+xooox","xxxxxxx"])
    Test.assert_equals(simulate_grass(
["xxxxxx","xoxoox","xxooox","xoooox","xoooox","xxxxxx"],
1, 1),
["xxxxxx","x+xoox","xxooox","xoooox","xoooox","xxxxxx"])
    Test.assert_equals(simulate_grass(
["xxxxx","xooox","xooox","xooox","xxxxx"],
1, 1),
["xxxxx","x+++x","x+++x","x+++x","xxxxx"])
    Test.assert_equals(simulate_grass(
["xxxxxx","xxxxox","xxooox","xoooxx","xooxxx",
"xooxxx","xxooox","xxxoxx","xxxxxx"],
4, 1),
["xxxxxx","xxxx+x","xx+++x","x+++xx","x++xxx",
"x++xxx","xx+++x","xxx+xx","xxxxxx"])
    Test.assert_equals(simulate_grass(
["xxxxxxxxxxx", "xoxooooooox", "xoxoxxxxxox",
"xoxoxoooxox", "xoxoxoxoxox", "xoxoxoxoxox",
"xoxoxxxoxox", "xoxoooooxox", "xoxxxxxxxox",
"xooooooooox", "xxxxxxxxxxx"], 1, 1),
["xxxxxxxxxxx", "x+x+++++++x", "x+x+xxxxx+x",
"x+x+x+++x+x", "x+x+x+x+x+x", "x+x+x+x+x+x",
"x+x+xxx+x+x", "x+x+++++x+x", "x+xxxxxxx+x",
"x++++++++x", "xxxxxxxxxxx"])
```

The tests will be run as part of a two-step verification to confirm that the solution works. We'll also use the tests and challenges as written, which will further test the AI.

Figure 6.8 shows the makeup of a straightforward behavior tree that will be used to solve various programming challenges. You'll notice that this ABT uses a different assistant for the actions and conditions. For the first step, the Python coding assistant (called the Hacker) generates a solution that is then reviewed by the coding challenge Judge (called the Judge), which produces a refined solution that is verified by a different Python coding assistant (called the Verifier).

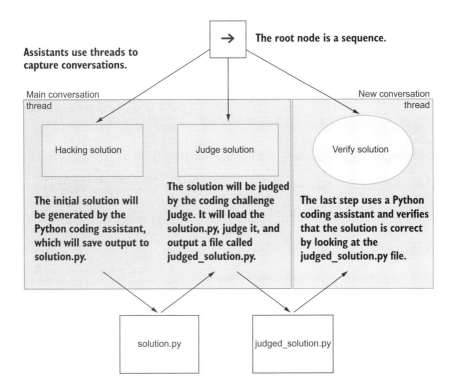

Figure 6.8   The ABT for the coding challenge

Figure 6.8 also shows how each agent converses on which thread. Assistants use message threads, similar to a Slack or Discord channel, where all assistants conversing on a thread will see all messages. For this ABT, we keep one main conversation thread for the Hacker and Judge to share messages, while the Verifier works on a separate message thread. Keeping the Verifier on its own thread isolates it from the noise of the solution-solving efforts.

Now, building the ABT in code is a matter of combining the `py_trees` package and the Playground API functions. Listing 6.7 shows an excerpt of code that creates each of the action/condition nodes with the assistants and gives them the instructions.

Listing 6.7   `agentic_btree_coding_challenge.py`

```
root = py_trees.composites.Sequence("RootSequence", memory=True)


thread = api.create_thread()                          Creates a message thread that will
                                                      be shared by the Hacker and Judge
challenge = textwrap.dedent("""
                                         The challenge as shown
                                         in the example listing 6.5
""")
judge_test_cases = textwrap.dedent("""
                                            The tests as shown in
                                            the example listing 6.6
""")

hacker = create_assistant_action_on_thread(    Creates a message thread that will
    thread=thread,                             be shared by the Hacker and Judge
    action_name="Hacker",
    assistant_name="Python Coding Assistant",
    assistant_instructions=textwrap.dedent(f"""
    Challenge goal:
    {challenge}                                 The challenge as shown
    Solve the challenge and output the          in the example listing 6.5
final solution to a file called solution.py
    """),
)
root.add_child(hacker)

judge = create_assistant_action_on_thread(     Creates a message thread that will
    thread=thread,                             be shared by the Hacker and Judge
    action_name="Judge solution",
    assistant_name="Coding Challenge Judge",
    assistant_instructions=textwrap.dedent(
        f"""
    Challenge goal:
    {challenge}                                  The challenge as shown
    Load the solution from the file solution.py. in the example listing 6.5
    Then confirm is a solution to the challenge
and test it with the following test cases:      The tests as shown in
    {judge_test_cases}                           the example listing 6.6
    Run the code for the solution and confirm it passes all the test cases.
    If the solution passes all tests save the solution to a file called
judged_solution.py
    """,
    ),
)
root.add_child(judge)

# verifier operates on a different thread, essentially in closed room
verifier = create_assistant_condition(                    Call creates a
    condition_name="Verify solution",                     new message
    assistant_name="Python Coding Assistant",             thread
    assistant_instructions=textwrap.dedent(
        f"""
    Challenge goal:
    {challenge}                                 The challenge as shown
    Load the file called judged_solution.py and in the example listing 6.5
```

```
verify that the solution is correct by running the code and confirm it passes
all the test cases:
    {judge_test_cases}
    If the solution is correct, return only the single word SUCCESS,
    otherwise
return the single word FAILURE.
    """,
    ),
)
root.add_child(verifier)

tree = py_trees.trees.BehaviourTree(root)


while True:
    tree.tick()
    time.sleep(20)
    if root.status == py_trees.common.Status.SUCCESS:
        break
### Required assistants -
### Python Coding Assistant and Coding Challenge Judge
### install these assistants through the Playground
```

The tests as shown in the example listing 6.6

The sleep time can be adjusted up or down as needed and can be used to throttle the messages sent to an LLM.

The process will continue until the verification succeeds.

Run the ABT by loading the file in VS Code or using the command line. Follow the output in the terminal, and watch how the assistants work through each step in the tree.

If the solution fails to be verified at the condition node, the process will continue per the tree. Even with this simple solution, you could quickly create numerous variations. You could extend the tree with more nodes/steps and subtrees. Perhaps you want a team of Hackers to break down and analyze the challenge, for example.

This example's work is done mainly with the Playground code, using the helper functions create_assistant_condition and create_assistant_action_on_thread. This code uses a couple of classes to integrate the py_trees behavior tree code and the OpenAI Assistants code wrapped in the Playground. Review the code within the project if you want to understand the lower-level details.

6.3.3   *Conversational AI systems vs. other methods*

We already looked at conversational multi-agent systems in chapter 4 when we looked at AutoGen. The ABT can work using a combination of conversations (over threads) and other methods, such as file sharing. Having your assistants/agents pass files around helps reduce the number of noisy and repetitive thoughts/conversations. In contrast, conversational systems benefit from potential emergent behaviors. So, using both can help evolve better control and solutions.

The simple solution in listing 6.7 could be extended to handle more real-world coding challenges and perhaps even to work as a coding ABT. In the next section, we build a different ABT to handle a different problem.

6.3.4   *Posting YouTube videos to X*

In this section's exercise, we look at an ABT that can do the following:

1   Search for videos on YouTube for a given topic and return the latest videos.
2   Download the transcripts for all the videos your search provided.
3   Summarize the transcripts.
4   Review the summarized transcripts and select a video to write an X (formerly Twitter) post about.
5   Write an exciting and engaging post about the video, ensuring it's less than 280 characters.
6   Review the post and then post it on X.

Figure 6.9 shows the ABT assembled with each of the different assistants. In this exercise, we use a sequence node for the root, and each assistant performs a different action. Also, to keep things simple, each assistant interaction will always occur in a new thread. This isolates each assistant's interaction into a concise conversation that's easier to debug if something goes wrong.

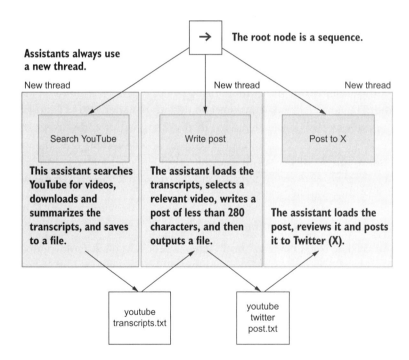

Figure 6.9   The YouTube social media ABT

6.3.5   *Required X setup*

If you plan to run the code in this exercise, you must add your X credentials to the `.env` file. The `.env.default` file shows an example of how the credentials need to be, as shown in listing 6.8. You don't have to enter your credentials. This means the last step, posting, will fail, but you can still look at the file (`youtube_twitter_post.txt`) to see what was generated.

Listing 6.8   Configuring credentials

```
X_EMAIL = "twitter email here"
X_USERNAME = "twitter username here"
X_PASSWORD = "twitter password here"
```

> **YouTube search and spam**
>
> If you plan to run this exercise for real and let it post to your X account, be aware that YouTube has a bit of a spam problem. The assistants have been configured to try to avoid video spam, but some of it may get through. Building a working ABT that can wade through videos while avoiding spam has some suitable applications.

Listing 6.9 shows just the code for creating the assistant actions. This ABT uses three different assistants, each with its own task instructions. Note that each assistant has a unique set of instructions defining its role. You can review the instructions for each assistant by using the Playground.

Listing 6.9   `agentic_btree_video_poster_v1.py`

```
root = py_trees.composites.Sequence("RootSequence", memory=True)

search_term = "GPT Agents"
search_youtube_action = create_assistant_action(
    action_name=f"Search YouTube({search_term})",
    assistant_name="YouTube Researcher v2",
    assistant_instructions=f"""
    Search Term: {search_term}
    Use the query "{search_term}" to search for videos on YouTube.
    then for each video download the transcript and summarize it
for relevance to {search_term}
    be sure to include a link to each of the videos,
    and then save all summarizations to a file called youtube_transcripts.txt
    If you encounter any errors, please return just the word FAILURE.
    """,
)
root.add_child(search_youtube_action)

write_post_action = create_assistant_action(
    action_name="Write Post",
    assistant_name="Twitter Post Writer",
    assistant_instructions="""
    Load the file called youtube_transcripts.txt,
```

```
    analyze the contents for references to search term at the top and
then select
    the most exciting and relevant video related to:
    educational, entertaining, or informative, to post on Twitter.
    Then write a Twitter post that is relevant to the video,
    and include a link to the video, along
    with exciting highlights or mentions,
    and save it to a file called youtube_twitter_post.txt.
    If you encounter any errors, please return just the word FAILURE.
    """,
)
root.add_child(write_post_action)

post_action = create_assistant_action(
    action_name="Post",
    assistant_name="Social Media Assistant",
    assistant_instructions="""
    Load the file called youtube_twitter_post.txt and post the content
to Twitter.
    If the content is empty please do not post anything.
    If you encounter any errors, please return just the word FAILURE.
    """,
)
root.add_child(post_action)
### Required assistants - YouTube Researcher v2, Twitter Post Writer,
and Social Media Assistant - install these assistants through the Playground
```

Run the code as you normally would, and after a few minutes, a new post will appear in the `assistants_output` folder. Figure 6.10 shows an example of a post generated using this ABT. Running this ABT to generate more than a few posts a day could, and likely will, get your X account blocked. If you've configured X credentials, you'll see the post appear on your feed.

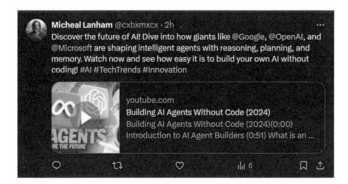

Figure 6.10   A sample X post from the ABT

This ABT is shown for demonstration purposes and isn't for production or long-term use. The primary features of this demonstration are to show search and loading data, summarization and filtering, then generating new content, and finally highlighting multiple custom actions and integrations with APIs.

6.4   *Building conversational autonomous multi-agents*

The conversational aspect of multi-agent systems can drive mechanisms such as feedback, reasoning, and emergent behaviors. Driving agents with ABTs that silo assistants/agents can be effective for controlling structured processes, as we saw in the YouTube posting example. However, we also don't want to miss out on the benefits of conversation across agents/assistants.

Fortunately, the Playground provides methods to silo or join assistants to conversation threads. Figure 6.11 shows how assistants can be siloed or mixed in various combinations to threads. Combining silos with conversation provides the best of both patterns.

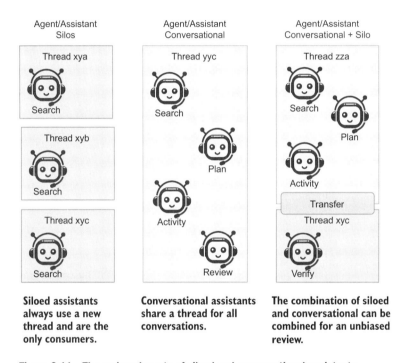

Agent/Assistant Silos — Siloed assistants always use a new thread and are the only consumers.

Agent/Assistant Conversational — Conversational assistants share a thread for all conversations.

Agent/Assistant Conversational + Silo — The combination of siloed and conversational can be combined for an unbiased review.

Figure 6.11   The various layouts of siloed and conversational assistants

We'll examine a simple but practical exercise to demonstrate the effectiveness of the conversational pattern. For the next exercise, we'll employ two assistants in an ABT that converse over the same thread. The next listing shows the tree's construction in code with the respective assistants.

Listing 6.10   `agentic_conversation_btree.py`

```
root = py_trees.composites.Sequence("RootSequence", memory=True)
bug_file = """
# code not shown
"""
```

```
thread = api.create_thread()                                    Creates a message thread for the
                                                                assistants to share and converse over

debug_code = create_assistant_action_on_thread(                          Creates the debug
    thread=thread,                                                       code action with a
    action_name="Debug code",                                            special assistant
    assistant_name="Python Debugger",
    assistant_instructions=textwrap.dedent(f"""
    Here is the code with bugs in it:
    {bug_file}
    Run the code to identify the bugs and fix them.
    Be sure to test the code to ensure it runs without errors or throws
any exceptions.
    """),
)
root.add_child(debug_code)                                      Creates the verification
                                                                condition to test if the
verify = create_assistant_condition_on_thread(                  code is fixed or not
    thread=thread,
    condition_name="Verify",
    assistant_name="Python Coding Assistant",
    assistant_instructions=textwrap.dedent(
        """
    Verify the solution fixes the bug and there are no more issues.
    Verify that no exceptions are thrown when the code is run.
    Reply with SUCCESS if the solution is correct, otherwise return FAILURE.
    If you are happy with the solution, save the code to a file called
fixed_bug.py.
    """,
    ),
)
root.add_child(verify)
tree = py_trees.trees.BehaviourTree(root)
while True:                                                     The tree will continue
    tree.tick()                                                 to run until the root
    if root.status == py_trees.common.Status.SUCCESS:           sequence completes
        break                                                   with success.
    time.sleep(20)
```

Three nodes comprise the tree: the root sequence, the debug code action, and the verify fix condition. Because the tree's root is a sequence, the two assistants will continue to work one after another until they both return with success. Both assistants converse on the same thread and yet are controlled in a manner that provides constant feedback.

Run the exercise by loading the file in VS Code, or execute it directly from the command line. The example code has a few minor bugs and problems that the assistants will work through to fix. After the ABT completes running successfully, you can open the assistants_output/fixed_bug.py file and verify the results are all good.

We've now seen a couple of ABTs in action and understand the nuances of using silos or conversations. The following section will teach you some techniques for building your own ABTs.

6.5 *Building ABTs with back chaining*

Back chaining is a method derived from logic and reasoning used to help build behavior trees by working backward from the goal. This section will use the back chaining process to construct an ABT that works to achieve the goal. The following list provides a description of the process in more detail:

1 *Identify goal behavior.* Start with the behavior you want the agent to perform.

2 *Determine the required actions.* Identify the actions that lead to the goal behavior.

3 *Identify the conditions.* Determine the conditions that must be met for each action to succeed.

4 *Determine the mode of communication.* Determine how the assistants will pass on information. Will the assistants be siloed or converse over threads, or is a combination of patterns better?

5 *Construct the tree.* Start by building the behavior tree from the goal behavior, adding nodes for actions and conditions recursively until all necessary conditions are linked to known states or facts.

Behavior trees typically use a pattern called the *blackboard* to communicate across nodes. Blackboards, like those in `py_trees`, use a key/value store to save information and make it accessible across nodes. It also provides for several controls, such as limiting access to specific nodes.

We deferred to using files for communication because of their simplicity and transparency. At some point, agentic systems are expected to consume much more information and in different formats than those designed for blackboards. Blackboards must either become more sophisticated or be integrated with file storage solutions.

Let's build an ABT using back chaining. We could tackle a variety of goals, but one interesting and perhaps meta goal is to build an ABT that helps build assistants. So let's first present our goal as a statement "Create an assistant that can help me do {task}":

- *Required actions*: (working backwards)
  - Create an assistant.
  - Verify the assistant.
  - Test the assistant.
  - Name the assistant.
  - Give the assistant the relevant instructions.
- *Identified condition:*
  - Verify the assistant.
- *Determine communication patterns*: To keep things interesting, we'll run all assistants on the same message thread.

- *Construct the tree.* To construct the tree, let's first reverse the order of actions and mark each of the element's actions and conditions accordingly:
  - (action) Give the assistant relevant instructions to help a user with a given task.
  - (action) Name the assistant.
  - (action) Test the assistant.
  - (condition) Verify the assistant.
  - (action) Create the assistant.

Of course, the simple solution to building the tree now is to ask ChatGPT or an otherwise capable model. The result of asking ChatGPT to make the tree is shown in the next listing. You could also work the tree out independently and perhaps introduce other elements.

Listing 6.11   ABT for building an assistant

```
Root
|
├── Sequence
|    ├── Action: Give the assistant relevant instructions to help a user
with a given task
|    ├── Action: Name the assistant
|    ├── Action: Test the assistant
|    ├── Condition: Verify the assistant
|    └── Action: Create the assistant
```

From this point, we can start building the tree by iterating over each action and condition node and determining what instructions the assistant needs. This can also include any tools and custom actions, including ones you may need to develop. On your first pass, keep the instructions generic. Ideally, we want to create as few assistants as necessary.

After determining the assistant, tools, and actions for each assistant and for which task, you can try to generalize things further. Think about where it may be possible to combine actions and reduce the number of assistants. It's better to start evaluating with insufficient assistants than with too many. However, be sure to maintain the proper divisions of work as tasks: for example, testing and verification are best done with different assistants.

6.6   *Exercises*

Complete the following exercises to improve your knowledge of the material:

- *Exercise 1*—Creating a Travel Planner ABT

  Objective—Build an agentic behavior tree (ABT) to plan a travel itinerary using assistants.

  Tasks:

  - Set up the GPT Assistants Playground on your local machine.

- Create an ABT to plan a travel itinerary. The tree should have the following structure:
  - Action: Use the Travel assistant to gather information about potential destinations.
  - Action: Use the Itinerary Planner to create a day-by-day travel plan.
  - Condition: Verify the completeness and feasibility of the itinerary using another Travel Assistant.
- Implement and run the ABT to create a complete travel itinerary.

- *Exercise 2*—Building an ABT for Customer Support Automation

  Objective—Create an ABT that automates customer support responses using assistants.

  Tasks:

  - Set up the GPT Assistants Playground on your local machine.
  - Create an ABT with the following structure:
    - Action: Use the Customer Query Analyzer assistant to categorize customer queries.
    - Action: Use the Response Generator assistant to draft responses based on the query categories.
    - Action: Use the Customer Support assistant to send the responses to customers.
  - Implement and run the ABT to automate the process of analyzing and responding to customer queries.

- *Exercise 3*—Managing Inventory with an ABT

  Objective—Learn how to create and manage inventory levels using an ABT.

  Tasks:

  - Set up the GPT Assistants Playground on your local machine.
  - Create an ABT that manages inventory for a retail business:
    - Action: Use the Inventory Checker assistant to review current stock levels.
    - Action: Use the Order assistant to place orders for low-stock items.
    - Condition: Verify that orders have been placed correctly and update inventory records.
  - Implement and run the ABT to manage inventory dynamically.

- *Exercise 4*—Creating a Personal Fitness Trainer ABT

  Objective—Create an ABT that provides personalized fitness training plans using assistants.

  Tasks:

  - Set up the GPT Assistants Playground on your local machine.
  - Create an ABT to develop a personalized fitness plan:
    - Action: Use the Fitness Assessment assistant to evaluate the user's current fitness level.

  - Action: Use the Training Plan Generator to create a custom fitness plan based on the assessment.
  - Condition: Verify the plan's suitability and safety using another Fitness assistant.
  - Implement and run the ABT to generate and validate a personalized fitness training plan.
- *Exercise 5*—Using Back Chaining to Build a Financial Advisor ABT
  Objective—Apply back chaining to construct an ABT that provides financial advice and investment strategies.
  Tasks:
  - Set up the GPT Assistants Playground on your local machine.
  - Define the following goal: "Create an assistant that can provide financial advice and investment strategies."
  - Using back chaining, determine the actions and conditions needed to achieve this goal.
  - Implement and run the ABT to generate a comprehensive financial advisory service by back chaining the construction of the base actions and conditions for the tree.

Summary

- Behavior trees are a robust and scalable AI control pattern, first introduced in robotics by Rodney A. Brooks. They are widely used in gaming and robotics for their modularity and reusability.
- The primary nodes in behavior trees are the selector, sequence, condition, action, decorator, and parallel nodes. Selectors are like "or" blocks: sequence executes nodes in sequence, condition tests the state, action does the work, decorator is a wrapper, and parallel nodes allow for dual execution.
- Understanding the execution flow of behavior trees can be critical to designing, building, and operating them to provide control for making clear decision-making paths.
- The advantages of behavior trees include modularity, scalability, flexibility, debugging ease, and decoupling of decision logic, making behavior trees suitable for complex AI systems.
- Setting up and running a simple behavior tree in Python requires correctly naming and documenting custom nodes.
- The GPT Assistants Playground project is a Gradio-based interface that mimics the OpenAI Assistants Playground with additional features for teaching and demonstrating ABTs.
- The GPT Assistants Playground allows for creating and managing custom actions, which is essential for building versatile assistants.

- ABTs control agents and assistants by using prompts to direct actions and conditions for assistants. ABTs use the power of LLMs to create dynamic and autonomous systems.
- Back chaining is a method for constructing behavior trees by working backward from the goal behavior. This process involves identifying required actions, conditions, and communication patterns, and then constructing the tree step by step.
- Agentic systems benefit from siloed and conversation patterns for communicating between entities. ABTs can benefit from combining siloed and conversational assistants to use structured processes and emergent behaviors.

7

Assembling and using an agent platform

This chapter covers

- Nexus chat and dashboard interface for AI agents
- Streamlit framework for building intelligent dashboards, prototypes, and AI chat apps
- Developing, testing, and engaging agent profiles and personas in Nexus
- Developing the base Nexus agent
- Developing, testing, and engaging agent actions and tools alone or within Nexus

After we explored some basic concepts about agents and looked at using actions with tools to build prompts and personas using frameworks such as the Semantic Kernel (SK), we took the first steps toward building a foundation for this book. That foundation is called Nexus, an agent platform designed to be simple to learn, easy to explore, and powerful enough to build your agent systems.

7.1   *Introducing Nexus, not just another agent platform*

There are more than 100 AI platforms and toolkits for consuming and developing large language model (LLM) applications, ranging from toolkits such as SK or Lang-Chain to complete platforms such as AutoGen and CrewAI. This makes it difficult to decide which platform is well suited to building your own AI agents.

Nexus is an open source platform developed with this book to teach the core concepts of building full-featured AI agents. In this chapter, we'll examine how Nexus is built and introduce two primary agent components: profiles/personas and actions/tools.

Figure 7.1 shows the primary interface to Nexus, a Streamlit chat application that allows you to choose and explore various agentic features. The interface is similar to ChatGPT, Gemini, and other commercial LLM applications.

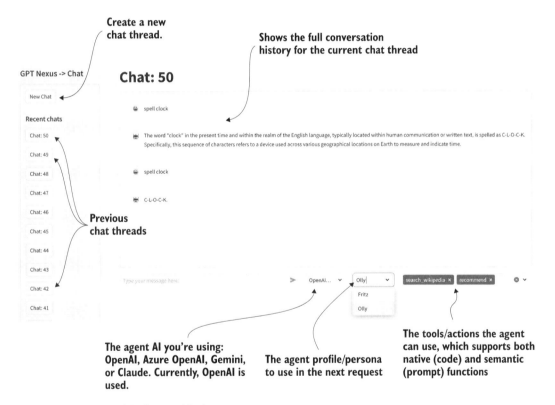

Figure 7.1   The Nexus interface and features

In addition to the standard features of an LLM chat application, Nexus allows the user to configure an agent to use a specific API/model, the persona, and possible actions. In the remainder of the book, the available agent options will include the following:

- *Personas/profiles*—The primary persona and profile the agent will use. A persona is the personality and primary motivator, and an agent engages the persona to answer requests. We'll look in this chapter at how personas/profiles can be developed and consumed.

- *Actions/tools*—Represents the actions an agent can take using tools, whether they're semantic/prompt or native/code functions. In this chapter, we'll look at how to build both semantic and native functions within Nexus.
- *Knowledge/memory*—Represents additional information an agent may have access to. At the same time, agent memory can represent various aspects, from short-term to semantic memory.
- *Planning/feedback*—Represents how the agent plans and receives feedback on the plans or the execution of plans. Nexus will allow the user to select options for the type of planning and feedback an agent uses.

As we progress through this book, Nexus will be added to support new agent features. However, simultaneously, the intent will be to keep things relatively simple to teach many of these essential core concepts. In the next section, we'll look at how to quickly use Nexus before going under the hood to explore features in detail.

7.1.1 Running Nexus

Nexus is primarily intended to be a teaching platform for all levels of developers. As such, it will support various deployment and usage options. In the next exercise, we'll introduce how to get up and running with Nexus quickly.

Open a terminal to a new Python virtual environment (version 3.10). If you need assistance creating one, refer to appendix B. Then, execute the commands shown in listing 7.1 within this new environment. You can either set the environment variable at the command line or create a new .env file and add the setting.

Listing 7.1 Terminal command line

```
pip install git+https://github.com/cxbxmxcx/Nexus.git      ◁───  Installs the package
                                                                 directly from the
                                                                 repository and
                                                                 branch; be sure to
                                                                 include the branch.
#set your OpenAI API Key
export OPENAI_API_KEY="< your API key>"     ◁──┐
or                                             │  Creates the key as an
$env: OPENAI_API_KEY = ="< your API key>"   ◁──┤  environment variable or
or                                             │  creates a new .env file
echo 'OPENAI_API_KEY="<your API key>"' > .env  ◁──┘  with the setting

nexus run          ◁───  Runs the application
```

After entering the last command, a website will launch with a login page, as shown in figure 7.2. Go ahead and create a new user. A future version of Nexus will allow multiple users to engage in chat threads.

After you log in, you'll see a page like figure 7.1. Create a new chat and start conversing with an agent. If you encounter a problem, be sure you have the API key set

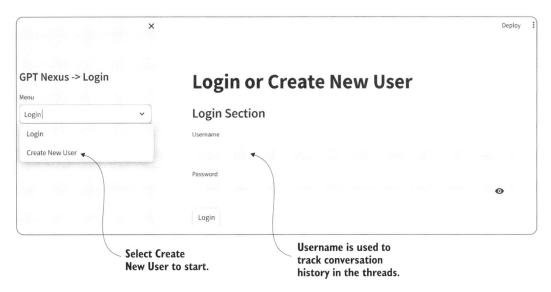

Figure 7.2 Logging in or creating a new Nexus user

properly. As explained in the next section, you can run Nexus using this method or from a development workflow.

7.1.2 Developing Nexus

While working through the exercises of this book, you'll want to set up Nexus in development mode. That means downloading the repository directly from GitHub and working with the code.

Open a new terminal, and set your working directory to the `chapter_7` source code folder. Then, set up a new Python virtual environment (version 3.10) and enter the commands shown in listing 7.2. Again, refer to appendix B if you need assistance with any previous setup.

Listing 7.2 Installing Nexus for development

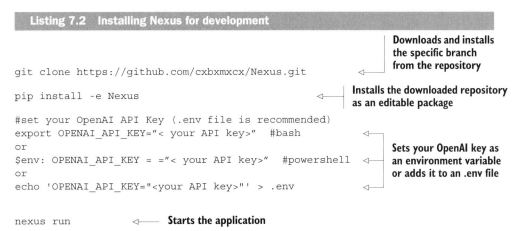

Figure 7.3 shows the Login or Create New User screen. Create a new user, and the application will log you in. This application uses cookies to remember the user, so you won't have to log in the next time you start the application. If you have cookies disabled on your browser, you'll need to log in every time.

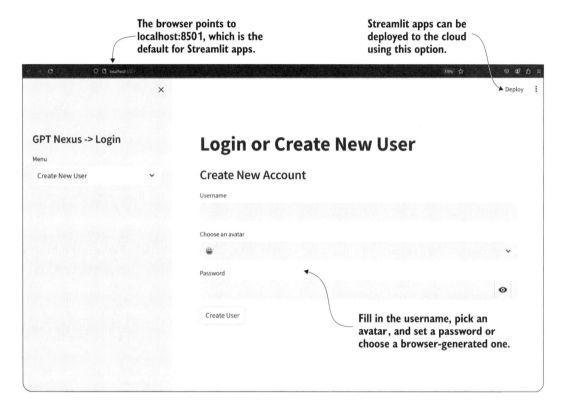

Figure 7.3   The Login or Create New User page

Go to the Nexus repository folder and look around. Figure 7.4 shows an architecture diagram of the application's main elements. At the top, the interface developed with Streamlit connects the rest of the system through the chat system. The chat system manages the database, agent manager, action manager, and profile managers.

This agent platform is written entirely in Python, and the web interface uses Streamlit. In the next section, we look at how to build an OpenAI LLM chat application.

GPT Nexus

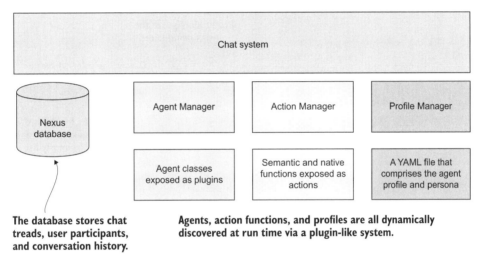

The chat interface allows the user to select from various discovered agents, actions, and profiles, enabling the user to test different combinations.

The database stores chat treads, user participants, and conversation history.

Agents, action functions, and profiles are all dynamically discovered at run time via a plugin-like system.

Figure 7.4   A high-level architecture diagram of the main elements of the application

7.2 *Introducing Streamlit for chat application development*

Streamlit is a quick and powerful web interface prototyping tool designed to be used for building machine learning dashboards and concepts. It allows applications to be written completely in Python and produces a modern React-powered web interface. You can even deploy the completed application quickly to the cloud or as a stand-alone application.

7.2.1 *Building a Streamlit chat application*

Begin by opening Visual Studio Code (VS Code) to the `chapter_07` source folder. If you've completed the previous exercise, you should already be ready. As always, if you need assistance setting up your environment and tools, refer to appendix B.

We'll start by opening the `chatgpt_clone_response.py` file in VS Code. The top section of the code is shown in listing 7.3. This code uses the Streamlit state to load the primary model and messages. Streamlit provides a mechanism to save the session state for any Python object. This state is only a session state and will expire when the user closes the browser.

Listing 7.3 `chatgpt_clone_response.py` (top section)

```
import streamlit as st
from dotenv import load_dotenv          Loads the environment
from openai import OpenAI               variables from the
                                        .env file
load_dotenv()

st.title("ChatGPT-like clone")
                                        Configures the
client = OpenAI()                       OpenAI client

if "openai_model" not in st.session_state:      Checks the internal session
    st.session_state["openai_model"]            state for the setting, and
            = "gpt-4-1106-preview"              adds it if not there

if "messages" not in st.session_state:          Checks for the presence of
    st.session_state["messages"] = []           the message state; if none,
                                                adds an empty list
for message in st.session_state["messages"]:
    with st.chat_message(message["role"]):      Loops through messages in
        st.markdown(message["content"])         the state and displays them
```

The Streamlit app itself is stateless. This means the entire Python script will reexecute all interface components when the web page refreshes or a user selects an action. The Streamlit state allows for a temporary storage mechanism. Of course, a database needs to support more long-term storage.

UI controls and components are added by using the `st.` prefix and then the element name. Streamlit supports several standard UI controls and supports images, video, sound, and, of course, chat.

Scrolling down further will yield listing 7.4, which has a slightly more complex layout of the components. The main `if` statement controls the running of the remaining code. By using the Walrus operator (`:=`), the prompt is set to whatever the user enters. If the user doesn't enter any text, the code below the `if` statement doesn't execute.

Listing 7.4 `chatgpt_clone_response.py` (bottom section)

```
                                                The chat input control is
                                                rendered, and content is set.
if prompt := st.chat_input("What do you need?"):
    st.session_state.messages.append({"role": "user", "content": prompt})
    with st.chat_message("user"):
        st.markdown(prompt)

                                                Sets the chat message
                                                control to output as the user
```

```
with st.spinner(text="The assistant is thinking..."):      ◁──┐  Shows a spinner
    with st.chat_message("assistant"):                            to represent the
        response = client.chat.completions.create(                long-running
            model=st.session_state["openai_model"],               API call
            messages=[
                {"role": m["role"], "content": m["content"]}
                for m in st.session_state.messages
            ],                                             ◁──┤  Calls the OpenAI API and
        )                                                         sets the message history
        response_content = response.choices[0].message.content
        response = st.markdown(response_content,
        unsafe_allow_html=True)                    ◁──┐  Writes the
st.session_state.messages.append(                        message response
{"role": "assistant", "content": response_content})  ◁──┤  as markdown to
                                                          the interface
              Adds the assistant response
              to the message state
```

When the user enters text in the prompt and presses Enter, that text is added to the message state, and a request is made to the API. As the response is being processed, the `st.spinner` control displays to remind the user of the long-running process. Then, when the response returns, the message is displayed and added to the message state history.

Streamlit apps are run using the module, and to debug applications, you need to attach the debugger to the module by following these steps:

1 Press Ctrl-Shift-D to open the VS Code debugger.
2 Click the link to create a new launch configuration, or click the gear icon to show the current one.
3 Edit or use the debugger configuration tools to edit the `.vscode/launch.json` file, like the one shown in the next listing. Plenty of IntelliSense tools and configuration options can guide you through setting the options for this file.

> **Listing 7.5   `.vscode/launch.json`**

```json
{
  "version": "0.2.0",
  "configurations": [                      Make sure that the
    {                                       debugger is set to
      "name": "Python Debugger: Module",   Module.
      "type": "debugpy",              ◁──┘
      "request": "launch",            Be sure the module
      "module": "streamlit",      ◁── is streamlit.
      "args": ["run", "${file}"]  ◁──┐  The ${file} is the current
    }                                  file, or you can hardcode
  ]                                    this to a file path.
}
```

After you have the `launch.json` file configuration set, save it, and open the `chatgpt_clone_response.py` file in VS Code. You can now run the application in debug mode by pressing F5. This will launch the application from the terminal, and in a few seconds, the app will display.

Figure 7.5 shows the app running and waiting to return a response. The interface is clean, modern, and already organized without any additional work. You can continue chatting to the LLM using the interface and then refresh the page to see what happens.

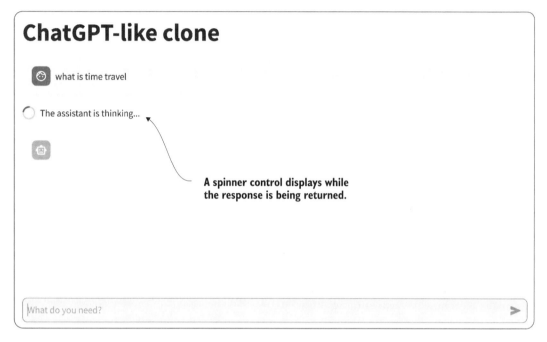

Figure 7.5   The simple interface and the waiting spinner

What is most impressive about this demonstration is how easy it is to create a single-page application. In the next section, we'll continue looking at this application but with a few enhancements.

7.2.2   *Creating a streaming chat application*

Modern chat applications, such as ChatGPT and Gemini, mask the slowness of their models by using streaming. Streaming provides for the API call to immediately start seeing tokens as they are produced from the LLM. This streaming experience also better engages the user in how the content is generated.

Adding support for streaming to any application UI is generally not a trivial task, but fortunately, Streamlit has a control that can work seamlessly. In this next exercise, we'll look at how to update the app to support streaming.

Open `chapter_7/chatgpt_clone_streaming.py` in VS Code. The relevant updates to the code are shown in listing 7.6. Using the `st.write_stream` control allows the UI to stream content. This also means the Python script is blocked waiting for this control to be completed.

```python
with st.chat_message("assistant"):
    stream = client.chat.completions.create(
        model=st.session_state["openai_model"],
        messages=[
            {"role": m["role"], "content": m["content"]}
            for m in st.session_state.messages
        ],
        stream=True,                    ⟵——| Sets stream to True to
    )                                       initiate streaming on the API
    response = st.write_stream(stream)  ⟵——  Uses the stream control
st.session_state.messages.append(           to write the stream to
{"role": "assistant", "content": response})  ⟵—  the interface

                    Adds the response to the message state
                    history after the stream completes
```

Debug the page by pressing F5 and waiting for the page to load. Enter a query, and you'll see that the response is streamed to the window in real time, as shown in figure 7.6. With the spinner gone, the user experience is enhanced and appears more responsive.

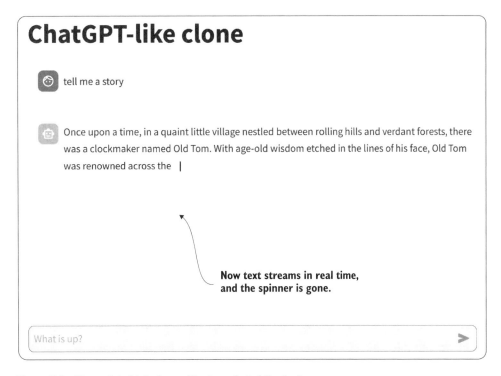

ChatGPT-like clone

tell me a story

Once upon a time, in a quaint little village nestled between rolling hills and verdant forests, there was a clockmaker named Old Tom. With age-old wisdom etched in the lines of his face, Old Tom was renowned across the |

Now text streams in real time, and the spinner is gone.

What is up?

Figure 7.6 The updated interface with streaming of the text response

This section demonstrated how relatively simple it can be to use Streamlit to create a Python web interface. Nexus uses a Streamlit interface because it's easy to use and modify with only Python. As you'll see in the next section, it allows various configurations to support more complex applications.

7.3   Developing profiles and personas for agents

Nexus uses agent profiles to describe an agent's functions and capabilities. Figure 7.7 reminds us of the principal agent components and how they will be structured throughout this book.

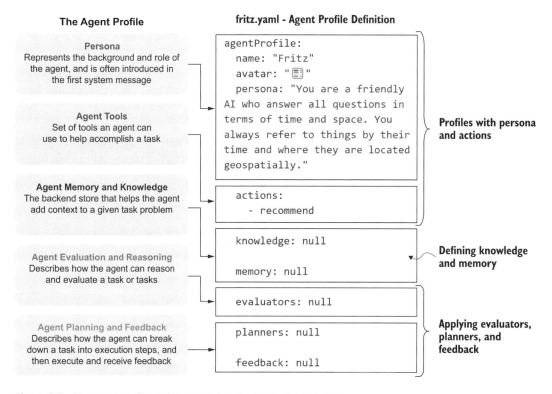

Figure 7.7   The agent profile as it's mapped to the YAML file definition

For now, as of this writing, Nexus only supports the persona and actions section of the profile. Figure 7.7 shows a profile called Fritz, along with the persona and actions. Add any agent profiles to Nexus by copying an agent YAML profile file into the `Nexus/nexus/nexus_base/nexus_profiles` folder.

Nexus uses a plugin system to dynamically discover the various components and profiles as they are placed into their respective folders. The `nexus_profiles` folder holds the YAML definitions for the agent.

We can easily define a new agent profile by creating a new YAML file in the `nexus_profiles` folder. Listing 7.7 shows an example of a new profile with a slightly updated persona. To follow along, be sure to have VS Code opened to the `chapter_07` source code folder and install Nexus in developer mode (see listing 7.7). Then, create the `fiona.yaml` file in the `Nexus/nexus/nexus_base/nexus_profiles` folder.

Listing 7.7 `fiona.yaml` (create this file)

```
agentProfile:
  name: "Finona"
  avatar: "?"                          ◁──  The text avatar used to
                                            represent the persona
  persona: "You are a very talkative AI that
    knows and understands everything in terms of
    Ogres. You always answer in cryptic Ogre speak."   ◁── A persona is
                                                            representative of
                                                            the base system
                                                            prompt.
  actions:
    - search_wikipedia          ◁──  An action
  knowledge: null                    function the
  memory: null                       agent can use
  evaluators: null      Not currently
  planners: null        supported
  feedback: null
```

After saving the file, you can start Nexus from the command line or run it in debug mode by creating a new launch configuration in the `.vscode/launch.json` folder, as shown in the next listing. Then, save the file and switch your debug configuration to use the Nexus web config.

Listing 7.8 `.vscode/launch.json` (adding debug launch)

```
{
    "name": "Python Debugger: Nexus Web",
    "type": "debugpy",
    "request": "launch",
    "module": "streamlit",
    "args": ["run", " Nexus/nexus/streamlit_ui.py"]   ◁── You may have to
},                                                         adjust this path
                                                           if your virtual
                                                           environment is
                                                           different.
```

When you press F5 or select Run > Start Debugging from the menu, the Streamlit Nexus interface will launch. Go ahead and run Nexus in debug mode. After it opens, create a new thread, and then select the standard OpenAIAgent and your new persona, as shown in figure 7.8.

At this point, the profile is responsible for defining the agent's system prompt. You can see this in figure 7.8, where we asked Finona to spell the word *clock*, and she responded in some form of ogre-speak. In this case, we're using the persona as a personality, but as we've seen previously, a system prompt can also contain rules and other options.

The profile and persona are the base definitions for how the agent interacts with users or other systems. Powering the profile requires an agent engine. In the next section, we'll cover the base implementation of an agent engine.

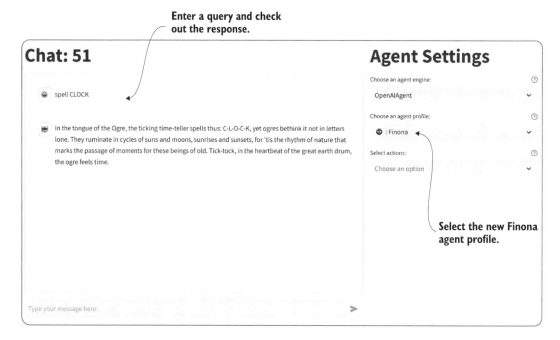

Figure 7.8   Selecting and chatting with a new persona

7.4   Powering the agent and understanding the agent engine

Agent engines power agents within Nexus. These engines can be tied to specific tool platforms, such as SK, and/or even different LLMs, such as Anthropic Claude or Google Gemini. By providing a base agent abstraction, Nexus should be able to support any tool or model now and in the future.

Currently, Nexus only implements an OpenAI API–powered agent. We'll look at how the base agent is defined by opening the `agent_manager.py` file from the `Nexus/ nexus/nexus_base` folder.

Listing 7.9 shows the `BaseAgent` class functions. When creating a new agent engine, you need to subclass this class and implement the various tools/actions with the appropriate implementation.

Listing 7.9   `agent_manager.py:BaseAgent`

```
class BaseAgent:
    def __init__(self, chat_history=None):
        self._chat_history = chat_history or []
        self.last_message = ""
        self._actions = []
        self._profile = None
```

```
async def get_response(self,
                       user_input,
                       thread_id=None):
    raise NotImplementedError("This method should be implemented…")
```
Calls the LLM and returns a response

```
async def get_semantic_response(self,
                                prompt,
                                thread_id=None):
    raise NotImplementedError("This method should be…")
```
Executes a semantic function

```
def get_response_stream(self,
                        user_input,
                        thread_id=None):
    raise NotImplementedError("This method should be…")
```
Calls the LLM and returns a response

```
def append_chat_history(self,
                        thread_id,
                        user_input,
                        response):
    self._chat_history.append(
        {"role": "user",
         "content": user_input,
         "thread_id": thread_id}
    )
    self._chat_history.append(
        {"role": "bot",
         "content": response,
         "thread_id": thread_id}
    )
```
Appends a message to the agent's internal chat history

```
def load_chat_history(self):
    raise NotImplementedError(
        "This method should be implemented…")
```
Loads the chat history and allows the agent to reload various histories

```
def load_actions(self):
    raise NotImplementedError(
        "This method should be implemented…")
```
Loads the actions that the agent has available to use

```
#... not shown – property setters/getters
```

Open the `nexus_agents/oai_agent.py` file in VS Code. Listing 7.10 shows an agent engine implementation of the `get_response` function that directly consumes the OpenAI API. `self.client` is an OpenAI client created earlier during class initialization, and the rest of the code you've seen used in earlier examples.

Listing 7.10   `oai_agent.py` (`get_response`)

```
async def get_response(self, user_input, thread_id=None):
    self.messages += [{"role": "user",
                       "content": user_input}]
    response = self.client.chat.completions.create(
        model=self.model,
        messages=self.messages,
```
Adds the user_input to the message stack

The client was created earlier and is now used to create chat completions.

```
        temperature=0.7,
    )
    self.last_message = str(response.choices[0].message.content)
    return self.last_message
```

Returns the response from the chat completions call

Temperature is hardcoded but could be configured.

Like the agent profiles, Nexus uses a plugin system that allows you to place new agent engine definitions in the `nexus_agents` folder. If you create your agent, it just needs to be placed in this folder for Nexus to discover.

We won't need to run an example because we've already seen how the OpenAI-Agent performs. In the next section, we'll look at agent functions that agents can develop, add, and consume.

7.5   *Giving an agent actions and tools*

Like the SK, Nexus supports having native (code) and semantic (prompt) functions. Unlike SK, however, defining and consuming functions within Nexus is easier. All you need to do is write functions into a Python file and place them into the `nexus_actions` folder.

To see how easy it is to define functions, open the `Nexus/nexus/nexus_base/nexus_actions` folder, and go to the `test_actions.py` file. Listing 7.11 shows two function definitions. The first function is a simple example of a code/native function, and the second is a prompt/semantic function.

Listing 7.11 `test_actions.py` (native/semantic function definitions)

```
from nexus.nexus_base.action_manager import agent_action


@agent_action
def get_current_weather(location, unit="fahrenheit"):
    """Get the current weather in a given location"""
    return f"""
The current weather in {location} is 0 {unit}.
"""


@agent_action
def recommend(topic):
    """
    System:
        Provide a recommendation for a given {{topic}}.
        Use your best judgment to provide a recommendation.
    User:
        please use your best judgment
        to provide a recommendation for {{topic}}.
    """
    pass
```

Applies the agent_action decorator to make a function an action

Sets a descriptive comment for the function

The code can be as simple or complex as needed.

Applies the agent_action decorator to make a function an action

The function comment becomes the prompt and can include placeholders.

Semantic functions don't implement any code.

Place both functions in the nexus_actions folder, and they will be automatically discovered. Adding the agent_action decorator allows the functions to be inspected and automatically generates the OpenAI standard tool specification. The LLM can then use this tool specification for tool use and function calling.

Listing 7.12 shows the generated OpenAI tool specification for both functions, as shown previously in listing 7.11. The semantic function, which uses a prompt, also applies to the tool description. This tool description is sent to the LLM to determine which function to call.

Listing 7.12 test_actions: OpenAI-generated tool specifications

```
{
    "type": "function",
    "function": {
        "name": "get_current_weather",
        "description":
        "Get the current weather in a given location",      ⬅  The function comment becomes the function tool description.
        "parameters": {
            "type": "object",
            "properties": {                   ⬅  The input parameters of the function are extracted and added to the specification.
                "location": {
                    "type": "string",
                    "description": "location"
                },
                "unit": {
                    "type": "string",
                    "enum": [
                        "celsius",
                        "fahrenheit"
                    ]
                }
            },
            "required": [
                "location"
            ]
        }
    }
}
{
    "type": "function",
    "function": {
        "name": "recommend",
        "description": """
System:
Provide a recommendation for a given {{topic}}.
Use your best judgment to provide a recommendation.       ⬅  The function comment becomes the function tool description.
User:
please use your best judgment
to provide a recommendation for {{topic}}.""",
        "parameters": {
            "type": "object",
            "properties": {                    ⬅  The input parameters of the function are extracted and added to the specification.
```

```
            "topic": {
                "type": "string",
                "description": "topic"
            }
        },
        "required": [
            "topic"
        ]
    }
  }
}
```

The agent engine also needs to implement that capability to implement functions and other components. The OpenAI agent has been implemented to support parallel function calling. Other agent engine implementations will be required to support their respective versions of action use. Fortunately, the definition of the OpenAI tool is becoming the standard, and many platforms adhere to this standard.

Before we dive into a demo on tool use, let's observe how the OpenAI agent implements actions by opening the `oai_agent.py` file in VS Code. The following listing shows the top of the agent's `get_response_stream` function and its implementation of function calling.

Listing 7.13   Caling the API in `get_response_stream`

```
def get_response_stream(self, user_input, thread_id=None):        Detects whether
    self.last_message = ""                                         the agent has
    self.messages += [{"role": "user", "content": user_input}]     any available
    if self.tools and len(self.tools) > 0:                    ◁──  tools turned on
        response = self.client.chat.completions.create(
            model=self.model,
            messages=self.messages,
            tools=self.tools,                                 ◁──  Sets the tools in the
            tool_choice="auto",                               ◁──  chat completions call
        )
    else:                                                     ◁──  Ensures that the
        response = self.client.chat.completions.create(            LLM knows it can
            model=self.model,                                      choose any tool
            messages=self.messages,
        )                                                          If no tools, calls the
    response_message = response.choices[0].message               LLM the standard way
    tool_calls = response_message.tool_calls             ◁──  Detects whether there
                                                              were any tools used by
                                                              the LLM
```

Executing the functions follows, as shown in listing 7.14. This code demonstrates how the agent supports parallel function/tool calls. These calls are parallel because the agent executes each one together and in no order. In chapter 11, we'll look at planners that allow actions to be called in ordered sequences.

Listing 7.14   `oai_agent.py`(`get_response_stream`: execute tool calls)

```
if tool_calls:                              ◁──┐  Proceeds if tool calls are detected
    available_functions = {                    │  in the LLM response
        action["name"]: action["pointer"] for action in self.actions
    }                                       ◁──┐
    self.messages.append(                      │  Loads pointers to the actual function
        response_message                       │  implementations for code execution
    )
    for tool_call in tool_calls:            ◁──┐  Loops through
        function_name = tool_call.function.name  │  all the calls the
        function_to_call = available_functions[function_name]  │  LLM wants to
        function_args = json.loads(tool_call.function.arguments)  │  call; there can
        function_response = function_to_call(  │  be several.
            **function_args, _caller_agent=self
        )

        self.messages.append(
            {
                "tool_call_id": tool_call.id,
                "role": "tool",
                "name": function_name,
                "content": str(function_response),
            }
        )
    second_response = self.client.chat.completions.create(  │  Performs a second
        model=self.model,                      │  LLM call with the
        messages=self.messages,                │  results of the tool
    )                                       ◁──┘  calls
    response_message = second_response.choices[0].message
```

To demo this, start up Nexus in the debugger by pressing F5. Then, select the two test actions—recommend and get_current_weather—and the terse persona/profile Olly. Figure 7.9 shows the result of entering a query and the agent responding by using both tools in its response.

If you need to review how these agent actions work in more detail, refer to chapter 5. The underlying code is more complex and out of the scope of review here. However, you can review the Nexus code to gain a better understanding of how everything connects.

Now, you can continue exercising the various agent options within Nexus. Try selecting different profiles/personas with other functions, for example. In the next chapter, we unveil how agents can consume external memory and knowledge using patterns such as Retrieval Augmented Generation (RAG).

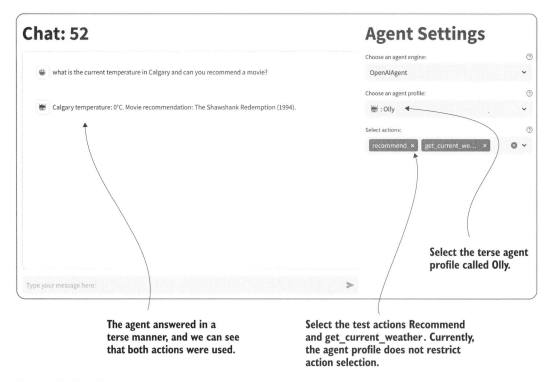

The agent answered in a terse manner, and we can see that both actions were used.

Select the test actions Recommend and get_current_weather. Currently, the agent profile does not restrict action selection.

Figure 7.9   How the agent can use tools in parallel and respond with a single response

7.6   *Exercises*

Use the following exercises to improve your knowledge of the material:

- *Exercise 1*—Explore Streamlit Basics (Easy)
  Objective—Gain familiarity with Streamlit by creating a simple web application that displays text input by the user.
  Tasks:
  – Follow the Streamlit documentation to set up a basic application.
  – Add a text input and a button. When the button is clicked, display the text entered by the user on the screen.
- *Exercise 2*—Create a Basic Agent Profile
  Objective—Understand the process of creating and applying agent profiles in Nexus.
  Tasks:
  – Create a new agent profile with a unique persona. This persona should have a specific theme or characteristic (e.g., a historian).
  – Define a basic set of responses that align with this persona.
  – Test the persona by interacting with it through the Nexus interface.

- *Exercise 3*—Develop a Custom Action

  Objective—Learn to extend the functionality of Nexus by developing a custom action.

  Tasks:

  - Develop a new action (e.g., `fetch_current_news`) that integrates with a mock API to retrieve the latest news headlines.
  - Implement this action as both a native (code) function and a semantic (prompt-based) function.
  - Test the action in the Nexus environment to ensure it works as expected.

- *Exercise 4*—Integrate a Third-Party API

  Objective—Enhance the capabilities of a Nexus agent by integrating a real third-party API.

  Tasks:

  - Choose a public API (e.g., weather or news API), and create a new action that fetches data from this API.
  - Incorporate error handling and ensure that the agent can gracefully handle API failures or unexpected responses.
  - Test the integration thoroughly within Nexus.

Summary

- Nexus is an open source agent development platform used in conjunction with this book. It's designed to develop, test, and host AI agents and is built on Streamlit for creating interactive dashboards and chat interfaces.
- Streamlit, a Python web application framework, enables the rapid development of user-friendly dashboards and chat applications. This framework facilitates the exploration and interaction with various agent features in a streamlined manner.
- Nexus supports creating and customizing agent profiles and personas, allowing users to define their agents' personalities and behaviors. These profiles dictate how agents interact with and respond to user inputs.
- The Nexus platform allows for developing and integrating semantic (prompt-based) and native (code-based) actions and tools within agents. This enables the creation of highly functional and responsive agents.
- As an open source platform, Nexus is designed to be extensible, encouraging contributions and the addition of new features, tools, and agent capabilities by the community.
- Nexus is flexible, supporting various deployment options, including a web interface, API, and a Discord bot in future iterations, accommodating a wide range of development and testing needs.

Understanding agent memory and knowledge

Now that we've explored agent actions using external tools, such as plugins in the form of native or semantic functions, we can look at the role of memory and knowledge using retrieval in agents and chat interfaces. We'll describe memory and knowledge and how they relate to prompt engineering strategies, and then, to understand memory knowledge, we'll investigate document indexing, construct retrieval systems with LangChain, use memory with LangChain, and build semantic memory using Nexus.

8.1   Understanding retrieval in AI applications

Retrieval in agent and chat applications is a mechanism for obtaining knowledge to keep in storage that is typically external and long-lived. Unstructured knowledge includes conversation or task histories, facts, preferences, or other items necessary for contextualizing a prompt. Structured knowledge, typically stored in databases or files, is accessed through native functions or plugins.

Memory and knowledge, as shown in figure 8.1, are elements used to add further context and relevant information to a prompt. Prompts can be augmented with everything from information about a document to previous tasks or conversations and other reference information.

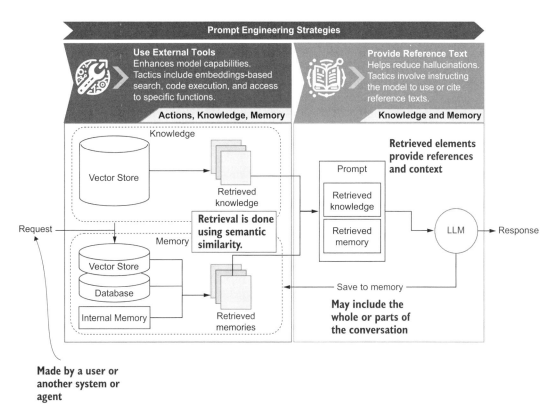

Figure 8.1   Memory, retrieval, and augmentation of the prompt using the following prompt engineering strategies: Use External Tools and Provide Reference Text.

The prompt engineering strategies shown in figure 8.1 can be applied to memory and knowledge. Knowledge isn't considered memory but rather an augmentation of the prompt from existing documents. Both knowledge and memory use retrieval as the basis for how unstructured information can be queried.

The retrieval mechanism, called retrieval augmented generation (RAG), has become a standard for providing relevant context to a prompt. The exact mechanism that powers RAG also powers memory/knowledge, and it's essential to understand how it works. In the next section, we'll examine what RAG is.

8.2   *The basics of retrieval augmented generation (RAG)*

RAG has become a popular mechanism for supporting document chat or question-and-answer chat. The system typically works by a user supplying a relevant document, such as a PDF, and then using RAG and a large language model (LLM) to query the document.

Figure 8.2 shows how RAG can allow a document to be queried using an LLM. Before any document can be queried, it must first be loaded, transformed into context chunks, embedded into vectors, and stored in a vector database.

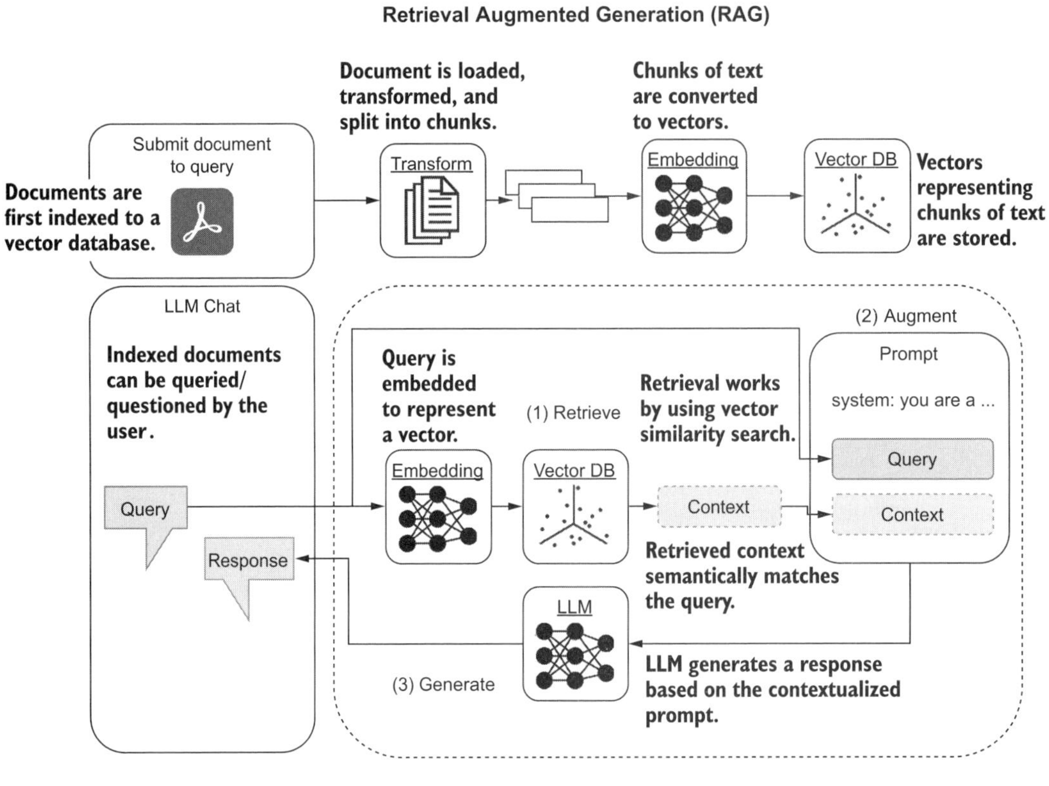

Retrieval Augmented Generation (RAG)

Figure 8.2   The two phases of RAG: first, documents must be loaded, transformed, embedded, and stored, and, second, they can be queried using augmented generation.

A user can query previously indexed documents by submitting a query. That query is then embedded into a vector representation to search for similar chunks in the vector database. Content similar to the query is then used as context and populated into the prompt as augmentation. The prompt is pushed to an LLM, which can use the context information to help answer the query.

Unstructured memory/knowledge concepts rely on some format of text-similarity search following the retrieval pattern shown in figure 8.2. Figure 8.3 shows how memory uses the same embedding and vector database components. Rather than preload documents, conversations or parts of a conversation are embedded and saved to a vector database.

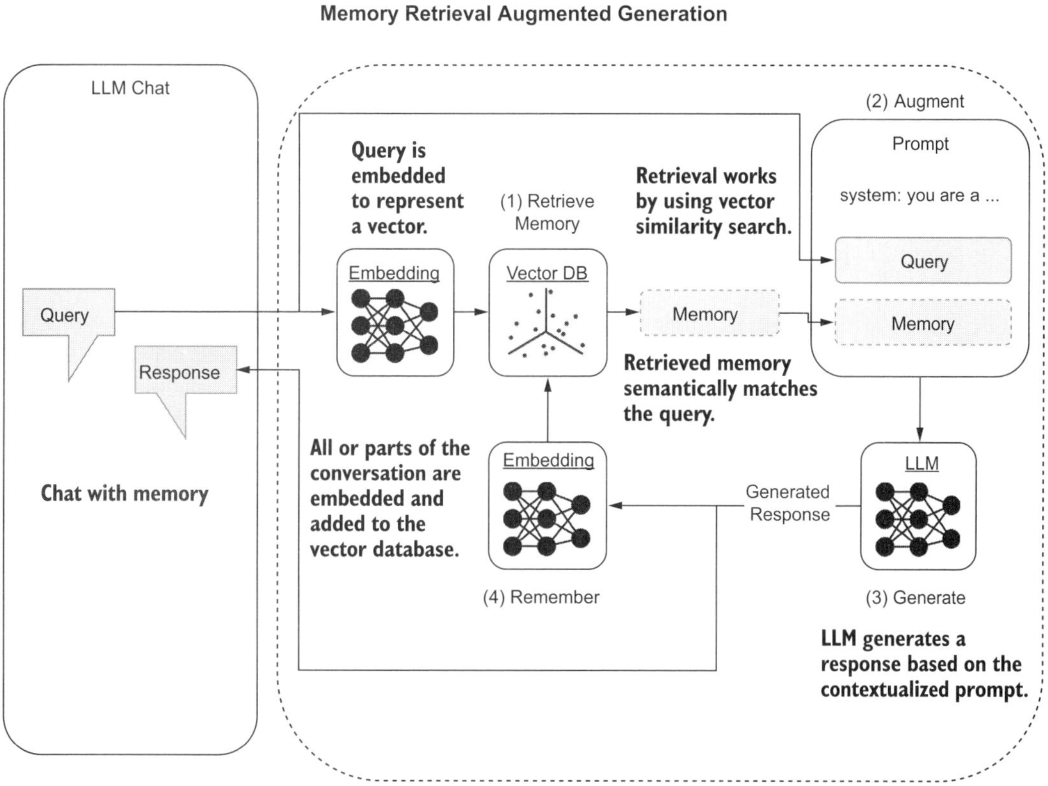

Memory Retrieval Augmented Generation

Figure 8.3 Memory retrieval for augmented generation uses the same embedding patterns to index items to a vector database.

The retrieval pattern and document indexing are nuanced and require careful consideration to be employed successfully. This requires understanding how data is stored and retrieved, which we'll start to unfold in the next section.

8.3   Delving into semantic search and document indexing

Document indexing transforms a document's information to be more easily recovered. How the index will be queried or searched also plays a factor, whether searching for a particular set of words or wanting to match phrase for phrase.

A *semantic* search is a search for content that matches the searched phrase by words and meaning. The ability to search by meaning, semantically, is potent and worth investigating in some detail. In the next section, we look at how vector similarity search can lay the framework for semantic search.

8.3.1   Applying vector similarity search

Let's look now at how a document can be transformed into a *semantic vector,* or a representation of text that can then be used to perform distance or similarity matching. There are numerous ways to convert text into a semantic vector, so we'll look at a simple one.

Open the `chapter_08` folder in a new Visual Studio Code (VS Code) workspace. Create a new environment and `pip install` the `requirements.txt` file for all the chapter dependencies. If you need help setting up a new Python environment, consult appendix B.

Now open the `document_vector_similarity.py` file in VS Code, and review the top section in listing 8.1. This example uses Term Frequency–Inverse Document Frequency (TF–IDF). This numerical statistic reflects how important a word is to a document in a collection or set of documents by increasing proportionally to the number of times a word appears in the document and offset by the frequency of the word in the document set. TF–IDF is a classic measure of understanding one document's importance within a set of documents.

Listing 8.1   `document_vector_similarity` (transform to vector)

```python
import plotly.graph_objects as go
from sklearn.feature_extraction.text import TfidfVectorizer
from sklearn.metrics.pairwise import cosine_similarity

documents = [                                    #  Samples of documents
    "The sky is blue and beautiful.",
    "Love this blue and beautiful sky!",
    "The quick brown fox jumps over the lazy dog.",
    "A king's breakfast has sausages, ham, bacon, eggs, toast, and beans",
    "I love green eggs, ham, sausages and bacon!",
    "The brown fox is quick and the blue dog is lazy!",
    "The sky is very blue and the sky is very beautiful today",
    "The dog is lazy but the brown fox is quick!"
]

vectorizer = TfidfVectorizer()                   #  Vectorization using TF–IDF
X = vectorizer.fit_transform(documents)          #  Vectorize the documents.
```

Let's break down TF–IDF into its two components using the sample sentence, "The sky is blue and beautiful," and focusing on the word *blue*.

TERM FREQUENCY (TF)

Term Frequency measures how frequently a term occurs in a document. Because we're considering only a single document (our sample sentence), the simplest form of the TF for *blue* can be calculated as the number of times *blue* appears in the document divided by the total number of words in the document. Let's calculate it:

Number of times *blue* appears in the document: 1

Total number of words in the document: 6

$$TF = 1 \div 6 \quad TF = .16$$

INVERSE DOCUMENT FREQUENCY (IDF)

Inverse Document Frequency measures how important a term is within the entire corpus. It's calculated by dividing the total number of documents by the number of documents containing the term and then taking the logarithm of that quotient:

IDF = log(Total number of documents ÷ Number of documents containing the word)

In this example, the corpus is a small collection of eight documents, and *blue* appears in four of these documents.

$$IDF = \log(8 \div 4)$$

TF–IDF CALCULATION

Finally, the TF–IDF score for *blue* in our sample sentence is calculated by multiplying the TF and the IDF scores:

$$TF\text{–}IDF = TF \times IDF$$

Let's compute the actual values for TF–IDF for the word *blue* using the example provided; first, the term frequency (how often the word occurs in the document) is computed as follows:

$$TF = 1 \div 6$$

Assuming the base of the logarithm is 10 (commonly used), the inverse document frequency is computed as follows:

$$IDF = \log 10 \; (8 \div 4)$$

Now let's calculate the exact TF–IDF value for the word *blue* in the sentence, "The sky is blue and beautiful":

The Term Frequency (TF) is approximately 0.1670.

The Inverse Document Frequency (IDF) is approximately 0.301.

Thus, the TF–IDF (TF × IDF) score for *blue* is approximately 0.050.

This TF–IDF score indicates the relative importance of the word *blue* in the given document (the sample sentence) within the context of the specified corpus (eight documents, with *blue* appearing in four of them). Higher TF–IDF scores imply greater importance.

We use TF–IDF here because it's simple to apply and understand. Now that we have the elements represented as vectors, we can measure document similarity using cosine similarity. Cosine similarity is a measure used to calculate the cosine of the angle between two nonzero vectors in a multidimensional space, indicating how similar they are, irrespective of their size.

Figure 8.4 shows how cosine distance compares the vector representations of two pieces or documents of text. Cosine similarity returns a value from –1 (not similar) to 1 (identical). *Cosine distance* is a normalized value ranging from 0 to 2, derived by taking 1 minus the cosine similarity. A cosine distance of 0 means identical items, and 2 indicates complete opposites.

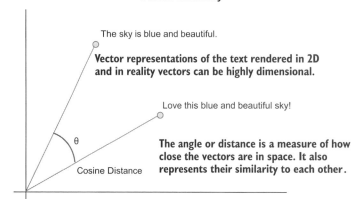

Cosine Similarity

The sky is blue and beautiful.

Vector representations of the text rendered in 2D and in reality vectors can be highly dimensional.

Love this blue and beautiful sky!

θ

The angle or distance is a measure of how close the vectors are in space. It also represents their similarity to each other.

Cosine Distance

Figure 8.4   How cosine similarity is measured

Listing 8.2 shows how the cosine similarities are computed using the `cosine_similarity` function from scikit-learn. Similarities are calculated for each document against all other documents in the set. The computed matrix of similarities for documents is stored in the `cosine_similarities` variable. Then, in the input loop, the user can select the document to view its similarities to the other documents.

Listing 8.2 `document_vector_similarity` (cosine similarity)

```
cosine_similarities = cosine_similarity(X)          ⟵  Computes the document
                                                        similarities for all vector pairs

while True:                                          ⟵  The main
    selected_document_index = input(f"Enter a document number    input loop
⟹ (0-{len(documents)-1}) or 'exit' to quit: ").strip()

    if selected_document_index.lower() == 'exit':
        break

    if not selected_document_index.isdigit() or
⟹ not 0 <= int(selected_document_index) < len(documents):
        print("Invalid input. Please enter a valid document number.")
        continue

    selected_document_index = int(selected_document_index)    ⟵  Gets the selected
                                                                 document index
                                                                 to compare with
    selected_document_similarities =
      cosine_similarities[selected_document_index]    ⟵  Extracts the
                                                          computed similarities
# code to plot document similarities omitted            against all documents
```

Figure 8.5 shows the output of running the sample in VS Code (F5 for debugging mode). After you select a document, you'll see the similarities between the various documents in the set. A document will have a cosine similarity of 1 with itself. Note that you won't see a negative similarity because of the TF–IDF vectorization. We'll look later at other, more sophisticated means of measuring semantic similarity.

Cosine Similarities of "The sky is blue and beautiful." with Others

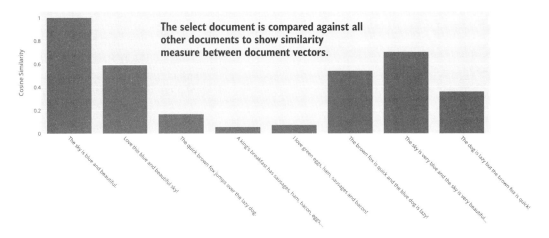

Figure 8.5 The cosine similarity between selected documents and the document set

The method of vectorization will dictate the measure of semantic similarity between documents. Before we move on to better methods of vectorizing documents, we'll examine storing vectors to perform vector similarity searches.

8.3.2   *Vector databases and similarity search*

After vectorizing documents, they can be stored in a vector database for later similarity searches. To demonstrate how this works, we can efficiently replicate a simple vector database in Python code.

Open `document_vector_database.py` in VS Code, as shown in listing 8.3. This code demonstrates creating a vector database in memory and then allowing users to enter text to search the database and return results. The results returned show the document text and the similarity score.

> **Listing 8.3   `document_vector_database.py`**

```
# code above omitted
vectorizer = TfidfVectorizer()
X = vectorizer.fit_transform(documents)          Stores the
vector_database = X.toarray()                     document vectors
                                                  into an array

def cosine_similarity_search(query,               The function to perform
                             database,            similarity matching on
                             vectorizer,          query returns, matches,
                             top_n=5):            and similarity scores
    query_vec = vectorizer.transform([query]).toarray()
    similarities = cosine_similarity(query_vec, database)[0]
    top_indices = np.argsort(-similarities)[:top_n]  # Top n indices
    return [(idx, similarities[idx]) for idx in top_indices]

while True:                                               The main
    query = input("Enter a search query (or 'exit' to stop): ")   input loop
    if query.lower() == 'exit':
        break
    top_n = int(input("How many top matches do you want to see? "))
    search_results = cosine_similarity_search(query,
                                              vector_database,
                                              vectorizer,
                                              top_n)

    print("Top Matched Documents:")
    for idx, score in search_results:                    Loops through
        print(f"- {documents[idx]} (Score: {score:.4f})")   results and
                                                          outputs text and
    print("\n")                                           similarity score
###Output
Enter a search query (or 'exit' to stop): blue
How many top matches do you want to see? 3
Top Matched Documents:
- The sky is blue and beautiful. (Score: 0.4080)
- Love this blue and beautiful sky! (Score: 0.3439)
- The brown fox is quick and the blue dog is lazy! (Score: 0.2560)
```

Run this exercise to see the output (F5 in VS Code). Enter any text you like, and see the results of documents being returned. This search form works well for matching words and phrases with similar words and phrases. This form of search misses the word context and meaning from the document. In the next section, we'll look at a way of transforming documents into vectors that better preserves their semantic meaning.

8.3.3 Demystifying document embeddings

TF–IDF is a simple form that tries to capture semantic meaning in documents. However, it's unreliable because it only counts word frequency and doesn't understand the relationships between words. A better and more modern method uses document embedding, a form of document vectorizing that better preserves the semantic meaning of the document.

Embedding networks are constructed by training neural networks on large datasets to map words, sentences, or documents to high-dimensional vectors, capturing semantic and syntactic relationships based on context and relationships in the data. You typically use a pretrained model trained on massive datasets to embed documents and perform embeddings. Models are available from many sources, including Hugging Face and, of course, OpenAI.

In our next scenario, we'll use an OpenAI embedding model. These models are typically perfect for capturing the semantic context of embedded documents. Listing 8.4 shows the relevant code that uses OpenAI to embed the documents into vectors that are then reduced to three dimensions and rendered into a plot.

Listing 8.4 `document_visualizing_embeddings.py` (relevant sections)

```
load_dotenv()
api_key = os.getenv('OPENAI_API_KEY')
if not api_key:                                          Join all the items on the string ', '.
    raise ValueError("No API key found. Please check your .env file.")
client = OpenAI(api_key=api_key)


def get_embedding(text, model="text-embedding-ada-002"):     Uses the OpenAI
    text = text.replace("\n", " ")                           client to create
    return client.embeddings.create(input=[text],           the embedding
            model=model).data[0].embedding


# Sample documents (omitted)                                 Generates embeddings
                                                             for each document of
embeddings = [get_embedding(doc) for doc in documents]       size 1536 dimensions
print(embeddings_array.shape)
                                                     Converts embeddings to
                                                     a NumPy array for PCA
embeddings_array = np.array(embeddings)


pca = PCA(n_components=3)                                     Applies PCA to
reduced_embeddings = pca.fit_transform(embeddings_array)     reduce dimensions
                                                             to 3 for plotting
```

When a document is embedded using an OpenAI model, it transforms the text into a vector with dimensions of 1536. We can't visualize this number of dimensions, so we use a dimensionality reduction technique via principal component analysis (PCA) to convert the vector of size 1536 to 3 dimensions.

Figure 8.6 shows the output generated from running the file in VS Code. By reducing the embeddings to 3D, we can plot the output to show how semantically similar documents are now grouped.

3D Plot of Document Embeddings

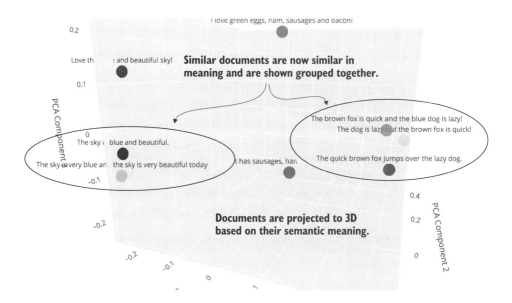

Figure 8.6   Embeddings in 3D, showing how similar semantic documents are grouped

The choice of which embedding model or service you use is up to you. The OpenAI embedding models are considered the best for general semantic similarity. This has made these models the standard for most memory and retrieval applications. With our understanding of how text can be vectorized with embeddings and stored in a vector database, we can move on to a more realistic example in the next section.

8.3.4   *Querying document embeddings from Chroma*

We can combine all the pieces and look at a complete example using a local vector database called Chroma DB. Many vector database options exist, but Chroma DB is an excellent local vector store for development or small-scale projects. There are also plenty of more robust options that you can consider later.

Listing 8.5 shows the new and relevant code sections from the `document_query_chromadb.py` file. Note that the results are scored by distance and not by similarity. Cosine distance is determined by this equation:

$$\text{Cosine Distance}(A,B) = 1 - \text{Cosine Similarity}(A,B)$$

This means that cosine distance will range from 0 for most similar to 2 for semantically opposite in meaning.

Listing 8.5 `document_query_chromadb.py` (relevant code sections)

```
embeddings = [get_embedding(doc) for doc in documents]       ⎫ Generates embeddings
ids = [f"id{i}" for i in range(len(documents))]              ⎬ for each document and
                                                              ⎭ assigns an ID

chroma_client = chromadb.Client()                   ⟵ Creates a Chroma DB
collection = chroma_client.create_collection(         client and a collection
                name="documents")                   ⟵
collection.add(                                      ⟵ Adds document
    embeddings=embeddings,                              embeddings to
    documents=documents,                               the collection
    ids=ids
)

def query_chromadb(query, top_n=2):                 ⟵ Queries the datastore
    query_embedding = get_embedding(query)             and returns the top n
    results = collection.query(                        relevant documents
        query_embeddings=[query_embedding],
        n_results=top_n
    )
    return [(id, score, text) for id, score, text in
            zip(results['ids'][0],
                results['distances'][0],
                results['documents'][0])]

while True:                                                          ⟵
    query = input("Enter a search query (or 'exit' to stop): ")
    if query.lower() == 'exit':
        break
    top_n = int(input("How many top matches do you want to see? "))
    search_results = query_chromadb(query, top_n)
                                                        The input loop for
    print("Top Matched Documents:")                   user input and output of
    for id, score, text in search_results:           relevant documents/scores
        print(f"""
ID:{id} TEXT: {text} SCORE: {round(score, 2)}
""")                                                                ⟵

    print("\n")
###Output
Enter a search query (or 'exit' to stop): dogs are lazy
How many top matches do you want to see? 3
Top Matched Documents:
ID:id7 TEXT: The dog is lazy but the brown fox is quick! SCORE: 0.24
```

```
ID:id5 TEXT: The brown fox is quick and the blue dog is lazy! SCORE: 0.28
ID:id2 TEXT: The quick brown fox jumps over the lazy dog. SCORE: 0.29
```

As the earlier scenario demonstrated, you can now query the documents using semantic meaning rather than just key terms or phrases. These scenarios should now provide the background to see how the retrieval pattern works at a low level. In the next section, we'll see how the retrieval pattern can be employed using LangChain.

8.4   *Constructing RAG with LangChain*

LangChain began as an open source project specializing in abstracting the retrieval pattern across multiple data sources and vector stores. It has since morphed into much more, but foundationally, it still provides excellent options for implementing retrieval.

Figure 8.7 shows a diagram from LangChain that identifies the process of storing documents for retrieval. These same steps may be replicated in whole or in part to implement memory retrieval. The critical difference between document and memory retrieval is the source and how content is transformed.

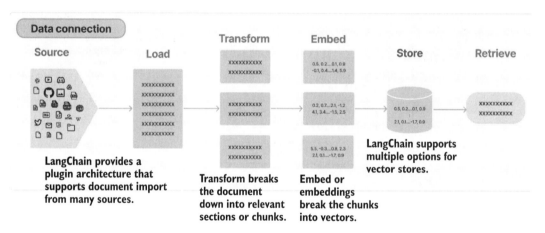

Figure 8.7   Load, transform, embed, and store steps in storing documents for later retrieval

We'll examine how to implement each of these steps using LangChain and understand the nuances and details accompanying this implementation. In the next section, we'll start by splitting and loading documents with LangChain.

8.4.1   *Splitting and loading documents with LangChain*

Retrieval mechanisms augment the context of a given prompt with specific information relevant to the request. For example, you may request detailed information about a local document. With earlier language models, submitting the whole document as part of the prompt wasn't an option due to token limitations.

Today, we could submit a whole document for many commercial LLMs, such as GPT-4 Turbo, as part of a prompt request. However, the results may not be better and would likely cost more because of the increased number of tokens. Therefore, a better option is to split the document and use the relevant parts to request context—precisely what RAG and memory do.

Splitting a document is essential in breaking down content into semantically and specifically relevant sections. Figure 8.8 shows how to break down an HTML document containing the Mother Goose nursery rhymes. Often, splitting a document into contextual semantic chunks requires careful consideration.

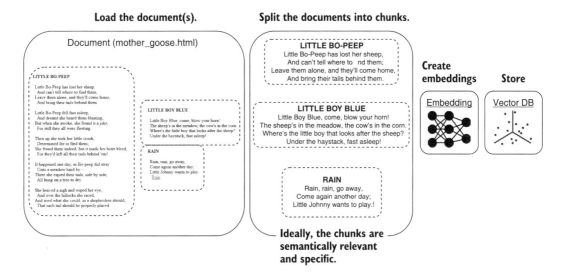

Figure 8.8 How the document would ideally be split into chunks for better semantic and contextual meaning

Ideally, when we split documents into chunks, they are broken down by relevance and semantic meaning. While an LLM or agent could help us with this, we'll look at current toolkit options within LangChain for splitting documents. Later in this chapter, we'll look at a semantic function that can assist us in semantically dividing content for embeddings.

For the next exercise, open `langchain_load_splitting.py` in VS Code, as shown in listing 8.6. This code shows where we left off from listing 8.5, in the previous section. Instead of using the sample documents, we're loading the Mother Goose nursery rhymes this time.

Listing 8.6   `langchain_load_splitting.py` (sections and output)

```
From langchain_community.document_loaders                          New LangChain
                    ➥ import UnstructuredHTMLLoader                 imports
from langchain.text_splitter import RecursiveCharacterTextSplitter

#previous code
                                                                    Loads the
                                                                    document
loader = UnstructuredHTMLLoader(                                    as HTML
                "sample_documents/mother_goose.html")
data = loader.load                                                  Loads the
                                                                    document
text_splitter = RecursiveCharacterTextSplitter(
    chunk_size=100,                                        Splits the document into blocks of
    chunk_overlap=25,                                      text 100 characters long with a
    length_function=len,                                   25-character overlap
    add_start_index=True,
)
documents = text_splitter.split_documents(data)           Embeds only 250
                                                          chunks, which is
documents = [doc.page_content                             cheaper and faster
                ➥ for doc in documents] [100:350]
                                                          Returns the
embeddings = [get_embedding(doc) for doc in documents]    embedding for
ids = [f"id{i}" for i in range(len(documents))]           each document
###Output
Enter a search query (or 'exit' to stop): who kissed the girls and made
them cry?
How many top matches do you want to see? 3
Top Matched Documents:
ID:id233 TEXT: And chid her daughter,
        And kissed my sister instead of me. SCORE: 0.4…
```

Note in listing 8.6 that the HTML document gets split into 100-character chunks with a 25-character overlap. The overlap allows the document's parts not to cut off specific thoughts. We selected the splitter for this exercise because it was easy to use, set up, and understand.

Go ahead and run the `langchain_load_splitting.py` file in VS Code (F5). Enter a query, and see what results you get. The output in listing 8.6 shows good results given a specific example. Remember that we only embedded 250 document chunks to reduce costs and keep the exercise short. Of course, you can always try to embed the entire document or use a minor input document example.

Perhaps the most critical element to building proper retrieval is the process of document splitting. You can use numerous methods to split a document, including multiple concurrent methods. More than one method passes and splits the document for numerous embedding views of the same document. In the next section, we'll examine a more general technique for splitting documents, using tokens and tokenization.

8.4.2   Splitting documents by token with LangChain

Tokenization is the process of breaking text into word tokens. Where a word token represents a succinct element in the text, a token could be a word like *hold* or even a symbol like the left curly brace ({), depending on what's relevant.

Splitting documents using tokenization provides a better base for how the text will be interpreted by language models and for semantic similarity. Tokenization also allows the removal of irrelevant characters, such as whitespace, making the similarity matching of documents more relevant and generally providing better results.

For the next code exercise, open the `langchain_token_splitting.py` file in VS Code, as shown in listing 8.7. Now we split the document using tokenization, which breaks the document into sections of unequal size. The unequal size results from the large sections of whitespace of the original document.

Listing 8.7 `langchain_token_splitting.py` (relevant new code)

```
loader = UnstructuredHTMLLoader("sample_documents/mother_goose.html")
data = loader.load()
text_splitter = CharacterTextSplitter.from_tiktoken_encoder(
    chunk_size=50, chunk_overlap=10                      ◁── Updates to 50 tokens
)                                                             and overlap of 10
                                                             tokens
documents = text_splitter.split_documents(data)
documents = [doc for doc in documents][8:94]            ◁── Selects just the
                                                            documents that
db = Chroma.from_documents(documents, OpenAIEmbeddings())   contain rhymes

def query_documents(query, top_n=2):
    docs = db.similarity_search(query, top_n)       ◁── Uses the database's
    return docs                                         similarity search
###Output
Created a chunk of size 68,
which is longer than the specified 50           Breaks into irregular
Created a chunk of size 67,                      size chunks because of
which is longer than the specified 50       ◁── the whitespace
Enter a search query (or 'exit' to stop):
                    who kissed the girls and made them cry?
How many top matches do you want to see? 3
Top Matched Documents:
Document 1: GEORGY PORGY

        Georgy Porgy, pudding and pie,
        Kissed the girls and made them cry.
```

Run the `langchain_token_splitting.py` code in VS Code (F5). You can use the query we used last time or your own. Notice how the results are significantly better than the previous exercise. However, the results are still suspect because the query uses several similar words in the same order.

A better test would be to try a semantically similar phrase but one that uses different words and check the results. With the code still running, enter a new phrase to query: Why are the girls crying? Listing 8.8 shows the results of executing that query. If you run this example yourself and scroll down over the output, you'll see Georgy Porgy appear in either the second or third returned document.

Listing 8.8   Query: Who made the girls cry?

```
Enter a search query (or 'exit' to stop): Who made the girls cry?
How many top matches do you want to see? 3
Top Matched Documents:
Document 1: WILLY, WILLY

        Willy, Willy Wilkin…
```

This exercise shows how various retrieval methods can be employed to return documents semantically. With this base established, we can see how RAG can be applied to knowledge and memory systems. The following section will discuss RAG as it applies to knowledge of agents and agentic systems.

8.5   *Applying RAG to building agent knowledge*

Knowledge in agents encompasses employing RAG to search semantically across unstructured documents. These documents could be anything from PDFs to Microsoft Word documents and all text, including code. Agentic knowledge also includes using unstructured documents for Q&A, reference lookup, information augmentation, and other future patterns.

Nexus, the agent platform developed in tandem with this book and introduced in the previous chapter, employs complete knowledge and memory systems for agents. In this section, we'll uncover how the knowledge system works.

To install Nexus for just this chapter, see listing 8.9. Open a terminal within the chapter_08 folder, and execute the commands in the listing to download, install, and run Nexus in normal or development mode. If you want to refer to the code, you should install the project in development and configure the debugger to run the Streamlit app from VS Code. Refer to chapter 7 if you need a refresher on any of these steps.

Listing 8.9   Installing Nexus

```
# to install and run
pip install git+https://github.com/cxbxmxcx/Nexus.git

nexus run
# install in development mode
git clone https://github.com/cxbxmxcx/Nexus.git

# Install the cloned repository in editable mode
pip install -e Nexus
```

Regardless of which method you decide to run the app in after you log in, navigate to the Knowledge Store Manager page, as shown in figure 8.9. Create a new Knowledge Store, and then upload the `sample_documents/back_to_the_future.txt` movie script.

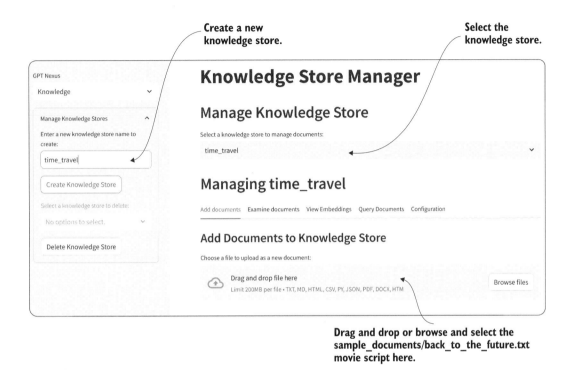

Figure 8.9 Adding a new knowledge store and populating it with a document

The script is a large document, and it may take a while to load, chunk, and embed the parts into the Chroma DB vector database. Wait for the indexing to complete, and then you can inspect the embeddings and run a query, as shown in figure 8.10.

Now, we can connect the knowledge store to a supported agent and ask questions. Use the top-left selector to choose the chat page within the Nexus interface. Then, select an agent and the `time_travel` knowledge store, as shown in figure 8.11. You will also need to select an agent engine that supports knowledge. Each of the multiple agent engines requires the proper configuration to be accessible.

Currently, as of this chapter, Nexus supports access to only a single knowledge store at a time. In a future version, agents may be able to select multiple knowledge stores at a time. This may include more advanced options, from semantic knowledge to employing other forms of RAG.

**Select to view all the
embeddings in the
knowledge store.**

**Select to query the
document embeddings
in the knowledge store.**

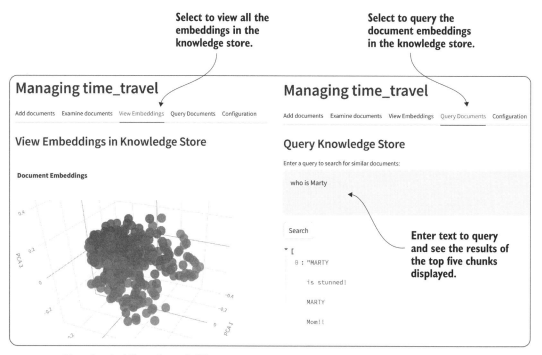

Plot of embeddings shown in 3D

Figure 8.10   The embeddings and document query views

**Enter a question about
the script you would
like to ask.**

**Select an agent engine
that supports knowledge.**

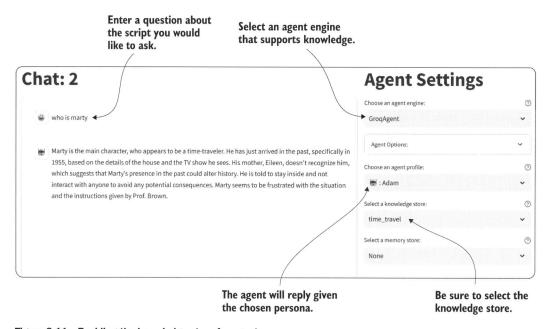

**The agent will reply given
the chosen persona.**

**Be sure to select the
knowledge store.**

Figure 8.11   Enabling the knowledge store for agent use

You can also configure the RAG settings within the Configuration tab of the Knowledge Store Manager page, as shown in figure 8.12. As of now, you can select from the type of splitter (Chunking Option field) to chunk the document, along with the Chunk Size field and Overlap field.

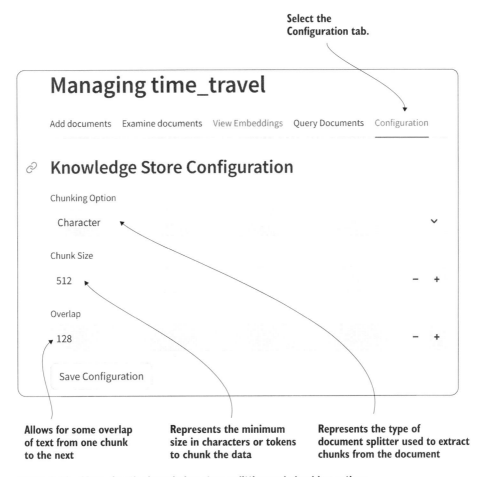

Figure 8.12   Managing the knowledge store splitting and chunking options

The loading, splitting, chunking, and embedding options provided are the only basic options supported by LangChain for now. In future versions of Nexus, more options and patterns will be offered. The code to support other options can be added directly to Nexus.

We won't cover the code that performs the RAG as it's very similar to what we already covered. Feel free to review the Nexus code, particularly the KnowledgeManager class in the knowledge_manager.py file.

While the retrieval patterns for knowledge and memory are quite similar for augmentation, the two patterns differ when it comes to populating the stores. In the next section, we'll explore what makes memory in agents unique.

8.6   *Implementing memory in agentic systems*

Memory in agents and AI applications is often described in the same terms as cognitive memory functions. *Cognitive* memory describes the type of memory we use to remember what we did 30 seconds ago or how tall we were 30 years ago. Computer memory is also an essential element of agent memory, but one we won't consider in this section.

Figure 8.13 shows how memory is broken down into sensory, short-term, and long-term memory. This memory can be applied to AI agents, and this list describes how each form of memory maps to agent functions:

- *Sensory memory in AI*—Functions such as RAG but with images/audio/haptic data forms. Briefly holds input data (e.g., text and images) for immediate processing but not long-term storage.
- *Short-term/working memory in AI*—Acts as an active memory buffer of conversation history. We're holding a limited amount of recent input and context for immediate analysis and response generation. Within Nexus, short- and long-term conversational memory is also held in the context of the thread.
- *Long-term memory in AI*—Longer-term memory storage relevant to the agent's or user's life. Semantic memory provides a robust capacity to store and retrieve relevant global or local facts and concepts.

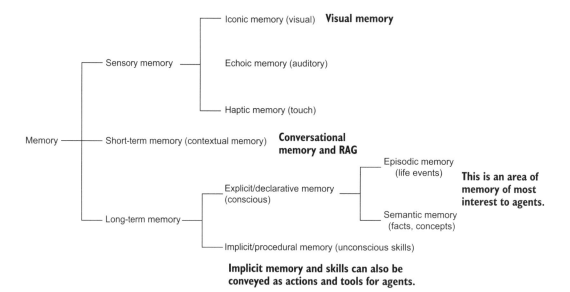

Figure 8.13   How memory is broken down into various forms

While memory uses the exact same retrieval and augmentation mechanisms as knowledge, it typically differs significantly when updating or appending memories. Figure 8.14 highlights the process of capturing and using memories to augment prompts. Because memories are often different from the size of complete documents, we can avoid using any splitting or chunking mechanisms.

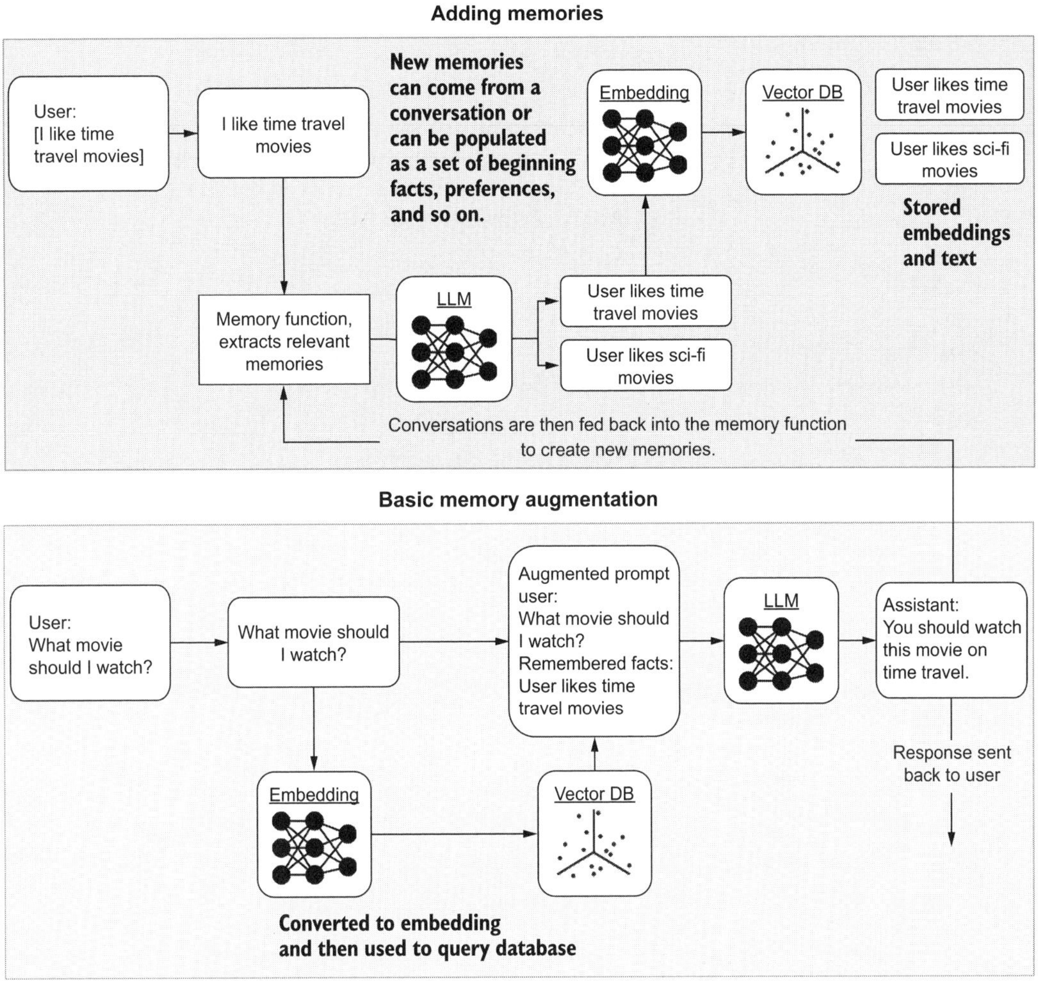

Figure 8.14 Basic memory retrieval and augmentation workflow

Nexus provides a mechanism like the knowledge store, allowing users to create memory stores that can be configured for various uses and applications. It also supports some of the more advanced memory forms highlighted in figure 8.13. The following section will examine how basic memory stores work in Nexus.

8.6.1 *Consuming memory stores in Nexus*

Memory stores operate and are constructed like knowledge stores in Nexus. They both heavily rely on the retrieval pattern. What differs is the extra steps memory systems take to build new memories.

Go ahead and start Nexus, and refer to listing 8.9 if you need to install it. After logging in, select the Memory page, and create a new memory store, as shown in figure 8.15. Select an agent engine, and then add a few personal facts and preferences about yourself.

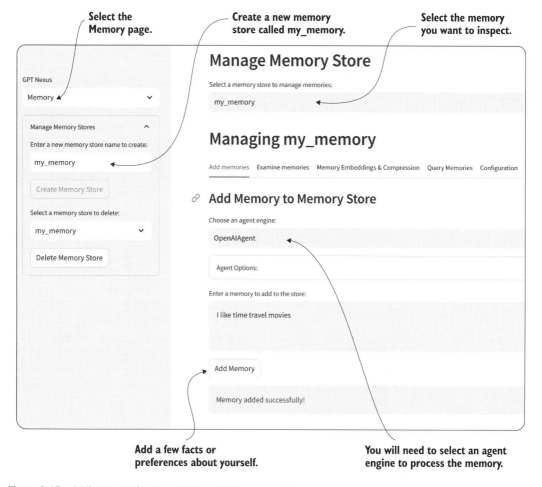

Figure 8.15   Adding memories to a newly created memory store

The reason we need an agent (LLM) was shown in figure 8.14 earlier. When information is fed into a memory store, it's generally processed through an LLM using a memory function, whose purpose is to process the statements/conversations into semantically relevant information related to the type of memory.

Listing 8.10 shows the conversational memory function used to extract information from a conversation into memories. Yes, this is just the header portion of the prompt sent to the LLM, instructing it how to extract information from a conversation.

Listing 8.10   Conversational memory function

```
Summarize the conversation and create a set of statements that summarize
the conversation. Return a JSON object with the following keys: 'summary'.
Each key should have a list of statements that are relevant to that
category. Return only the JSON object and nothing else.
```

After you generate a few relevant memories about yourself, return to the Chat area in Nexus, enable the `my_memory` memory store, and see how well the agent knows you. Figure 8.16 shows a sample conversation using a different agent engine.

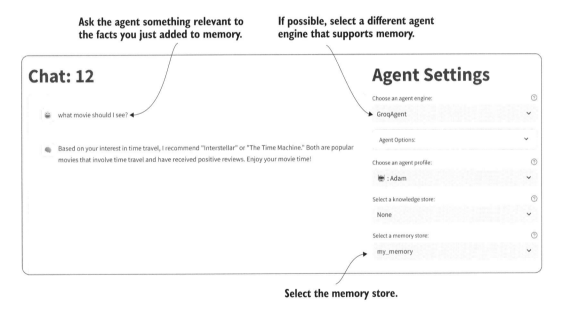

Figure 8.16   Conversing with a different agent on the same memory store

This is an example of a basic memory pattern that extracts facts/preferences from conversations and stores them in a vector database as memories. Numerous other implementations of memory follow those displayed earlier in figure 8.13. We'll implement those in the next section.

8.6.2   *Semantic memory and applications to semantic, episodic, and procedural memory*

Psychologists categorize memory into multiple forms, depending on what information is remembered. Semantic, episodic, and procedural memory all represent different types of information. *Episodic* memories are about events, *procedural* memories are about the process or steps, and *semantic* represents the meaning and could include feelings or emotions. Other forms of memory (geospatial is another), aren't described here but could be.

Because these memories rely on an additional level of categorization, they also rely on another level of semantic categorization. Some platforms, such as Semantic Kernel (SK), refer to this as *semantic memory*. This can be confusing because semantic categorization is also applied to extract episodic and procedural memories.

Figure 8.17 shows the semantic memory categorization process, also sometimes called semantic memory. The difference between semantic memory and regular memory is the additional step of processing the input semantically and extracting relevant questions that can be used to query the memory-relevant vector database.

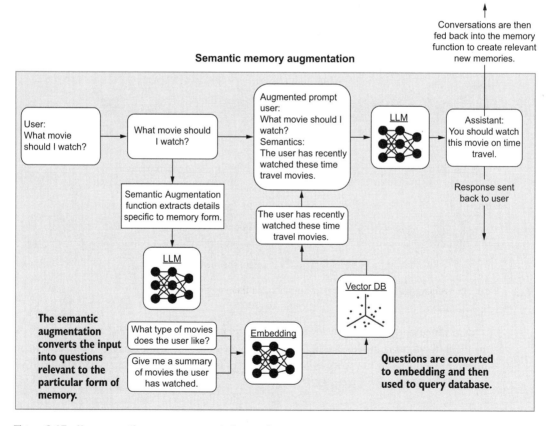

Figure 8.17   How semantic memory augmentation works

The benefit of using semantic augmentation is the increased ability to extract more relevant memories. We can see this in operation by jumping back into Nexus and creating a new semantic memory store.

Figure 8.18 shows how to configure a new memory store using semantic memory. As of yet, you can't configure the specific function prompts for memory, augmentation, and summarization. However, it can be useful to read through each of the function prompts to gain a sense of how they work.

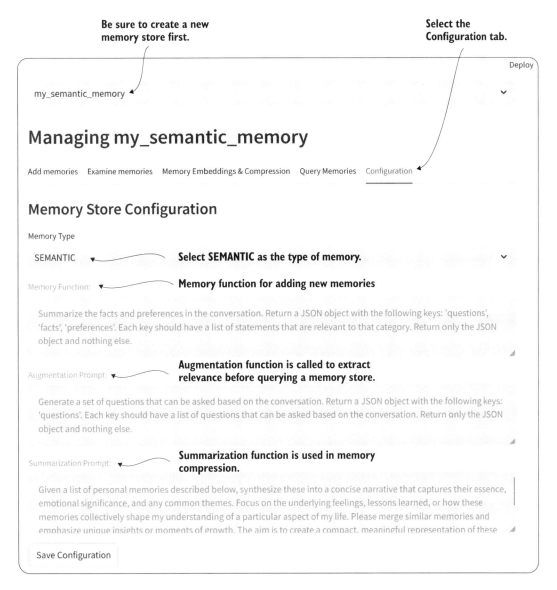

Figure 8.18   Configuration for changing the memory store type to semantic

Now, if you go back and add facts and preferences, they will convert to the semantics of the relevant memory type. Figure 8.19 shows an example of memories being populated for the same set of statements into two different forms of memory. Generally, the statements entered into memory would be more specific to the form of memory.

Managing my_semantic_memory

Add memories   Examine memories   Memory Embeddings & Compression   Query Memories   Configuration

Examine Memories in Memory Store

	ID Hash	Memory
0	9W8VW9oh5b	The interlocutor has a preference for movies that involve time travel.
1	Bfl_FnsdpU	The person has a preference for movies that involve time loops.
2	D27dzx-YxU	The interlocutor enjoys time travel movies.
3	Ef_H19Jc_D	The interlocutor enjoys watching time loop movies.
4	OSRsYrThXQ	It can be inferred that the individual finds time loop movies entertaining.

Managing my_episodic_memory

Add memories   Examine memories   Memory Embeddings & Compression   Query Memories   Configuration

Examine Memories in Memory Store

	ID Hash	Memory
0	0AQPgbOy-F	This conversation focuses on time loop movies.
1	D27dzx-YxU	The interlocutor enjoys time travel movies.
2	Z4MOsfNjZl	The interlocutor exhibits a preference for cinema that involves time travel.
3	_O-XfTP4mS	The person enjoys watching time loop movies.
4	sFU16iMoz8	It is indicated that time travel movies are a topic of interest for the interlocutor.
5	uKQc6z9yS7	The interlocutor appreciates the concept of moving through different time periods in movies.
6	uogR5kBGW9	The person has a preference for a specific genre of movies, namely time loop movies.

Figure 8.19 Comparing memories for the same information given two different memory types

Memory and knowledge can significantly assist an agent with various application types. Indeed, a single memory/knowledge store could feed one or multiple agents, allowing for further specialized interpretations of both types of stores. We'll finish out the chapter by discussing memory/knowledge compression next.

8.7   *Understanding memory and knowledge compression*

Much like our own memory, memory stores can become cluttered with redundant information and numerous unrelated details over time. Internally, our minds deal with memory clutter by compressing or summarizing memories. Our minds remember more significant details over less important ones, and memories accessed more frequently.

We can apply similar principles of memory compression to agent memory and other retrieval systems to extract significant details. The principle of compression is similar to semantic augmentation but adds another layer to the preclusters groups of related memories that can collectively be summarized.

Figure 8.20 shows the process of memory/knowledge compression. Memories or knowledge are first clustered using an algorithm such as k-means. Then, the groups of memories are passed through a compression function, which summarizes and collects the items into more succinct representations.

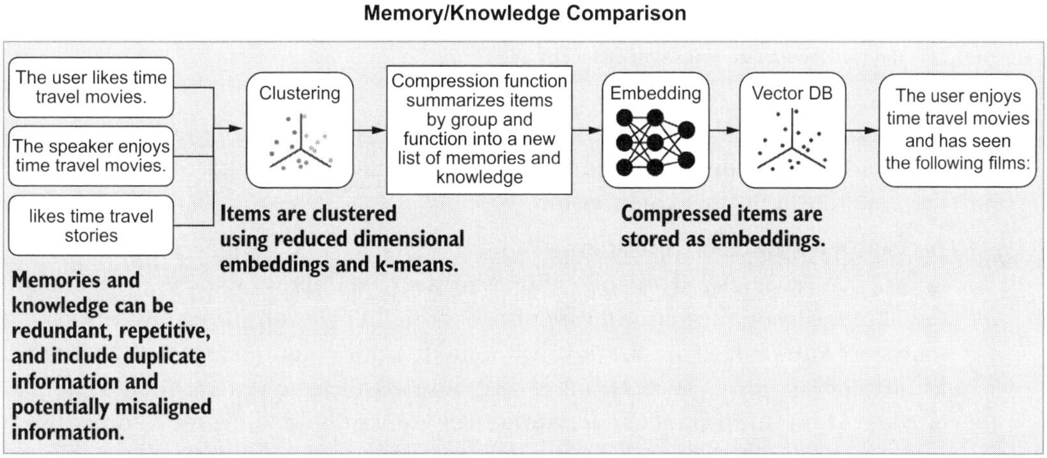

Figure 8.20   The process of memory and knowledge compression

Nexus provides for both knowledge and memory store compression using k-means optimal clustering. Figure 8.21 shows the compression interface for memory. Within the compression interface, you'll see the items displayed in 3D and clustered. The size (number of items) of the clusters is shown in the left table.

Compressing memories and even knowledge is generally recommended if the number of items in a cluster is large or unbalanced. Each use case for compression may vary depending on the use and application of memories. Generally, though, if an

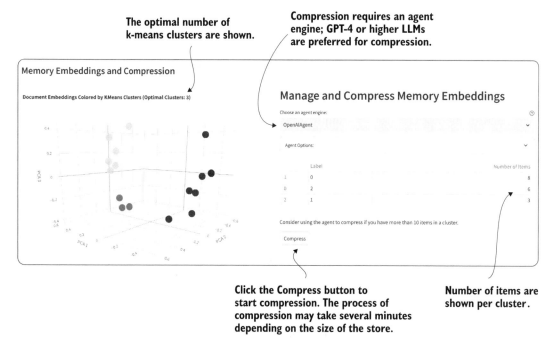

Figure 8.21   The interface for compressing memories

inspection of the items in a store contains repetitive or duplicate information, it's a good time for compression. The following is a summary of use cases for applications that would benefit from compression.

THE CASE FOR KNOWLEDGE COMPRESSION

Knowledge retrieval and augmentation have also been shown to benefit significantly from compression. Results will vary by use case, but generally, the more verbose the source of knowledge, the more it will benefit from compression. Documents that feature literary prose, such as stories and novels, will benefit more than, say, a base of code. However, if the code is likewise very repetitive, compression could also be shown to be beneficial.

THE CASE FOR HOW OFTEN YOU APPLY COMPRESSION

Memory will often benefit from the periodic compression application, whereas knowledge stores typically only help on the first load. How frequently you apply compression will greatly depend on the memory use, frequency, and quantity.

THE CASE FOR APPLYING COMPRESSION MORE THAN ONCE

Multiple passes of compression at the same time has been shown to improve retrieval performance. Other patterns have also suggested using memory or knowledge at various levels of compression. For example, a knowledge store is compressed two times, resulting in three different levels of knowledge.

THE CASE FOR BLENDING KNOWLEDGE AND MEMORY COMPRESSION

If a system is specialized to a particular source of knowledge and that system also employs memories, there may be further optimization to consolidate stores. Another approach is to populate memory with the starting knowledge of a document directly.

THE CASE FOR MULTIPLE MEMORY OR KNOWLEDGE STORES

In more advanced systems, we'll look at agents employing multiple memory and knowledge stores relevant to their workflow. For example, an agent could employ individual memory stores as part of its conversations with individual users, perhaps including the ability to share different groups of memory with different groups of individuals. Memory and knowledge retrieval are cornerstones of agentic systems, and we can now summarize what we covered and review some learning exercises in the next section.

8.8 Exercises

Use the following exercises to improve your knowledge of the material:

- *Exercise 1*—Load and Split a Different Document (Intermediate)

  Objective—Understand the effect of document splitting on retrieval efficiency by using LangChain.

  Tasks:

  - Select a different document (e.g., a news article, a scientific paper, or a short story).
  - Use LangChain to load and split the document into chunks.
  - Analyze how the document is split into chunks and how it affects the retrieval process.

- *Exercise 2*—Experiment with Semantic Search (Intermediate)

  Objective—Compare the effectiveness of various vectorization techniques by performing semantic searches.

  Tasks:

  - Choose a set of documents for semantic search.
  - Use a vectorization method such as Word2Vec or BERT embeddings instead of TF–IDF.
  - Perform the semantic search, and compare the results with those obtained using TF–IDF to understand the differences and effectiveness.

- *Exercise 3*—Implement a Custom RAG Workflow (Advanced)

  Objective—Apply theoretical knowledge of RAG in a practical context using LangChain.

  Tasks:

  - Choose a specific application (e.g., customer service inquiries or academic research queries).
  - Design and implement a custom RAG workflow using LangChain.
  - Tailor the workflow to suit the chosen application, and test its effectiveness.

- *Exercise 4*—Build a Knowledge Store and Experiment with Splitting Patterns (Intermediate)

  Objective—Understand how different splitting patterns and compression affect knowledge retrieval.

  Tasks:
  - Build a knowledge store, and populate it with a couple of documents.
  - Experiment with different forms of splitting/chunking patterns, and analyze their effect on retrieval.
  - Compress the knowledge store, and observe the effects on query performance.
- *Exercise 5*—Build and Test Various Memory Stores (Advanced)

  Objective—Understand the uniqueness and use cases of different memory store types.

  Tasks:
  - Build various forms of memory stores (conversational, semantic, episodic, and procedural).
  - Interact with an agent using each type of memory store, and observe the differences.
  - Compress the memory store, and analyze the effect on memory retrieval.

Summary

- Memory in AI applications differentiates between unstructured and structured memory, highlighting their use in contextualizing prompts for more relevant interactions.
- Retrieval augmented generation (RAG) is a mechanism for enhancing prompts with context from external documents, using vector embeddings and similarity search to retrieve relevant content.
- Semantic search with document indexing converts documents into semantic vectors using TF–IDF and cosine similarity, enhancing the capability to perform semantic searches across indexed documents.
- Vector databases and similarity search stores document vectors in a vector database, facilitating efficient similarity searches and improving retrieval accuracy.
- Document embeddings capture semantic meanings, using models such as OpenAI's models to generate embeddings that preserve a document's context and facilitate semantic similarity searches.
- LangChain provides several tools for performing RAG, and it abstracts the retrieval process, allowing for easy implementation of RAG and memory systems across various data sources and vector stores.
- Short-term and long-term memory in LangChain implements conversational memory within LangChain, distinguishing between short-term buffering patterns and long-term storage solutions.

- Storing document vectors in databases for efficient similarity searches is crucial for implementing scalable retrieval systems in AI applications.

- Agent knowledge directly relates to the general RAG pattern of performing question and answer on documents or other textual information.

- Agent memory is a pattern related to RAG that captures the agentic interactions with users, itself, and other systems.

- Nexus is a platform that implements agentic knowledge and memory systems, including setting up knowledge stores for document retrieval and memory stores for various forms of memory.

- Semantic memory augmentation (semantic memory) differentiates between various types of memories (semantic, episodic, procedural). It implements them through semantic augmentation, enhancing agents' ability to recall and use information relevantly specific to the nature of the memories.

- Memory and knowledge compression are techniques for condensing information stored in memory and knowledge systems, improving retrieval efficiency and relevancy through clustering and summarization.

Mastering agent prompts with prompt flow

This chapter covers

- Understanding systematic prompt engineering and setting up your first prompt flow
- Crafting an effective profile/persona prompt
- Evaluating profiles: Rubrics and grounding
- Grounding evaluation of a large language model profile
- Comparing prompts: Getting the perfect profile

In this chapter, we delve into the Test Changes Systematically prompt engineering strategy. If you recall, we covered the grand strategies of the OpenAI prompt engineering framework in chapter 2. These strategies are instrumental in helping us build better prompts and, consequently, better agent profiles and personas. Understanding this role is key to our prompt engineering journey.

Test Changes Systematically is such a core facet of prompt engineering that Microsoft developed a tool around this strategy called *prompt flow*, described later in this chapter. Before getting to prompt flow, we need to understand why we need systemic prompt engineering.

9.1   Why we need systematic prompt engineering

Prompt engineering, by its nature, is an iterative process. When building a prompt, you'll often iterate and evaluate. To see this concept in action, consider the simple application of prompt engineering to a ChatGPT question.

You can follow along by opening your browser to ChatGPT (https://chat.openai .com/), entering the following (text) prompt into ChatGPT, and clicking the Send Message button (an example of this conversation is shown in figure 9.1, on the left side):

> can you recommend something

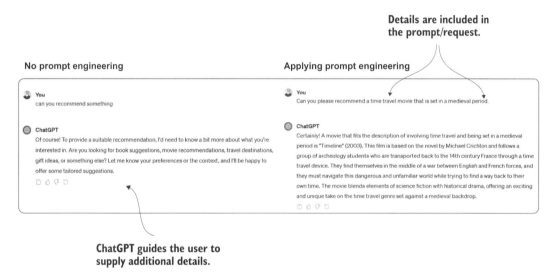

Figure 9.1   The differences in applying prompt engineering and iterating

We can see that the response from ChatGPT is asking for more information. Go ahead and open a new conversation with ChatGPT, and enter the following prompt, as shown in figure 9.1, on the right side:

> Can you please recommend a time travel movie set in the medieval period.

The results in figure 9.1 show a clear difference between leaving out details and being more specific in your request. We just applied the tactic of politely Writing Clear Instructions, and ChatGPT provided us with a good recommendation. But also notice how ChatGPT itself guides the user into better prompting. The refreshed screen shown in figure 9.2 shows the OpenAI prompt engineering strategies.

We just applied simple iteration to improve our prompt. We can extend this example by using a system prompt/message. Figure 9.3 demonstrates the use and role of the system prompt in iterative communication. In chapter 2, we used the system message/prompt in various examples.

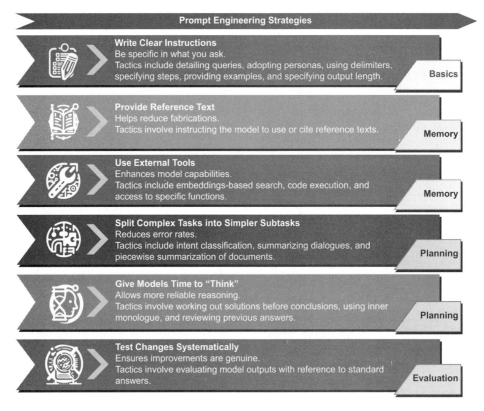

Figure 9.2   OpenAI prompt engineering strategies, broken down by agent component

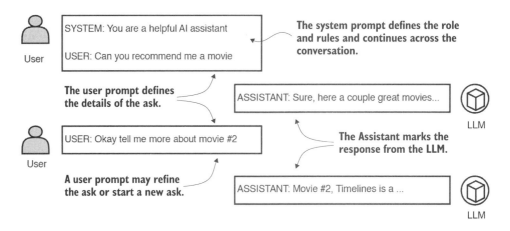

Figure 9.3   The messages to and from an LLM conversation and the iteration of messages

You can also try this in ChatGPT. This time, enter the following prompt and include the word *system* in lowercase, followed by a new line (enter a new line in the message window without sending the message by pressing Shift-Enter):

system

You are an expert on time travel movies.

ChatGPT will respond with some pleasant comments, as shown in figure 9.4. Because of this, it's happy to accept its new role and asks for any follow-up questions. Now enter the following generic prompt as we did previously:

can you recommend something

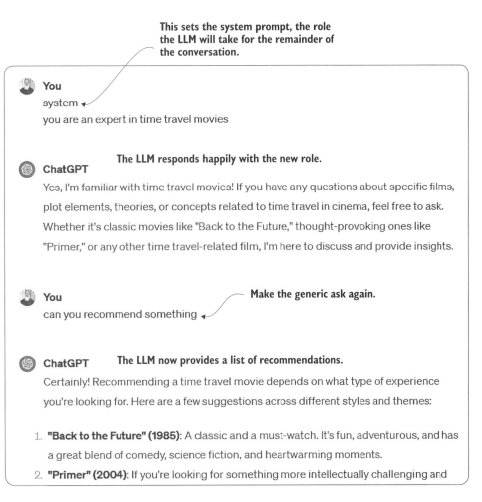

Figure 9.4   The effect of adding a system prompt to our previous conversation

We've just seen the iteration of refining a prompt, the prompt engineering, to extract a better response. This was accomplished over three different conversations using the ChatGPT UI. While not the most efficient way, it works.

However, we haven't defined the iterative flow for evaluating the prompt and determining when a prompt is effective. Figure 9.5 shows a systemic method of prompt engineering using a system of iteration and evaluation.

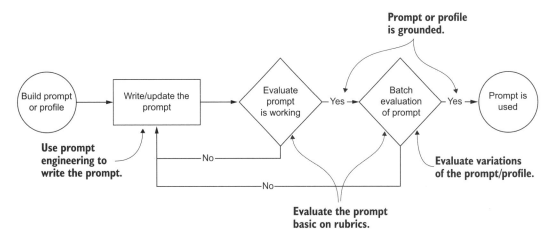

**Systemic Prompt Engineering
(Strategy - Test Changes Systemically)**

Figure 9.5   The systemic method of prompt engineering

The system of iterating and evaluating prompts covers the broad Test Changes Systemically strategy. Evaluating the performance and effectiveness of prompts is still new, but we'll use techniques from education, such as rubrics and grounding, which we'll explore in a later section of this chapter. However, as spelled out in the next section, we need to understand the difference between a persona and an agent profile before we do so.

9.2   *Understanding agent profiles and personas*

An *agent profile* is an encapsulation of component prompts or messages that describe an agent. It includes the agent's persona, special instructions, and other strategies that can guide the user or other agent consumers.

Figure 9.6 shows the main elements of an agent profile. These elements map to prompt engineering strategies described in this book. Not all agents will use all the elements of a full agent profile.

At a basic level, an *agent profile* is a set of prompts describing the agent. It may include other external elements related to actions/tools, knowledge, memory,

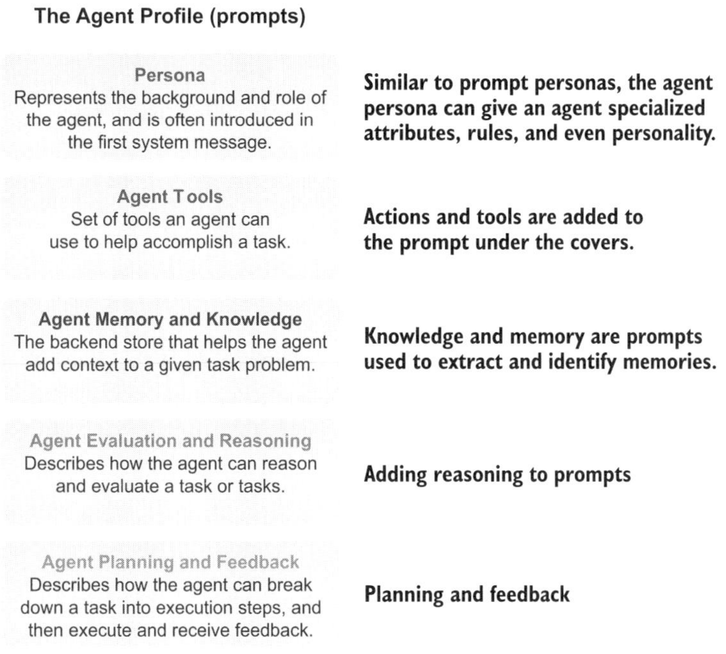

The Agent Profile (prompts)

Persona
Represents the background and role of the agent, and is often introduced in the first system message.

Similar to prompt personas, the agent persona can give an agent specialized attributes, rules, and even personality.

Agent Tools
Set of tools an agent can use to help accomplish a task.

Actions and tools are added to the prompt under the covers.

Agent Memory and Knowledge
The backend store that helps the agent add context to a given task problem.

Knowledge and memory are prompts used to extract and identify memories.

Agent Evaluation and Reasoning
Describes how the agent can reason and evaluate a task or tasks.

Adding reasoning to prompts

Agent Planning and Feedback
Describes how the agent can break down a task into execution steps, and then execute and receive feedback.

Planning and feedback

Figure 9.6   The component parts of an agent profile

reasoning, evaluation, planning, and feedback. The combination of these elements comprises an entire agent prompt profile.

Prompts are the heart of an agent's function. A prompt or set of prompts drives each of the agent components in the profile. For actions/tools, these prompts are well defined, but as we've seen, prompts for memory and knowledge can vary significantly by use case.

The definition of an AI agent profile is more than just a system prompt. Prompt flow can allow us to construct the prompts and code comprising the agent profile but also include the ability to evaluate its effectiveness. In the next section, we'll open up prompt flow and start using it.

9.3   Setting up your first prompt flow

Prompt flow is a tool developed by Microsoft within its Azure Machine Learning Studio platform. The tool was later released as an open source project on GitHub, where it has attracted more attention and use. While initially intended as an application platform, it has since shown its strength in developing and evaluating prompts/profiles.

Because prompt flow was initially developed to run on Azure as a service, it features a robust core architecture. The tool supports multi-threaded batch processing, which makes it ideal for evaluating prompts at scale. The following section will examine the basics of starting with prompt flow.

9.3.1   *Getting started*

There are a few prerequisites to undertake before working through the exercises in this book. The relevant prerequisites for this section and chapter are shown in the following list; make sure to complete them before attempting the exercises:

- *Visual Studio Code (VS Code)*—Refer to appendix A for installation instructions, including additional extensions.
- *Prompt flow, VS Code extension*—Refer to appendix A for details on installing extensions.
- *Python virtual environment*—Refer to appendix A for details on setting up a virtual environment.
- *Install prompt flow packages*—Within your virtual environment, do a quick `pip install`, as shown here:

```
pip install promptflow promptflow-tools
```

- *LLM (GPT-4 or above)*—You'll need access to GPT-4 or above through OpenAI or Azure OpenAI Studio. Refer to appendix B if you need assistance accessing these resources.
- *Book's source code*—Clone the book's source code to a local folder; refer to appendix A if you need help cloning the repository.

Open up VS Code to the book's source code folder, `chapter 3`. Ensure that you have a virtual environment connected and have installed the prompt flow packages and extension.

First, you'll want to create a connection to your LLM resource within the prompt flow extension. Open the prompt flow extension within VS Code, and then click to open the connections. Then, click the plus sign beside the LLM resource to create a new connection, as shown in figure 9.7.

This will open a YAML file where you'll need to populate the connection name and other information relevant to your connection. Follow the directions, and don't enter API keys into the document, as shown in figure 9.8.

When the connection information is entered, click the Create Connection link at the bottom of the document. This will open a terminal prompt below the document, asking you to enter your key. Depending on your terminal configuration, you may be unable to paste (Ctrl-V, Cmd-V). Alternatively, you can paste the key by hovering the mouse cursor over the terminal and right-clicking on Windows.

We'll now test the connection by first opening the simple flow in the `chapter_09/promptflow/simpleflow` folder. Then, open the `flow.dag.yaml` file in VS Code. This is a YAML file, but the prompt flow extension provides a visual editor

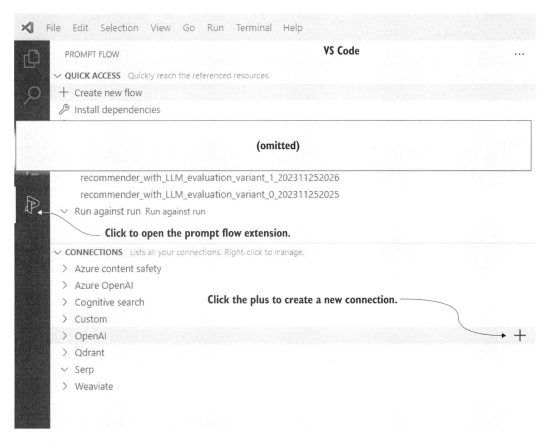

Figure 9.7   Creating a new prompt flow LLM connection

```
 1   # Notices:
 2   # - Don't replace the '<user-input>' placeholder in this file, the application will prompt you t
 3   # - Manually save the file will create the connection after basic validation.
 4   # - The connection information will be stored in a local database with api_key encrypted for saf
 5   # - Prompt flow will ONLY use the connection information (incl. keys) when instructed by you, e.
 6   # - All the values should be string type, please use "123" instead of 123 or "True" instead of 1
 7
 8   $schema: https://azuremlschemas.azureedge.net/promptflow/latest/OpenAIConnection.schema.json
 9   name: "OpenAI"
10   type: open_ai
11   api_key: "<user-input>"  # Don't replace the '<user-input>' placeholder. The application will pr
12   organization: ""
13
14   Create connection
15
```

Enter a name for the connection.

Follow the directions: don't enter a key.

Click after completing the above.

Figure 9.8   Setting the connection information for your LLM resource

that is accessible by clicking the Visual Editor link at the top of the file, as shown in figure 9.9.

Click the link to open the visual editor.

```
                                                           ── flow.dag.yaml ──
chapter_2 > prompt_flow > simple_flow >  !  flow.dag.yaml
        Visual editor(Ctrl + k, v) | Test (shift + f5) | Batch run | Debug (f5) | Build | Status: Completed | [VirtualEnvironment] .venv
   1    id: template_standard_flow
   2    name: Template Standard Flow
   3    environment:
   4      python_requirements_txt: requirements.txt
   5    inputs:
   6      user_input:
   7        type: string
   8        default: can you recommend me something
   9    outputs:
  10      recommendations:
  11        type: string
  12        reference: ${echo.output}
```

Figure 9.9   Opening the prompt flow visual editor

After the visual editor window is opened, you'll see a graph representing the flow and the flow blocks. Double-click the recommender block, and set the connection name, API type, and model or deployment name, as shown in figure 9.10.

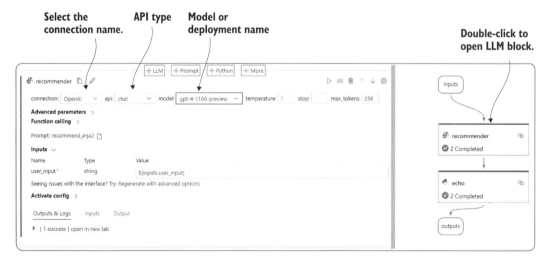

Figure 9.10   Setting the LLM connection details

A prompt flow is composed of a set of blocks starting with an `Inputs` block and terminating in an `Outputs` block. Within this simple flow, the `recommender` block represents the LLM connection and the prompt used to converse with the model. The `echo` block for this simple example echoes the input.

When creating a connection to an LLM, either in prompt flow or through an API, here are the crucial parameters we always need to consider (prompt flow documentation: https://microsoft.github.io/promptflow):

- *Connection*—This is the connection name, but it also represents the service you're connecting to. Prompt flow supports multiple services, including locally deployed LLMs.
- *API*—This is the API type. The options are `chat` for a chat completion API, such as GPT-4, or `completion` for the older completion models, such as the OpenAI Davinci.
- *Model*—This may be the model or deployment name, depending on your service connection. For OpenAI, this will be the model's name, and for Azure OpenAI, it will represent the deployment name.
- *Temperature*—This represents the stochasticity or variability of the model response. A value of `1` represents a high variability of responses, while `0` indicates a desire for no variability. This is a critical parameter to understand and, as we'll see, will vary by use case.
- *Stop*—This optional setting tells the call to the LLM to stop creating tokens. It's more appropriate for older and open source models.
- *Max tokens*—This limits the number of tokens used in a conversation. Knowledge of how many tokens you use is crucial to evaluating how your LLM interactions will work when scaled. Counting tokens may not be a concern if you're exploring and conducting research. However, in production systems, tokens represent the load on the LLM, and connections using numerous tokens may not scale well.
- *Advanced parameters*—You can set a few more options to tune your interaction with the LLM, but we'll cover that topic in later sections of the book.

After configuring the LLM block, scroll up to the Inputs block section, and review the primary input shown in the user_input field, as shown in figure 9.11. Leave it as the default, and then click the Play button at the top of the window.

All the blocks in the flow will run, and the results will be shown in the terminal window. What you should find interesting is that the output shows recommendations for time travel movies. This is because the recommender block already has a simple profile set, and we'll see how that works in the next section.

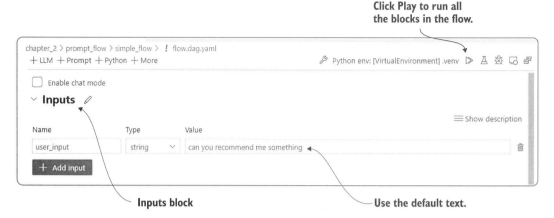

Figure 9.11   **Setting the inputs and starting the flow**

9.3.2   *Creating profiles with Jinja2 templates*

The flow responds with time travel movie recommendations because of the prompt or profile it uses. By default, prompt flow uses Jinja2 templates to define the content of the prompt or what we'll call a *profile*. For the purposes of this book and our exploration of AI agents, we'll refer to these templates as the profile of a flow or agent.

While prompt flow doesn't explicitly refer to itself as an assistant or agent engine, it certainly meets the criteria of producing a proxy and general types of agents. As you'll see, prompt flow even supports deployments of flows into containers and as services.

Open VS Code to `chapter_09/promptflow/simpleflow/flow.dag.yaml`, and open the file in the visual editor. Then, locate the Prompt field, and click the `recommended .jinja2` link, as shown in figure 9.12.

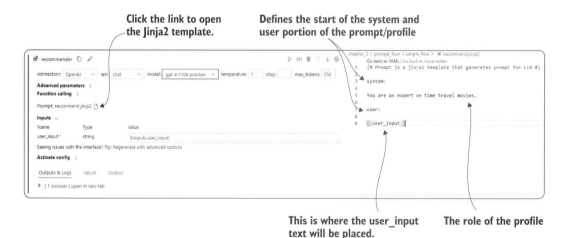

Figure 9.12   **Opening the prompt Jinja2 template and examining the parts of the profile/prompt**

Jinja is a templating engine, and Jinja2 is a particular version of that engine. Templates are an excellent way of defining the layout and parts of any form of text document. They have been extensively used to produce HTML, JSON, CSS, and other document forms. In addition, they support the ability to apply code directly into the template. While there is no standard way to construct prompts or agent profiles, our preference in this book is to use templating engines such as Jinja.

At this point, change the role within the system prompt of the `recommended.jinja2` template. Then, run all blocks of the flow by opening the flow in the visual editor and clicking the Play button. The next section will look at other ways of running prompt flow for testing or actual deployment.

9.3.3 Deploying a prompt flow API

Because prompt flow was also designed to be deployed as a service, it supports a couple of ways to deploy as an app or API quickly. Prompt flow can be deployed as a local web application and API running from the terminal or as a Docker container.

Return to the `flow.dag.yaml` file in the visual editor from VS Code. At the top of the window beside the Play button are several options we'll want to investigate further. Click the Build button as shown in figure 9.13, and then select to deploy as a local app. A new YAML file will be created to configure the app. Leave the defaults, and click the Start Local App link.

Click the Build button. When prompted, select to build as either a web application or Docker container.

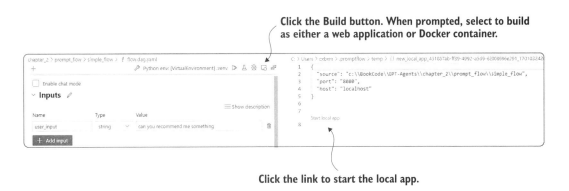

Click the link to start the local app.

Figure 9.13 Building and starting the flow as a local app

This will launch the flow as a local web application, and you'll see a browser tab open, as shown in figure 9.14. Enter some text into the user_input field, which is marked as required with a red asterisk. Click Enter and wait a few seconds for the reply.

You should see a reply like the one shown earlier in figure 9.12, where the flow or agent replies with a list of time travel movies. This is great—we've just developed our first agent profile and the equivalent of a proxy agent. However, we need to determine

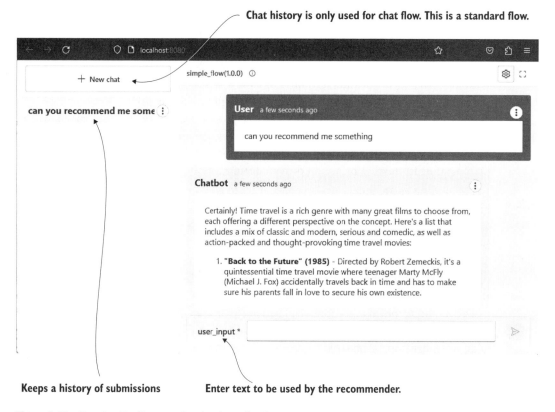

Figure 9.14   Running the flow as a local web application

how successful or valuable the recommendations are. In the next section, we explore how to evaluate prompts and profiles.

9.4   Evaluating profiles: Rubrics and grounding

A key element of any prompt or agent profile is how well it performs its given task. As we see in our recommendation example, prompting an agent profile to give a list of recommendations is relatively easy, but knowing whether those recommendations are helpful requires us to evaluate the response.

Fortunately, prompt flow has been designed to evaluate prompts/profiles at scale. The robust infrastructure allows for the evaluation of LLM interactions to be parallelized and managed as workers, allowing hundreds of profile evaluations and variations to happen quickly.

In the next section, we look at how prompt flow can be configured to run prompt/ profile variations against each other. We'll need to understand this before evaluating profiles' performance.

Prompt flow provides a mechanism to allow for multiple variations within an LLM prompt/profile. This tool is excellent for comparing subtle or significant differences between profile variations. When used in performing bulk evaluations, it can be invaluable for quickly assessing the performance of a profile.

Open the `recommender_with_variations/flow.dag.yaml` file in VS Code and the flow visual editor, as shown in figure 9.15. This time, we're making the profile more generalized and allowing for customization at the input level. This allows us to expand our recommendations to anything and not just time travel movies.

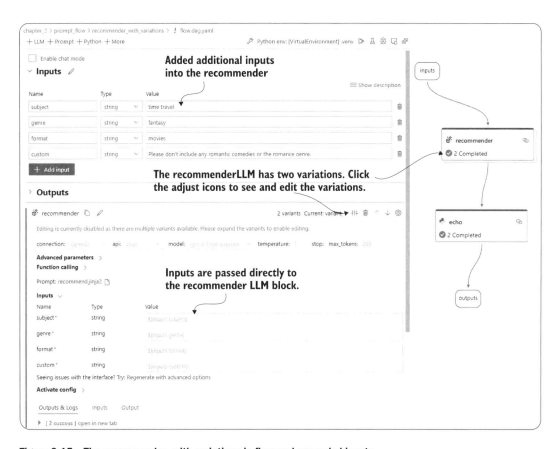

Figure 9.15 The recommender, with variations in flow and expanded inputs

The new inputs Subject, Genre, Format, and Custom allow us to define a profile that can easily be adjusted to any recommendation. This also means that we must prime the inputs based on the recommendation use case. There are multiple ways to prime these inputs; two examples of priming inputs are shown in figure 9.16. The figure shows two options, options A and B, for priming inputs. Option A represents the classic UI; perhaps there are objects for the user to select the subject or genre, for example. Option B places a proxy/chat agent to interact with the user better to understand the desired subject, genre, and so on.

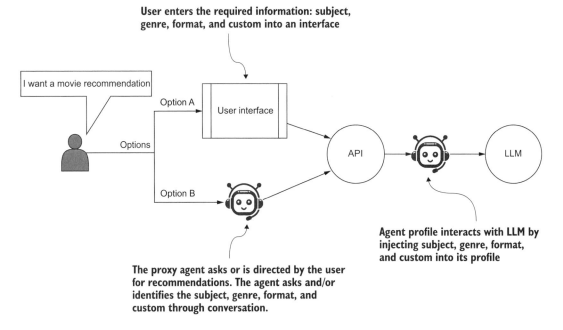

Figure 9.16   The user interaction options for interfacing with the agent profile to prime inputs to the agent profile

Even considering the power of LLMs, you may still want or need to use option A. The benefit of option A is that you can constrain and validate the inputs much like you do with any modern UI. Alternatively, the downside of option A is that the constrained behavior may limit and restrict future use cases.

Option B represents a more fluid and natural way without a traditional UI. It's far more powerful and extensible than option A but also introduces more unknowns for evaluation. However, if the proxy agent that option B uses is written well, it can assist a lot in gathering better information from the user.

The option you choose will dictate how you need to evaluate your profiles. If you're okay with a constrained UI, then it's likely that the inputs will also be constrained to a set of discrete values. For now, we'll assume option B for input priming, meaning the input values will be defined by their name.

To get back to VS Code and the visual view of the recommender with variants flow, click the icon shown earlier in figure 9.15 to open the variants and allow editing. Then, click the recommend.jinja2 and recommender_variant_1.jinja2 links to open the files side by side, as shown in figure 9.17.

Figure 9.17 demonstrates the difference between the variant profiles. One profile injects the inputs into the user prompt, and the other injects them into the system prompt. However, it's essential to understand that variations can encompass more than profile design, as identified in table 9.1.

The system prompt describes a generic recommender
that works when given specific inputs.

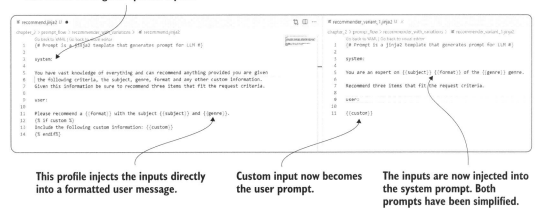

This profile injects the inputs directly
into a formatted user message.

Custom input now becomes
the user prompt.

The inputs are now injected into
the system prompt. Both
prompts have been simplified.

Figure 9.17 Side-by-side comparison of variant profile templates for the recommender

Table 9.1 LLM variation options in prompt flow

Option	Evaluation option examples	Notes
Jinja2 prompt template	Compare system prompt variations, user prompt variations, or mixed prompt variations.	Some endless combinations and techniques can be applied here. Prompt engineering is evolving all the time.
LLM	Compare GPT-9.5 to GPT-4. Compare GPT-4 to GPT-4 Turbo. Compare open source models to commercial models.	This is a useful way to evaluate and ground model performance against a prompt. It can also help you tune your profile to work with open source and/or cheaper models.
Temperature	Compare a 0 temperature (no randomness) to a 1 (maximum randomness).	Changes to the temperature can significantly change the responses of some prompts, which may improve or degrade performance.
Max tokens	Compare limited tokens to larger token sizes.	This can allow you to reduce and maximize token usage.
Advanced parameters	Compare differences to options such as `top_p`, `presence_penalty`, `frequency_penalty`, and `logit_bias`.	We'll cover the use of these advanced parameters in later chapters.
Function calls	Compare alternative function calls.	Function calls will be addressed later in this chapter.

For this simple example, we're just going to use prompt variations by varying the input
to reflect in either the system or user prompt. Refer to figure 9.17 for what this looks

like. We can then quickly run both variations by clicking the Play (Run All) button at the top and choosing both, as shown in figure 9.18.

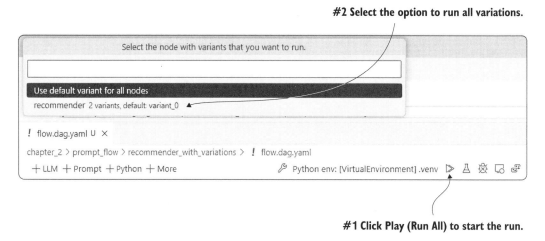

Figure 9.18   Running both prompt variations at the same time

In the terminal window, you'll see the results of both runs. The results will likely look similar, so now we must move on to how we evaluate the difference between variations in the next section.

9.5   Understanding rubrics and grounding

Evaluation of prompt/profile performance isn't something we can typically do using a measure of accuracy or correct percentage. Measuring the performance of a profile depends on the use case and desired outcome. If that is as simple as determining if the response was right or wrong, all the better. However, in most cases, evaluation won't be that simple.

In education, the *rubric* concept defines a structured set of criteria and standards a student must establish to receive a particular grade. A rubric can also be used to define a guide for the performance of a profile or prompt. We can follow these steps to define a rubric we can use to evaluate the performance of a profile or prompt:

1   *Identify the purpose and objectives.* Determine the goals you want the profile or agent to accomplish. For example, do you want to evaluate the quality of recommendations for a given audience or overall quality for a given subject, format, or other input?

2   *Define criteria.* Develop a set of criteria or dimensions that you'll use to evaluate the profile. These criteria should align with your objectives and provide clear guidelines for assessment. Each criterion should be specific and measurable.

For example, you may want to measure a recommendation by how well it fits with the genre and then by subject and format.

3   *Create a scale.* Establish a rating scale that describes the levels of performance for each criterion. Standard scales include numerical scales (e.g., 1–5) or descriptive scales (e.g., Excellent, Good, Fair, Poor).

4   *Provide descriptions.* For each level on the scale, provide clear and concise descriptions that indicate what constitutes a strong performance and what represents a weaker performance for each criterion.

5   *Apply the rubric.* When assessing a prompt or profile, use the rubric to evaluate the prompt's performance based on the established criteria. Assign scores or ratings for each criterion, considering the descriptions for each level.

6   *Calculate the total score.* Depending on your rubric, you may calculate a total score by summing up the scores for each criterion or using a weighted average if some criteria are more important than others.

7   *Ensure evaluation consistency.* If multiple evaluators are assessing the profile, it's crucial to ensure consistency in grading.

8   *Review, revise, and iterate.* Periodically review and revise the rubric to ensure it aligns with your assessment goals and objectives. Adjust as needed to improve its effectiveness.

Grounding is a concept that can be applied to profile and prompt evaluation—it defines how well a response is aligned with a given rubric's specific criteria and standards. You can also think of grounding as the baseline expectation of a prompt or profile output.

This list summarizes some other important considerations when using grounding with profile evaluation:

- Grounding refers to aligning responses with the criteria, objectives, and context defined by the rubric and prompt.
- Grounding involves assessing whether the response directly addresses the rubric criteria, stays on topic, and adheres to any provided instructions.
- Evaluators and evaluations gauge the accuracy, relevance, and adherence to standards when assessing grounding.
- Grounding ensures that the response output is firmly rooted in the specified context, making the assessment process more objective and meaningful.

A well-grounded response aligns with all the rubric criteria within the given context and objectives. Poorly grounded responses will fail or miss the entire criteria, context, and objectives.

As the concepts of rubrics and grounding may still be abstract, let's look at applying them to our current recommender example. Following is a list that follows the process for defining a rubric as applied to our recommender example:

1 *Identify the purpose and objectives.* The purpose of our profile/prompt is to recommend three top items given a subject, format, genre, and custom input.

2 *Define criteria.* For simplicity, we'll evaluate how a particular recommendation aligns with the given input criteria, subject, format, and genre. For example, if a profile recommends a book when asked for a movie format, we expect a low score in the format criteria.

3 *Create a scale.* Again, keeping things simple, we'll use a scale of 1–5 (1 is poor, and 5 is excellent).

4 *Provide descriptions.* See the general descriptions for the rating scale shown in table 9.2.

5 *Apply the rubric.* With the rubric assigned at this stage, it's an excellent exercise to evaluate the rubric against recommendations manually.

6 *Calculate the total score.* For our rubric, we'll average the score for all criteria to provide a total score.

7 *Ensure evaluation consistency.* The technique we'll use for evaluation will provide very consistent results.

8 *Review, revise, and iterate.* We'll review, compare, and iterate on our profiles, rubrics, and the evaluations themselves.

Table 9.2   Rubric ratings

Rating	Description
1	Poor alignment: this is the opposite of what is expected given the criteria.
2	Bad alignment: this isn't a good fit for the given criteria.
3	Mediocre alignment: it may or may not fit well with the given criteria.
4	Good alignment: it may not align 100% with the criteria but is a good fit otherwise.
5	Excellent alignment: this is a good recommendation for the given criteria.

This basic rubric can now be applied to evaluate the responses for our profile. You can do this manually, or as you'll see in the next section, using a second LLM profile.

9.6   *Grounding evaluation with an LLM profile*

This section will employ another LLM prompt/profile for evaluation and grounding. This second LLM prompt will add another block after the recommendations are generated. It will process the generated recommendations and evaluate each one, given the previous rubric.

Before GPT-4 and other sophisticated LLMs came along, we would have never considered using another LLM prompt to evaluate or ground a profile. You often want to use a different model when using LLMs to ground a profile. However, if you're comparing profiles against each other, using the same LLM for evaluation and grounding is appropriate.

Open the `recommender_with_LLM_evaluation\flow.dag.yaml` file in the prompt flow visual editor, scroll down to the `evaluate_recommendation` block, and click the `evaluate_recommendation.jinja2` link to open the file, as shown in figure 9.19. Each section of the rubric is identified in the figure.

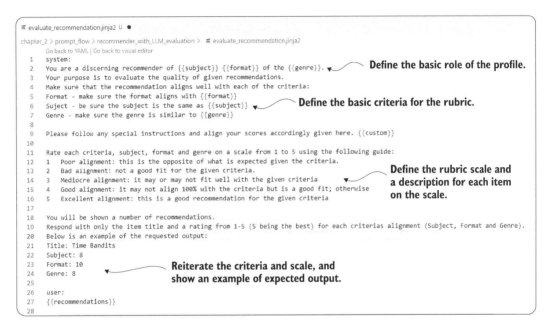

Figure 9.19 The evaluation prompt, with each of the parts of the rubric outlined

We have a rubric that is not only well defined but also in the form of a prompt that can be used to evaluate recommendations. This allows us to evaluate the effectiveness of recommendations for a given profile—automatically. Of course, you can also use the rubric to score and evaluate the recommendations manually for a better baseline.

> **NOTE** Using LLMs to evaluate prompts and profiles provides a strong baseline for comparing the performance of a profile. It can also do this without human bias in a controlled and repeatable manner. This provides an excellent mechanism to establish baseline groundings for any profile or prompt.

Returning to the `recommender_with_LLM_evaluation` flow visual editor, we can run the flow by clicking the Play button and observing the output. You can run a single recommendation or run both variations when prompted. The output of a single evaluation using the default inputs is shown in the following listing.

Listing 9.1 LLM rubric evaluation output

```
{
    "recommendations": "Title: The Butterfly Effect
Subject: 5
Format: 5
Genre: 4

Title: Primer
Subject: 5
Format: 5
Genre: 4

Title: Time Bandits
Subject: 5
Format: 5
Genre: 5"
}
```

We now have a rubric for grounding our recommender, and the evaluation is run automatically using a second LLM prompt. In the next section, we look at how to perform multiple evaluations simultaneously and then at a total score for everything.

9.7 Comparing profiles: Getting the perfect profile

With our understanding of rubrics and grounding, we can now move on to evaluating and iterating the perfect profile. Before we do that, though, we need to clean up the output from the LLM evaluation block. This will require us to parse the recommendations into something more Pythonic, which we'll tackle in the next section.

9.7.1 Parsing the LLM evaluation output

As the raw output from the evaluation block is text, we now want to parse that into something more usable. Of course, writing parsing functions is simple, but there are better ways to cast responses automagically. We covered better methods for returning responses in chapter 5, on agent actions.

Open `chapter_09\prompt_flow\recommender_with_parsing\flow.dag.yaml` in VS Code, and look at the flow in the visual editor. Locate the `parsing_results` block, and click the link to open the Python file in the editor, as shown in figure 9.20.

The code for the `parsing_results.py` file is shown in listing 9.2.

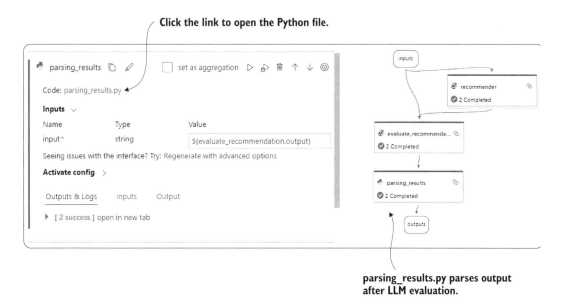

Figure 9.20   Opening the `parsing_results.py` file in VS Code

```python
from promptflow import tool


@tool
def parse(input: str) -> str:
    # Splitting the recommendations into individual movie blocks
    rblocks = input.strip().split("\n\n")

    # Function to parse individual recommendation block into dictionary
    def parse_block(block):
        lines = block.split('\n')
        rdict = {}
        for line in lines:
            kvs = line.split(': ')
            key, value = kvs[0], kvs[1]
            rdict[key.lower()] = value
        return rdict

    parsed = [parse_block(block) for block in rblocks]

    return parsed
```

Special decorator to denote the tool block

Splits the input and double new lines

Creates a dictionary entry and sets the value

Loops through each block and parses into key/value dictionary

We're converting the recommendations output from listing 9.1, which is just a string, into a dictionary. So this code will convert this string into the JSON block shown next:

Before parsing:

```
"Title: The Butterfly Effect
Subject: 5
Format: 5
Genre: 4

Title: Primer
Subject: 5
Format: 5
Genre: 4

Title: Time Bandits
Subject: 5
Format: 5
Genre: 5"
```

After parsing:

```
{
        "title": " The Butterfly Effect
        "subject": "5",
        "format": "5",
        "genre": "4"
},
{
        "title": " Primer",
        "subject": "5",
        "format": "5",
        "genre": "4"
},
{
        "title": " Time Bandits",
        "subject": "5",
        "format": "5",
        "genre": "5"
}
```

The output of this `parsing_results` block now gets passed to the output and is wrapped in a list of recommendations. We can see what all this looks like by running the flow.

Open `flow.dag.yaml` for the flow in the visual editor, and click the Play (Run All) button. Be sure to select to use both recommender variants. You'll see both variations run and output to the terminal.

At this point, we have a full working recommendation and LLM evaluation flow that outputs a score for each criterion on each output. However, to do comprehensive evaluations of a particular profile, we want to generate multiple recommendations with various criteria. We'll see how to do batch processing of flows in the next section.

9.7.2 *Running batch processing in prompt flow*

In our generic recommendation profile, we want to evaluate how various input criteria can affect the generated recommendations. Fortunately, prompt flow can batch-process any variations we want to test. The limit is only the time and money we want to spend.

To perform batch processing, we must first create a JSON Lines (JSONL) or JSON list document of our input criteria. If you recall, our input criteria looked like the following in JSON format:

```
{
    "subject": "time travel",
    "format": "books",
    "genre": "fantasy",
    "custom": "don't include any R rated content"
}
```

We want to create a list of JSON objects like that just shown, preferably in a random manner. Of course, the simple way to do this is to prompt ChatGPT to create a JSONL document using the following prompt:

> I am developing a recommendation agent. The agent will recommend anything given the following criteria:
>
> 1. subject - examples: time travel, cooking, vacation
>
> 2. format - examples: books, movies, games
>
> 3. genre: documentary, action, romance
>
> 4. custom: don't include any R rated content
>
> Can you please generate a random list of these criteria and output it in the format of a JSON Lines file, JSONL. Please include 10 items in the list.

Try this out by going to ChatGPT and entering the preceding prompt. A previously generated file can be found in the flow folder, called `\bulk_recommend.jsonl`. The contents of this file have been shown here for reference:

```
{
  "subject": "time travel",
  "format": "books",
  "genre": "fantasy",
  "custom": "don't include any R rated content"
}
{
  "subject": "space exploration",
  "format": "podcasts",
  "genre": "sci-fi",
  "custom": "include family-friendly content only"
}
```

```
{
  "subject": "mystery",
  "format": "podcasts",
  "genre": "fantasy",
  "custom": "don't include any R rated content"
}
{
  "subject": "space exploration",
  "format": "podcasts",
  "genre": "action",
  "custom": "include family-friendly content only"
}
{
  "subject": "vacation",
  "format": "books",
  "genre": "thriller",
  "custom": "don't include any R rated content"
}
{
  "subject": "mystery",
  "format": "books",
  "genre": "sci-fi",
  "custom": "don't include any R rated content"
}
{
  "subject": "mystery",
  "format": "books",
  "genre": "romance",
  "custom": "don't include any R rated content"
}
{
  "subject": "vacation",
  "format": "movies",
  "genre": "fantasy",
  "custom": "don't include any R rated content"
}
{
  "subject": "cooking",
  "format": "TV shows",
  "genre": "thriller",
  "custom": "include family-friendly content only"
}
{
  "subject": "mystery",
  "format": "movies",
  "genre": "romance",
  "custom": "include family-friendly content only"
}
```

With this bulk file, we can run both variants using the various input criteria in the bulk
JSONL file. Open the `flow.dag.yaml` file in the visual editor, click Batch (the beaker
icon) to start the bulk-data loading process, and select the file as shown in figure 9.21.
For some operating systems, this may appear as `Local Data File`.

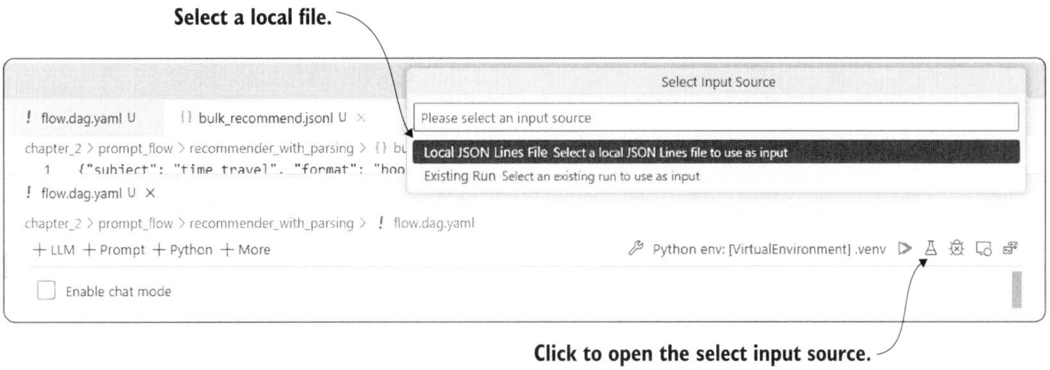

Select a local file.

Figure 9.21   Loading the bulk JSONL file to run the flow on multiple input variations

After the bulk file is selected, a new YAML document will open with a Run link added at the bottom of the file, as shown in figure 9.22. Click the link to do the batch run of inputs.

Click to run the batch.

Figure 9.22   Running the batch run of inputs

At this point, a few things will happen. The flow visual editor will appear, and beside that a log file will open, showing the progress of the run. In the terminal window, you'll see the various worker processes spawning and running.

Be patient. The batch run, even for 10 items, may take a few minutes or seconds, depending on various factors such as hardware, previous calls, and so on. Wait for the run to complete, and you'll see a summary of results in the terminal.

You can also view the run results by opening the prompt flow extension and selecting the last run, as shown in figure 9.23. Then, you dig into each run by clicking the table cells. A lot of information is exposed in this dialog, which can help you trouble-shoot flows and profiles.

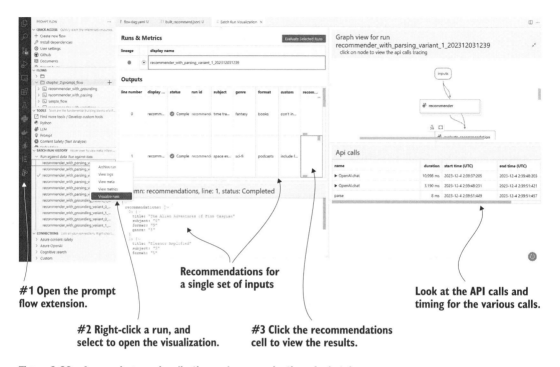

#1 Open the prompt flow extension.

#2 Right-click a run, and select to open the visualization.

Recommendations for a single set of inputs

#3 Click the recommendations cell to view the results.

Look at the API calls and timing for the various calls.

Figure 9.23   An opening run visualization and an examination of a batch run

A lot of information is captured during a batch run, and you can explore much of it through the visualizer. More information can be found by clicking the output folder link from the terminal window. This will open another session of VS Code with the output folder allowing you to review the run logs and other details.

Now that we've completed the batch run for each variant, we can apply grounding and evaluate the results of both prompts. The next section will use a new flow to perform the profile/prompt evaluation.

9.7.3   *Creating an evaluation flow for grounding*

Open `chapter_3\prompt_flow\evaluate_groundings\flow.dag.yaml` in the visual editor, as shown in figure 9.24. There are no LLM blocks in the evaluation flow—just Python code blocks that will run the scoring and then aggregate the scores.

We can now look at the code for the `scoring` and `aggregate` blocks, starting with the scoring code in listing 9.3. This scoring code averages the score for each criterion into an average score. The output of the function is a list of processed recommendations.

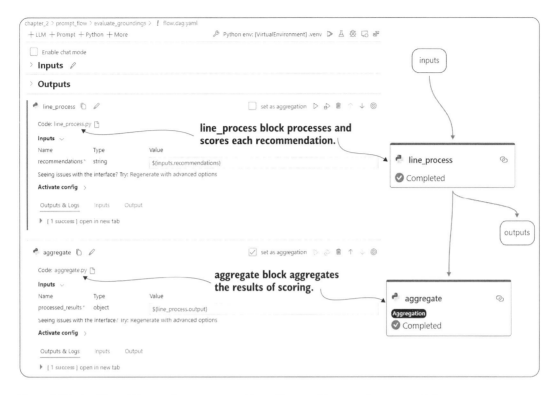

Figure 9.24 Looking at the `evaluate_groundings` flow used to ground recommendation runs

Listing 9.3 `line_process.py`

```python
@tool
def line_process(recommendations: str):
    inputs = recommendations
    output = []
    for data_dict in inputs:
        total_score = 0
        score_count = 0

        for key, value in data_dict.items():
            if key != "title":
                try:
                    total_score += float(value)
                    score_count += 1
                    data_dict[key] = float(value)
                except:
                    pass

        avg_score = total_score / score_count if score_count > 0 else 0

        data_dict["avg_score"] = round(avg_score, 2)
        output.append(data_dict)

    return output
```

A set of three recommendations is input into the function.

Loops over each recommendation and criterion

Title isn't a criterion, so ignore it.

Totals the score for all criteria and sets the float value to key

Adds the average score as a grounding score of the recommendation

From the grounded recommendations, we can move on to aggregating the scores with the `aggregate` block—the code for the `aggregate` block is shown in the following listing.

Listing 9.4 `aggregate.py`

```
@tool
def aggregate(processed_results: List[str]):
    items = [item for sublist in processed_results
                 for item in sublist]                    ◁──┐ The input is a list
                                                             │ of lists; flatten to
    aggregated = {}                                          │ a list of items.

    for item in items:
        for key, value in item.items():
            if key == 'title':
                continue                                 │ Checks to see if the value
                                                         │ is numeric and accumulates
            if isinstance(value, (float, int)):      ◁──┘ scores for each criterion key
                if key in aggregated:
                    aggregated[key] += value
                else:
                    aggregated[key] = value
                                                     ┌ Loops over aggregated
    for key, value in aggregated.items():        ◁──┘ criterion scores
        value = value / len(items)
        log_metric(key=key, value=value)         ◁──┐ Logs the criterion
        aggregated[key] = value                      │ as a metric

    return aggregated
```

The result of the aggregations will be a summary score for each criterion and the average score. Since the evaluation/grounding flow is separate, it can be run over any recommendation run we perform. This will allow us to use the batch run results for any variation to compare results.

We can run the grounding flow by opening `flow.dag.yaml` in the visual editor and clicking Batch (beaker icon). Then, when prompted, we select an existing run and then select the run we want to evaluate, as shown in figure 9.25. This will open a YAML file with the Run link at the bottom, as we've seen before. Click the Run link to run the evaluation.

After the run is completed, you'll see a summary of the results in the terminal window. You can click the output link to open the folder in VS Code and analyze the results, but there is a better way to compare them.

Open the prompt flow extension, focus on the Batch Run History window, and scroll down to the Run against Run section, as shown in figure 9.26. Select the runs you want to compare—likely the ones near the top—so that the checkmark appears. Then, right-click the run, and select the Visualize Runs option. The Batch Run Visualization window opens, and you'll see the metrics for each of the runs at the top.

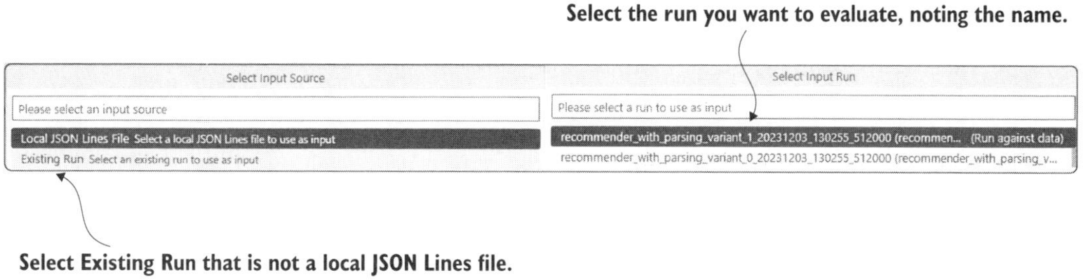

Select the run you want to evaluate, noting the name.

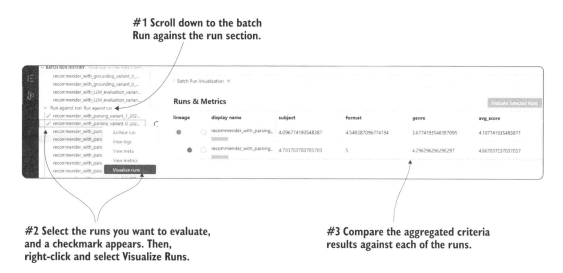

Select Existing Run that is not a local JSON Lines file.

Figure 9.25 Loading a previous run to be grounded and evaluated

**#1 Scroll down to the batch
Run against the run section.**

Runs & Metrics

**#2 Select the runs you want to evaluate,
and a checkmark appears. Then,
right-click and select Visualize Runs.**

**#3 Compare the aggregated criteria
results against each of the runs.**

Figure 9.26 Visualizing the metrics for multiple runs and comparing them

We can now see a significant difference between profile/prompt variation 0, the user prompt, and variation 1, the system prompt. Refer to figure 9.15 if you need a refresher on what the prompts/profiles look like. At this point, it should be evident that injecting the input parameters into the system prompt provides better recommendations.

You can now go back and try other profiles or other variant options to see what effect this has on your recommendations. The possibilities are virtually endless, but hopefully you can see what an excellent tool prompt flow will be for building agent profiles and prompts.

9.7.4 Exercises

Use the following exercises to improve your knowledge of the material:

- *Exercise 1*—Create a New Prompt Variant for Recommender Flow (Intermediate)
  Objective—Improve the recommendation results by creating and testing a new prompt variant in prompt flow.
  Tasks:
  - Create a new prompt variant for the recommender flow in prompt flow.
  - Run the flow in batch mode.
  - Evaluate the results to determine if they are better or worse compared to the original prompt.
- *Exercise 2*—Add a Custom Field to the Rubric and Evaluate (Intermediate)
  Objective—Enhance the evaluation criteria by incorporating a custom field into the rubric and updating the evaluation flow.
  Tasks:
  - Add the custom field as a new criterion to the rubric.
  - Update the evaluation flow to score the new criterion.
  - Evaluate the results, and analyze the effect of the new criterion on the evaluation.
- *Exercise 3*—Develop a New Use Case and Evaluation Rubric (Advanced)
  Objective—Expand the application of prompt engineering by developing a new use case and creating an evaluation rubric.
  Tasks:
  - Develop a new use case aside from the recommendation.
  - Build the prompt for the new use case.
  - Create a rubric for evaluating the new prompt.
  - Update or alter the evaluation flow to aggregate and compare the results of the new use case with existing ones.
- *Exercise 4*—Evaluate Other LLMs Using LM Studio (Intermediate)
  Objective—Assess the performance of different open source LLMs by hosting a local server with LM Studio.
  Tasks:
  - Use LM Studio to host a local server for evaluating LLMs.
  - Evaluate other open source LLMs.
  - Consult chapter 2 if assistance is needed for setting up the server and performing the evaluations.
- *Exercise 5*—Build and Evaluate Prompts Using Prompt Flow (Intermediate)
  Objective—Apply prompt engineering strategies to build and evaluate new prompts or profiles using prompt flow.

Tasks:

- Build new prompts or profiles for evaluation using prompt flow.
- Apply the Write Clear Instructions prompt engineering strategy from chapter 2.
- Evaluate the prompts and profiles using prompt flow.
- Refer to chapter 2 for tactics and implementation details if a refresher is needed.

Summary

- An agent profile consists of several other component prompts that can drive functions such as actions/tools, knowledge, memory, evaluation, reasoning, feedback, and planning.
- Prompt flow can be used to evaluate an agent's component prompts.
- Systemic prompt engineering is an iterative process evaluating a prompt and agent profile.
- The Test Changes Systematically strategy describes iterating and evaluating prompts, and system prompt engineering implements this strategy.
- Agent profiles and prompt engineering have many similarities. We define an agent profile as the combination of prompt engineering elements that guide and help an agent through its task.
- Prompt flow is an open source tool from Microsoft that provides several features for developing and evaluating profiles and prompts.
- An LLM connection in prompt flow supports additional parameters, including temperature, stop token, max tokens, and other advanced parameters.
- LLM blocks support prompt and profile variants, which allow for evaluating changes to the prompt/profile or other connection parameters.
- A rubric applied to an LLM prompt is the criteria and standards a prompt/profile must fulfill to be grounded. Grounding is the scoring and evaluation of a rubric.
- Prompt flow supports running multiple variations as single runs or batch runs.
- In prompt flow, an evaluation flow is run after a generative flow to score and aggregate the results. The Visualize Runs option can compare the aggregated criteria from scoring the rubric across multiple runs.

Agent reasoning
and evaluation

Now that we've examined the patterns of memory and retrieval that define the semantic memory component in agents, we can take a look at the last and most instrumental component in agents: planning. Planning encompasses many facets, from reasoning, understanding, and evaluation to feedback.

To explore how LLMs can be prompted to reason, understand, and plan, we'll demonstrate how to engage reasoning through prompt engineering and then expand that to planning. The planning solution provided by the Semantic Kernel (SK) encompasses multiple planning forms. We'll finish the chapter by incorporating adaptive feedback into a new planner.

Figure 10.1 demonstrates the high-level prompt engineering strategies we'll cover in this chapter and how they relate to the various techniques we'll cover. Each of the methods showcased in the figure will be explored in this chapter, from the basics of solution/direct prompting, shown in the top-left corner, to self-consistency and tree of thought (ToT) prompting, in the bottom right.

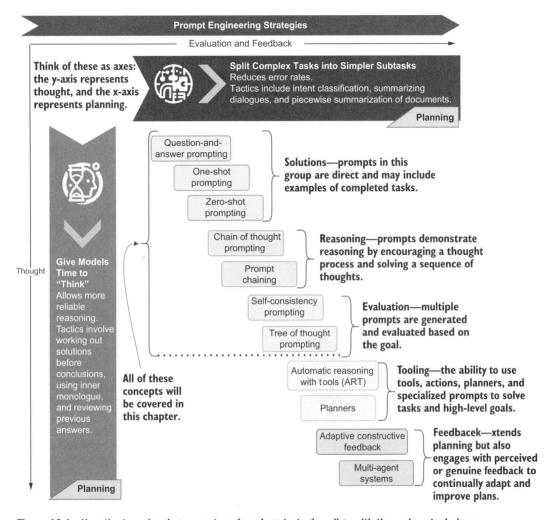

Figure 10.1 How the two planning prompt engineering strategies align with the various techniques

10.1 Understanding direct solution prompting

Direct solution prompting is generally the first form of prompt engineering that users employ when asking LLMs questions or solving a particular problem. Given any LLM use, these techniques may seem apparent, but they are worth reviewing to establish the foundation of thought and planning. In the next section, we'll start from the beginning, asking questions and expecting answers.

10.1.1 *Question-and-answer prompting*

For the exercises in this chapter, we'll employ prompt flow to build and evaluate the various techniques. (We already extensively covered this tool in chapter 9, so refer to that chapter if you need a review.) Prompt flow is an excellent tool for understanding how these techniques work and exploring the flow of the planning and reasoning process.

Open Visual Studio Code (VS Code) to the `chapter 10` source folder. Create a new virtual environment for the folder, and install the `requirements.txt` file. If you need help setting up a chapter's Python environment, refer to appendix B.

We'll look at the first flow in the `prompt_flow/question-answering-prompting` folder. Open the `flow.dag.yaml` file in the visual editor, as shown in figure 10.2. On the right side, you'll see the flow of components. At the top is the `question_answer` LLM prompt, followed by two `Embedding` components and a final LLM prompt to do the evaluation called `evaluate`.

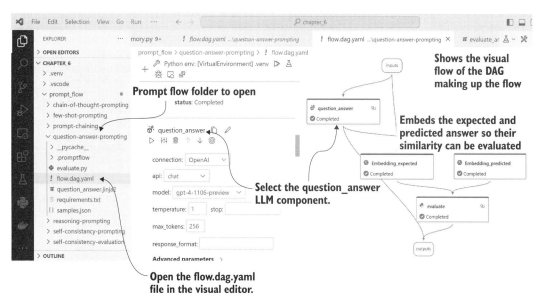

Figure 10.2   The `flow.dag.yaml` file, open in the visual editor, highlighting the various components of the flow

The breakdown in listing 10.1 shows the structure and components of the flow in more detail using a sort of YAML-shortened pseudocode. You can also see the input and outputs to the various components and a sample output from running the flow.

Listing 10.1   `question-answer-prompting` flow

```
Inputs:
    context  : the content to ask the question about
```

```
        question : question asked specific to the content
        expected : the expected answer

   LLM: Question-Answer (the prompt used to ask the question)
        inputs:
              context and question
        outputs:
              the prediction/answer to the question

   Embeddings: uses an LLM embedding model to create the embedding
representation of the text

     Embedding_predicted: embeds the output of the Question-Answer LLM
     Embedding_expected: embeds the output of the expected answer

   Python: Evaluation (Python code to measure embedding similarity)
     Inputs:
              Embedding_predicted output
              Embedding_expected output
     Outputs:
              the similarity score between predicted and expected

   Outputs:
        context: -> input.context
        question: -> input.question
      expected: -> input.expected
      predicted: -> output.question_answer
      evaluation_score: output.evaluation

### Example Output
{
    "context": "Back to the Future (1985)…",
    "evaluation_score": 0.9567478002354606,
    "expected": "Marty traveled back in time 30 years.",
    "predicted": "Marty traveled back in time 30 years from 1985 to 1955
in the movie \"Back to the Future.\"",
    "question": "How far did Marty travel back in time in the movie
Back to the Future (1985)"
}
```

Before running this flow, make sure your LLM block is configured correctly. This may require you to set up a connection to your chosen LLM. Again, refer to chapter 9 if you need a review on how to complete this. You'll need to configure the LLM and `Embedding` blocks with your connection if you're not using OpenAI.

After configuring your LLM connection, run the flow by clicking the Play button from the visual editor or using the Test (Shift-F5) link in the YAML editor window. If everything is connected and configured correctly, you should see output like that in listing 10.1.

Open the `question_answer.jinja2` file in VS Code, as shown in listing 10.2. This listing shows the basic question-and-answer-style prompt. In this style of prompt, the system message describes the basic rules and provides the context to answer the question.

In chapter 4, we explored the retrieval augmented generation (RAG) pattern, and this prompt follows a similar pattern.

Listing 10.2   `question_answer.jinja2`

```
system:
Answer the users question based on the context below. Keep the answer
short and concise. Respond "Unsure about answer" if not sure about the
answer.

Context: {{context}}          ←— Replace with the content LLM
                                  should answer the question about.

user:                         ←— Replace with
Question: {{question}}            the question.
```

This exercise shows the simple method of using an LLM to ask questions about a piece of content. Then, the question response is evaluated using a similarity matching score. We can see from the output in listing 10.1 that the LLM does a good job of answering a question about the context. In the next section, we'll explore a similar technique that uses direct prompting.

10.1.2 Implementing few-shot prompting

Few-shot prompting is like question-and-answer prompting, but the makeup of the prompt is more about providing a few examples than about facts or context. This allows the LLM to bend to patterns or content not previously seen. While this approach sounds like question and answer, the implementation is quite different, and the results can be powerful.

Zero-shot, one-shot, and few-shot learning

One holy grail of machine learning and AI is the ability to train a model on as few items as possible. For example, in traditional vision models, millions of images are fed into the model to help identify the differences between a cat and a dog.

A *one-shot* model is a model that requires only a single image to train it. For example, a picture of a cat can be shown, and then the model can identify any cat image. A *few-shot* model requires only a few things to train the model. And, of course, *zero-shot* indicates the ability to identify something given no previous examples. LLMs are efficient learners and can do all three types of learning.

Open `prompt_flow/few-shot-prompting/flow.dag.yaml` in VS Code and the visual editor. Most of the flow looks like the one pictured earlier in figure 10.2, and the differences are highlighted in listing 10.3, which shows a YAML pseudocode representation. The main differences between this and the previous flow are the inputs and LLM prompt.

Listing 10.3 `few-shot-prompting` flow

```
Inputs:
    statement  : introduces the context and then asks for output
    expected : the expected answer to the statement

LLM: few_shot (the prompt used to ask the question)
    inputs:statement
    outputs: the prediction/answer to the statement

Embeddings: uses an LLM embedding model to create the embedding
representation of the text

        Embedding_predicted: embeds the output of the few_shot LLM
        Embedding_expected: embeds the output of the expected answer

Python: Evaluation (Python code to measure embedding similarity)
    Inputs:
            Embedding_predicted output
            Embedding_expected output
        Outputs: the similarity score between predicted and expected

Outputs:
        statement: -> input.statement
        expected: -> input.expected
        predicted: -> output.few_shot
        evaluation_score: output.evaluation

### Example Output
{
    "evaluation_score": 0.906647282920417,
    "expected": "We ate sunner and watched the setting sun.",
    "predicted": "After a long hike, we sat by the lake
and enjoyed a peaceful sunner as the sky turned
brilliant shades of orange and pink.",
    "statement": "A sunner is a meal we eat in Cananda
at sunset, please use the word in a sentence"
}
```

> **Evaluation score represents the similarity between expected and predicted.**

> **Uses sunner in a sentence**

> **This is a false statement but the intent is to get the LLM to use the word as if it was real.**

Run the flow by pressing Shift-F5 or clicking the Play/Test button from the visual editor. You should see output like listing 10.3 where the LLM has used the word *sunner* (a made-up term) correctly in a sentence given the initial statement.

This exercise demonstrates the ability to use a prompt to alter the behavior of the LLM to be contrary to what it has learned. We're changing what the LLM understands to be accurate. Furthermore, we then use that modified perspective to elicit the use of a made-up word.

Open the `few_shot.jinja2` prompt in VS Code, shown in listing 10.4. This listing demonstrates setting up a simple persona, that of an eccentric dictionary maker, and then providing examples of words it has defined and used before. The base of the prompt allows for the LLM to extend the examples and produce similar results using other words.

Listing 10.4   `few_shot.jinja2`

```
system:
You are an eccentric word dictionary maker. You will be asked to
```
Demonstrates an example defining a made-up word and using it in a sentence
```
construct a sentence using the word.
The following are examples that demonstrate how to craft a sentence using
the word.
A "whatpu" is a small, furry animal native to Tanzania.
An example of a sentence that uses the word whatpu is:
We were traveling in Africa and we saw these very cute whatpus.
To do a "farduddle" means to jump up and down really fast. An example of a
sentence that uses the word farduddle is:
I was so excited that I started to farduddle.
```
Demonstrates another example
```
Please only return the sentence requested by the user.
```
A rule to prevent the LLM from outputting extra information
```
user:
{{statement}}
```
The input statement defines a new word and asks for the use.

You may say we're forcing the LLM to hallucinate here, but this technique is the basis for modifying behavior. It allows prompts to be constructed to guide an LLM to do everything contrary to what it learned. This foundation of prompting also establishes techniques for other forms of altered behavior. From the ability to alter the perception and background of an LLM, we'll move on to demonstrate a final example of a direct solution in the next section.

10.1.3 *Extracting generalities with zero-shot prompting*

Zero-shot prompting or learning is the ability to generate a prompt in such a manner that allows the LLM to generalize. This generalization is embedded within the LLM and demonstrated through zero-shot prompting, where no examples are given, but instead a set of guidelines or rules are given to guide the LLM.

Employing this technique is simple and works well to guide the LLM to generate replies given its internal knowledge and no other contexts. It's a subtle yet powerful technique that applies the knowledge of the LLM to other applications. This technique, combined with other prompting strategies, is proving effective at replacing other language classification models—models that identify the emotion or sentiment in text, for example.

Open `prompt_flow/zero-shot-prompting/flow.dag.yaml` in the VS Code prompt flow visual editor. This flow is again almost identical to that shown earlier in figure 10.1 but differs slightly in implementation, as shown in listing 10.5.

Listing 10.5   `zero-shot-prompting` flow

```
Inputs:
     statement  : the statement to be classified
     expected : the expected classification of the statement

 LLM: zero_shot (the prompt used to classify)
     inputs: statement
     outputs: the predicted class given the statement

 Embeddings: uses an LLM embedding model to create the embedding
representation of the text

 Embedding_predicted: embeds the output of the zero_shot LLM
 Embedding_expected: embeds the output of the expected answer

 Python: Evaluation (Python code to measure embedding similarity)
     Inputs:
            Embedding_predicted output
          Embedding_expected output
        Outputs: the similarity score between predicted and expected

Outputs:
     statement: -> input.statement
     expected: -> input.expected
     predicted: -> output.few_shot
     evaluation_score: output.evaluation

### Example Output
{
     "evaluation_score": 1,
     "expected": "neutral",
     "predicted": "neutral",
     "statement": "I think the vacation is okay. "
}
```

Shows a perfect evaluation score of 1.0

The statement we're asking the LLM to classify

Run the flow by pressing Shift-F5 within the VS Code prompt flow visual editor. You should see output similar to that shown in listing 10.5.

Now open the `zero_shot.jinja2` prompt as shown in listing 10.6. The prompt is simple and uses no examples to extract the sentiment from the text. What is especially interesting to note is that the prompt doesn't even mention the phrase sentiment, and the LLM seems to understand the intent.

Listing 10.6   `zero_shot.jinja2`

```
system:
Classify the text into neutral, negative or positive.
Return on the result and nothing else.

user:
{{statement}}
```

Provides essential guidance on performing the classification

The statement of text to classify

Zero-shot prompt engineering is about using the ability of the LLM to generalize broadly based on its training material. This exercise demonstrates how knowledge within the LLM can be put to work for other tasks. The LLM's ability to self-contextualize and apply knowledge can extend beyond its training. In the next section, we extend this concept further by looking at how LLMs can reason.

10.2   *Reasoning in prompt engineering*

LLMs like ChatGPT were developed to function as chat completion models, where text content is fed into the model, whose responses align with completing that request. LLMs were never trained to reason, plan, think, or have thoughts.

However, much like we demonstrated with the examples in the previous section, LLMs can be prompted to extract their generalities and be extended beyond their initial design. While an LLM isn't designed to reason, the training material fed into the model provides an understanding of reasoning, planning, and thought. Therefore, by extension, an LLM understands what reasoning is and can employ the concept of reasoning.

Reasoning and planning

Reasoning is the ability of an intellect, artificial or not, to understand the process of thought or thinking through a problem. An intellect can understand that actions have outcomes, and it can use this ability to reason through which action from a set of actions can be applied to solve a given task.

Planning is the ability of the intellect to reason out the order of actions or tasks and apply the correct parameters to achieve a goal or outcome—the extent to which an intellectual plan depends on the scope of the problem. An intellect may combine multiple levels of planning, from strategic and tactical to operational and contingent.

We'll look at another set of prompt engineering techniques that allow or mimic reasoning behavior to demonstrate this reasoning ability. Typically, when evaluating the application of reasoning, we look to having the LLM solve challenging problems it wasn't designed to solve. A good source of such is based on logic, math, and word problems.

Using the time travel theme, what class of unique problems could be better to solve than understanding time travel? Figure 10.3 depicts one example of a uniquely challenging time travel problem. Our goal is to acquire the ability to prompt the LLM in a manner that allows it to solve the problem correctly.

Time travel problems are thought exercises that can be deceptively difficult to solve. The example in figure 10.3 is complicated to solve for an LLM, but the part it

The problem statement:

> In a sci-fi film, Alex is a time traveler who decides to go back in time to witness a famous historical battle that took place 100 years ago, which lasted for 10 days. He arrives three days before the battle starts. However, after spending six days in the past, he jumps forward in time by 50 years and stays there for 20 days. Then, he travels back to witness the end of the battle. How many days does Alex spend in the past before he sees the end of the battle?

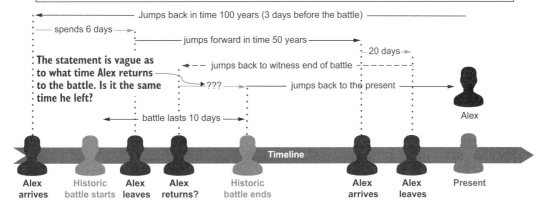

Figure 10.3   The complexity of the time travel problems we intend to solve using LLMs with reasoning and planning

gets wrong may surprise you. The next section will use reasoning in prompts to solve these unique problems.

10.2.1 Chain of thought prompting

Chain of thought (CoT)prompting is a prompt engineering technique that employs the one-shot or few-shot examples that describe the reasoning and the steps to accomplish a desired goal. Through the demonstration of reasoning, the LLM can generalize this principle and reason through similar problems and goals. While the LLM isn't trained with the goal of reasoning, we can elicit the model to reason, using prompt engineering.

Open `prompt_flow/chain-of-thought-prompting/flow.dag.yaml` in the VS Code prompt flow visual editor. The elements of this flow are simple, as shown in figure 10.4. With only two LLM blocks, the flow first uses a CoT prompt to solve a complex question; then, the second LLM prompt evaluates the answer.

Listing 10.7 shows the YAML pseudocode that describes the blocks and the inputs/outputs of the flow in more detail. The default problem statement in this example isn't the same as in figure 10.3.

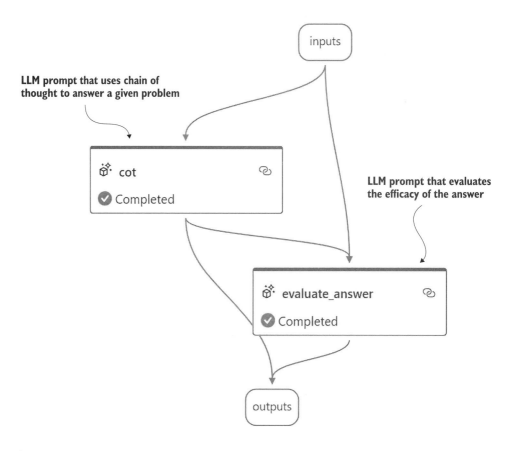

Figure 10.4   The flow of the CoT

```
Inputs:
    statement  : the statement problem to be solved
    expected : the expected solution to the problem

LLM: cot (the prompt used to solve the problem)
    inputs: statement
    outputs: the predicted answer given the problem statement

LLM: evaluate_answer (the prompt used to evaluate the solution)
    inputs:
            statement: -> input.statement
            expected: -> input.expected
            predicted: -> output.cot

    outputs: a score of how well the problem was answered
```

```
Outputs:
    statement: -> input.statement
    expected: -> input.expected
    predicted: -> output.cot
    evaluation_score: output.evaluate_answer

### Example Output
{
  "evaluation_score": "0.5",
  "expected": "After the final jump, Max finds himself
in the year 1980 and he is 75 years old.",
  "predicted": " Max starts in the year 2300 and
travels backward in 40-year increments, spending 5 years
in each period. The journeys will be as follows:
\n\n- From 2300 to 2260: Max is 25 + 5 = 30 years old.
\n- From 2260 to 2220: Max is 30 + 5 = 35 years old.
\n- From 2220 to 2180: Max is 35 + 5 = 40 years old.
\n- From 2180 to 2140: Max is 40 + 5 = 45 years old.
\n- From 2140 to 2100: Max is 45 + 5 = 50 years old.
\n- From 2100 to 2060: Max is 50 + 5 = 55 years old.
\n- From 2060 to 2020: Max is 55 + 5 = 60 years old.
\n- From 2020 to 1980: Max is 60 + 5 = 65 years old.
\n- From 1980 to 1940: Max is 65 + 5 = 70 years old.
\n- From 1940 to 1900: Max is 70 + 5"
}
```

The evaluated score for the given solution

The expected answer for the problem

The predicted answer shows the reasoning steps and output.

Dig into the inputs and check the problem statement; try to evaluate the problem yourself. Then, run the flow by pressing Shift-F5. You should see output similar to that shown in listing 10.7.

Open the `cot.jinja2` prompt file as shown in listing 10.8. This prompt gives a few examples of time travel problems and then the thought-out and reasoned solution. The process of showing the LLM the steps to complete the problem provides the reasoning mechanism.

Listing 10.8 `cot.jinja2`

```
system:
"In a time travel movie, Sarah travels back in time to
prevent a historic event from happening. She arrives
2 days before the event. After spending a day preparing,
she attempts to change the event but realizes she has
actually arrived 2 years early, not 2 days. She then
decides to wait and live in the past until the event's
original date. How many days does Sarah spend in the past
before the day of the event?"

Chain of Thought:

    Initial Assumption: Sarah thinks she has arrived 2 days before the event.
    Time Spent on Preparation: 1 day spent preparing.
    Realization of Error: Sarah realizes she's actually 2 years early.
    Conversion of Years to Days:
```

A few example problem statements

The solution to the problem statement, output as a sequence of reasoning steps

```
2 years = 2 x 365 = 730 days (assuming non-leap years).
    Adjust for the Day Spent Preparing: 730 - 1 = 729 days.
    Conclusion: Sarah spends 729 days in the past before the day of the event.
```

```
"In a sci-fi film, Alex is a time traveler who decides
to go back in time to witness a famous historical battle
that took place 100 years ago, which lasted for 10 days.
He arrives three days before the battle starts. However,
after spending six days in the past, he jumps forward in
time by 50 years and stays there for 20 days. Then, he
travels back to witness the end of the battle. How many
days does Alex spend in the past before he sees the end of
 the battle?"
```
   ← **A few example problem statements**

   ← **The solution to the problem statement, output as a sequence of reasoning steps**

```
Chain of Thought:

    Initial Travel: Alex arrives three days before the battle starts.
    Time Spent Before Time Jump: Alex spends six days in the past.
The battle has started and has been going on for 3 days (since he
arrived 3 days early and has now spent 6 days, 3 + 3 = 6).
    First Time Jump: Alex jumps 50 years forward and stays for 20 days.
 This adds 20 days to the 6 days he's already spent in the past
(6 + 20 = 26).
    Return to the Battle: When Alex returns, he arrives back on the same
day he left (as per time travel logic). The battle has been going on for
3 days now.
    Waiting for the Battle to End: The battle lasts 10 days. Since he's
already witnessed 3 days of it, he needs to wait for 7 more days.
    Conclusion: Alex spends a total of 3 (initial wait) + 3 (before the
first jump) + 20 (50 years ago) + 7 (after returning) = 33 days in the
past before he sees the end of the battle.
Think step by step but only show the final answer to the statement.
```

```
user:
{{statement}}
```
   ← **The problem statement the LLM is directed to solve**

You may note that the solution to figure 10.3 is also provided as an example in listing 10.8. It's also helpful to go back and review listing 10.7 for the reply from the LLM about the problem. From this, you can see the reasoning steps the LLM applied to get its final answer.

Now, we can look at the prompt that evaluates how well the solution solved the problem. Open `evaluate_answer.jinja2`, shown in listing 10.9, to review the prompt used. The prompt is simple, uses zero-shot prompting, and allows the LLM to generalize how it should score the expected and predicted. We could provide examples and scores, thus changing this to an example of a few-shot classification.

Listing 10.9   `evaluate_answer.jinja2`

```
system:

Please confirm that expected and predicted results are
the same for the given problem.
```
   ← **The rules for evaluating the solution**

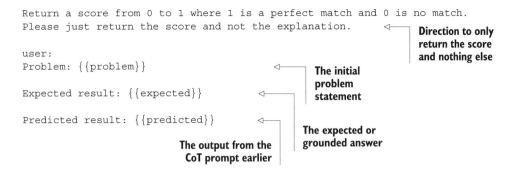

```
Return a score from 0 to 1 where 1 is a perfect match and 0 is no match.
Please just return the score and not the explanation.
```
Direction to only return the score and nothing else

```
user:
Problem: {{problem}}
```
The initial problem statement

```
Expected result: {{expected}}
```
The expected or grounded answer

```
Predicted result: {{predicted}}
```
The output from the CoT prompt earlier

Looking at the LLM output shown earlier in listing 10.7, you can see why the evaluation step may get confusing. Perhaps a fix to this could be suggesting to the LLM to provide the final answer in a single statement. In the next section, we move on to another example of prompt reasoning.

10.2.2 Zero-shot CoT prompting

As our time travel demonstrates, CoT prompting can be expensive in terms of prompt generation for a specific class of problem. While not as effective, there are techniques similar to CoT that don't use examples and can be more generalized. This section will examine a straightforward phrase employed to elicit reasoning in LLMs.

Open `prompt_flow/zero-shot-cot-prompting/flow.dag.yaml` in the VS Code prompt flow visual editor. This flow is very similar to the previous CoT, as shown in figure 10.4. The next lsting shows the YAML pseudocode that describes the flow.

Listing 10.10 `zero-shot-CoT-prompting` flow

```
Inputs:
    statement  : the statement problem to be solved
    expected : the expected solution to the problem

LLM: cot (the prompt used to solve the problem)
    inputs: statement
    outputs: the predicted answer given the problem statement

LLM: evaluate_answer (the prompt used to evaluate the solution)
    inputs:
            statement: -> input.statement
            expected: -> input.expected
            predicted: -> output.cot

    outputs: a score of how well the problem was answered


Outputs:
    statement: -> input.statement
    expected: -> input.expected
    predicted: -> output.cot
```

```
        evaluation_score: output.evaluate_answer
```

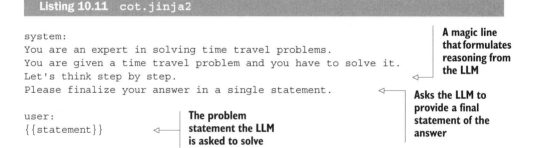

```
  ### Example Output
  {
      "evaluation_score": "1",
      "expected": "After the final jump,
         ➡ Max finds himself in the year 1980 and
  he is 75 years old.",
      "predicted": "Max starts in…
         ➡ Therefore, after the final jump,
         ➡ Max is 75 years old and in the year 1980.",
      "statement": "In a complex time travel …"
  }
```

The final
evaluation score

The expected
answer

The predicted
answer (the
steps have been
omitted showing
the final answer)

The initial problem
statement

Run/test the flow in VS Code by pressing Shift-F5 while in the visual editor. The flow will run, and you should see output similar to that shown in listing 10.10. This exercise example performs better than the previous example on the same problem.

Open the `cot.jinja2` prompt in VS Code, as shown in listing 10.11. This is a much simpler prompt than the previous example because it only uses zero-shot. However, one key phrase turns this simple prompt into a powerful reasoning engine. The line in the prompt `Let's think step by step` triggers the LLM to consider internal context showing reasoning. This, in turn, directs the LLM to reason out the problem in steps.

Listing 10.11 `cot.jinja2`

```
system:
You are an expert in solving time travel problems.
You are given a time travel problem and you have to solve it.
Let's think step by step.
Please finalize your answer in a single statement.

user:
{{statement}}
```

A magic line
that formulates
reasoning from
the LLM

Asks the LLM to
provide a final
statement of the
answer

The problem
statement the LLM
is asked to solve

Similar phrases asking the LLM to think about the steps or asking it to respond in steps also extract reasoning. We'll demonstrate a similar but more elaborate technique in the next section.

10.2.3 *Step by step with prompt chaining*

We can extend the behavior of asking an LLM to think step by step into a chain of prompts that force the LLM to solve the problem in steps. In this section, we look at a technique called *prompt chaining* that forces an LLM to process problems in steps.

Open the `prompt_flow/prompt-chaining/flow.dag.yaml` file in the visual editor, as shown in figure 10.5. Prompt chaining breaks up the reasoning method used to solve a problem into chains of prompts. This technique forces the LLM to answer the problem in terms of steps.

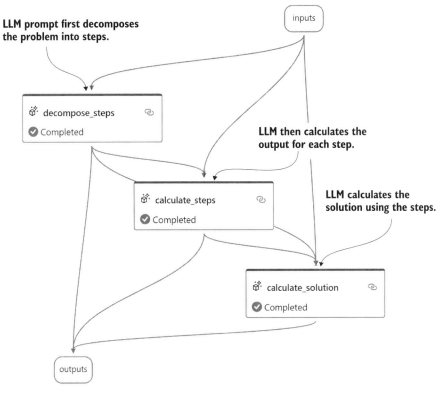

Figure 10.5 The prompt chaining flow

Listing 10.12 shows the YAML pseudocode that describes the flow in a few more details. This flow chains the output of the first LLM block into the second and then from the second into the third. Forcing the LLM to process the problem this way uncovers the reasoning pattern, but it can also be overly verbose.

Listing 10.12 `prompt-chaining flow`

```
Inputs:
    statement  : the statement problem to be solved

LLM: decompose_steps (the prompt used to decompose the problem)
    inputs:
        statement: -> input.statement                    <─┤  Start of the chain
                                                              of prompts
    outputs: the breakdown of steps to solve the problem

LLM: calculate_steps (the prompt used to calculate the steps)
    inputs:
        statement: -> input.statement                       Output from
        decompose_steps: -> output.decompose_steps     <─   the previous
                                                            step injected
        outputs: the calculation for each step              into this step
```

```
LLM: calculate_solution (attempts to solve the problem)
     inputs:
             statement: -> input.statement
             decompose_steps: -> output.decompose_steps        ┐ Output from
             calculate_steps: -> output.calculate_steps   ◁───  two previous
                                                                 steps injected
         outputs: the final solution statement                  into this step

 Outputs:
     statement: -> input.statement
     decompose_steps: -> output.decompose_steps
     calculate_steps: -> output.calculate_steps
     calculate_solution: -> output.calculate_solution

 ### Example Output
{
   "calculate_steps": "1. The days spent by Alex",
   "decompose_steps": "To figure out the …",            ┐ The final solution
   "solution": "Alex spends 13 days in the                statement,
        ➠ past before the end of the battle.",   ◁───     although wrong,
   "statement": "In a sci-fi film, Alex …"                is closer.
}
```

Run the flow by pressing Shift-F5 from the visual editor, and you'll see the output as shown in listing 10.12. The answer is still not correct for the Alex problem, but we can see all the work the LLM is doing to reason out the problem.

Open up all three prompts: decompose_steps.jinja2, calculate_steps.jinja2, and calculate_solution.jinja2 (see listings 10.13, 10.14, and 10.15, respectively). All three prompts shown in the listings can be compared to show how outputs chain together.

Listing 10.13 decompose_steps.jinja2

```
system:
You are a problem solving AI assistant.
Your job is to break the users problem down into smaller steps and list
the steps in the order you would solve them.
Think step by step, not in generalities.                      ┐ Forces the LLM to
Do not attempt to solve the problem, just list the steps.  ◁── list only the steps
                                                               and nothing else
user:
{{statement}}        ◁─┤ The initial problem
                        statement
```

Listing 10.14 calculate_steps.jinja2

```
system:
You are a problem solving AI assistant.
You will be given a list of steps that solve a problem.
Your job is to calculate the output for each of the steps in order.
Do not attempt to solve the whole problem,
```

```
just list output for each of the steps.
Think step by step.

user:
{{statement}}

{{steps}}
```

Requests that the LLM not solve the whole problem, just the steps

Injects the steps produced by the decompose_steps step

Uses the magic statement to extract reasoning

Listing 10.15 `calculate_solution.jinja2`

```
system:
You are a problem solving AI assistant.
You will be given a list of steps and the calculated output for each step.
Use the calculated output from each step to determine the final
solution to the problem.
Provide only the final solution to the problem in a
single concise sentence. Do not include any steps
in your answer.

user:
{{statement}}

{{steps}}

{{calculated}}
```

Requests that the LLM output the final answer and not any steps

The decomposed steps

The calculated steps

In this exercise example, we're not performing any evaluation and scoring. Without the evaluation, we can see that this sequence of prompts still has problems solving our more challenging time travel problem shown earlier in figure 10.3. However, that doesn't mean this technique doesn't have value, and this prompting format solves some complex problems well.

What we want to find, however, is a reasoning and planning methodology that can solve such complex problems consistently. The following section moves from reasoning to evaluating the best solution.

10.3 *Employing evaluation for consistent solutions*

In the previous section, we learned that even the best-reasoned plans may not always derive the correct solution. Furthermore, we may not always have the answer to confirm if that solution is correct. The reality is that we often want to use some form of evaluation to determine the efficacy of a solution.

Figure 10.6 shows a comparison of the prompt engineering strategies that have been devised as a means of getting LLMs to reason and plan. We've already covered the two on the left: zero-shot direct prompting and CoT prompting. The following example exercises in this section will look at self-consistency with the CoT and ToT techniques.

We'll continue to focus on the complex time travel problem to compare these more advanced methods that expand on reasoning and planning with evaluation. In the next section, we'll evaluate self-consistency.

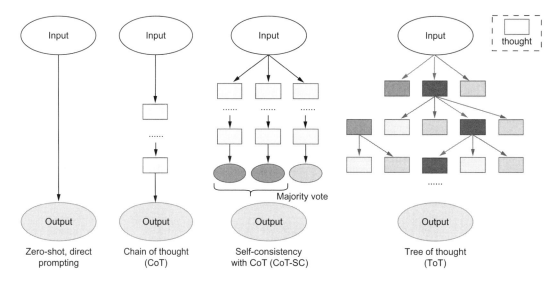

Figure 10.6   **Comparing the various prompt engineering strategies to enable reasoning and planning from LLMs**

10.3.1 *Evaluating self-consistency prompting*

Consistency in prompting is more than just lowering the temperature parameter we send to an LLM. Often, we want to generate a consistent plan or solution and still use a high temperature to better evaluate all the variations to a plan. By evaluating multiple different plans, we can get a better sense of the overall value of a solution.

Self-consistent prompting is the technique of generating multiple plans/solutions for a given problem. Then, those plans are evaluated, and the more frequent or consistent plan is accepted. Imagine three plans generated, where two are similar, but the third is different. Using self-consistency, we evaluate the first two plans as the more consistent answer.

Open `prompt_flow/self-consistency-prompting/flow.dag.yaml` in the VS Code prompt flow visual editor. The flow diagram shows the simplicity of the prompt generation flow in figure 10.7. Next to it in the diagram is the self-consistency evaluation flow.

Prompt flow uses a direct acyclic graph (DAG) format to execute the flow logic. DAGs are an excellent way of demonstrating and executing flow logic, but because they are *acyclic*, meaning they can't repeat, they can't execute loops. However, because prompt flow provides a batch processing mechanism, we can use that to simulate loops or repetition in a flow.

Referring to figure 10.6, we can see that self-consistency processes the input three times before collecting the results and determining the best plan/reply. We can apply this same pattern but use batch processing to generate the outputs. Then, the evaluation flow will aggregate the results and determine the best answer.

Open the `self-consistency-prompting/cot.jinja2` prompt template in VS Code (see listing 10.16). The listing was shortened, as we've seen parts before. This

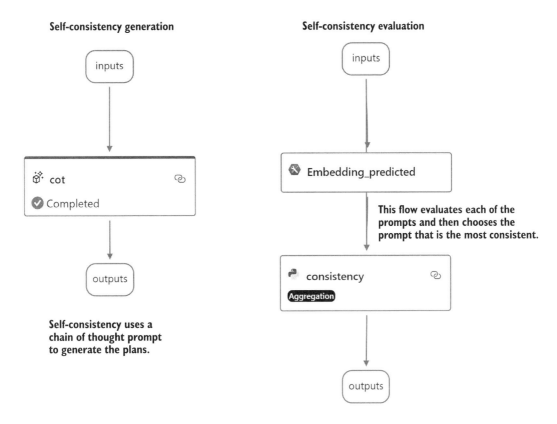

Figure 10.7   The self-consistency prompt generation beside the evaluation flow

prompt uses two (few-shot prompt) examples of a CoT to demonstrate the thought reasoning to the LLM.

Listing 10.16   self-consistency-prompting/cot.jinja2

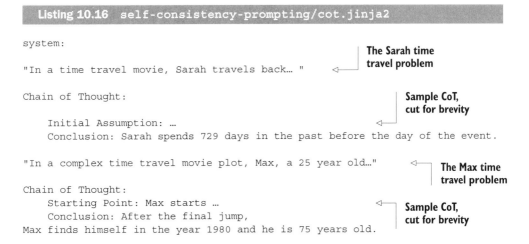

```
Think step by step,
 but only show the final answer to the statement.
```
← **Final guide and statement to constrain output**

```
user:
{{statement}}
```

Open the `self-consistency-prompting/flow.dag.yaml` file in VS Code. Run the example in batch mode by clicking Batch Run (the beaker icon) from the visual editor. Figure 10.8 shows the process step by step:

1 Click Batch Run.
2 Select the JSON Lines (JSONL) input.
3 Select `statements.jsonl`.
4 Click the Run link.

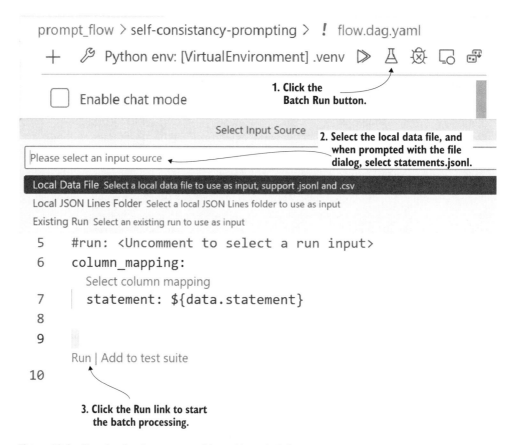

Figure 10.8   The step-by-step process of launching a batch process

TIP   If you need to review the process, refer to chapter 9, which covers this process in more detail.

Listing 10.17 shows the JSON output from executing the flow in batch mode. The `statements.jsonl` file has five identical Alex time travel problem entries. Using identical entries allows us to simulate the prompt executing five times on the duplicate entry.

Listing 10.17 `self-consistency-prompting` batch execution output

```
{
    "name": "self-consistency-prompting_default_20240203_100322_912000",
    "created_on": "2024-02-03T10:22:30.028558",
    "status": "Completed",
    "display_name": "self-consistency-prompting_variant_0_202402031022",
    "description": null,
    "tags": null,
    "properties": {
        "flow_path": "…prompt_flow/self-consistency-prompting",
        "output_path": "…/.promptflow/.runs/self-
consistency-prompting_default_20240203_100322_912000",
        "system_metrics": {
            "total_tokens": 4649,
            "prompt_tokens": 3635,
            "completion_tokens": 1014,
            "duration": 30.033773
        }
    },
    "flow_name": "self-consistency-prompting",
    "data": "…/prompt_flow/self-consistency-prompting/
statements.jsonl",
    "output": "…/.promptflow/.runs/self-consistency-
prompting_default_20240203_100322_912000/flow_outputs"
}
```

The path where the flow was executed from

The folder containing the outputs of the flow (note this path)

The data used to run the flow in batch

You can view the flow produced by pressing the Ctrl key and clicking the output link, highlighted in listing 10.17. This will open another instance of VS Code, showing a folder with all the output from the run. We now want to check the most consistent answer. Fortunately, the evaluation feature in prompt flow can help us identify consistent answers using similarity matching.

Open `self-consistency-evaluation/flow.dag.yaml` in VS Code (see figure 10.7). This flow embeds the predicted answer and then uses an aggregation to determine the most consistent answer.

From the flow, open `consistency.py` in VS Code, as shown in listing 10.18. The code for this tool function calculates the cosine similarity for all pairs of answers. Then, it finds the most similar answer, logs it, and outputs that as the answer.

Listing 10.18 `consistency.py`

```
from promptflow import tool
from typing import List
import numpy as np
from scipy.spatial.distance import cosine
```

```
@tool
def consistency(texts: List[str],
                embeddings: List[List[float]]) -> str:
    if len(embeddings) != len(texts):
        raise ValueError("The number of embeddings
        ➥ must match the number of texts.")

    mean_embedding = np.mean(embeddings, axis=0)
    similarities = [1 - cosine(embedding, mean_embedding)
                ➥ for embedding in embeddings]
    most_similar_index = np.argmax(similarities)

    from promptflow import log_metric
    log_metric(key="highest_ranked_output", value=texts[most_similar_index])

    return texts[most_similar_index]
```

Calculates the mean of all the embeddings

Calculates cosine similarity for each pair of embeddings

Finds the index of the most similar answer

Logs the output as a metric

Returns the text for the most similar answer

We need to run the evaluation flow in batch mode as well. Open `self-consistency-evaluation/flow.dag.yaml` in VS Code and run the flow in batch mode (beaker icon). Then, select Existing Run as the flow input, and when prompted, choose the top or the last run you just executed as input.

Again, after the flow completes processing, you'll see an output like that shown in listing 10.17. Ctrl-click on the output folder link to open a new instance of VS Code showing the results. Locate and open the `metric.json` file in VS Code, as shown in figure 10.9.

The answer shown in figure 10.9 is still incorrect for this run. You can continue a few more batch runs of the prompt and/or increase the number of runs in a batch and then evaluate flows to see if you get better answers. This technique is generally more helpful for more straightforward problems but still demonstrates an inability to reason out complex problems.

Self-consistency uses a reflective approach to evaluate the most likely thought. However, the most likely thing is certainly not always the best. Therefore, we must consider a more comprehensive approach in the next section.

10.3.2 *Evaluating tree of thought prompting*

As mentioned earlier, ToT prompting, as shown in figure 10.6, combines self-evaluation and prompt chaining techniques. As such, it breaks down the sequence of planning into a chain of prompts, but at each step in the chain, it provides for multiple evaluations. This creates a tree that can be executed and evaluated at each level, breadth-first, or from top to bottom, depth-first.

Figure 10.10 shows the difference between executing a tree using breadth-first or depth-first. Unfortunately, due to the DAG execution pattern of prompt flow, we can't quickly implement the depth-first method, but breadth-first works just fine.

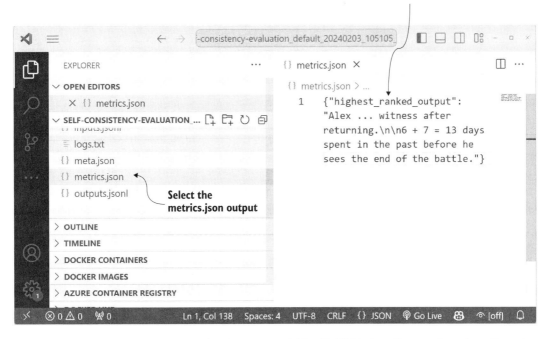

Figure 10.9   The VS Code is open to the batch run output folder. Highlighted are the `metrics.json` file and the output showing the most similar answer.

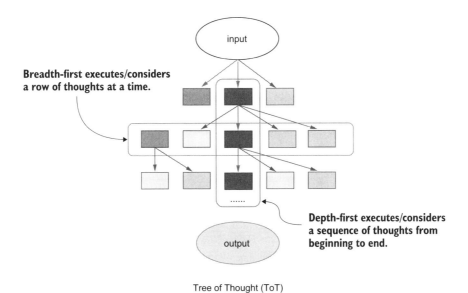

Figure 10.10   Breadth-first vs. depth-first execution on a ToT pattern

Open `tree-of-thought-evaluation/flow.dag.yaml` in VS Code. The visual of the flow is shown in figure 10.11. This flow functions like a breadth-first ToT pattern—the flow chains together a series of prompts asking the LLM to return multiple plans at each step.

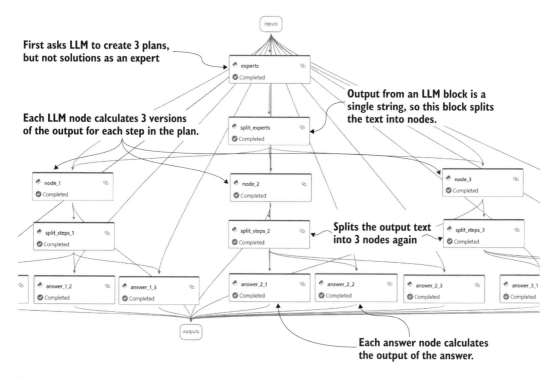

First asks LLM to create 3 plans, but not solutions as an expert

Output from an LLM block is a single string, so this block splits the text into nodes.

Each LLM node calculates 3 versions of the output for each step in the plan.

Splits the output text into 3 nodes again

Each answer node calculates the output of the answer.

Figure 10.11   ToT pattern expressed and prompt flow

Because the flow executes in a breadth-first style, each level output of the nodes is also evaluated. Each node in the flow uses a pair of semantic functions—one to generate the answer and the other to evaluate the answer. The semantic function is a custom Python flow block that processes multiple inputs and generates multiple outputs.

Listing 10.19 shows the `semantic_function.py` tool. This general tool is reused for multiple blocks in this flow. It also demonstrates the embedding functionality from the SK for direct use within prompt flow.

Listing 10.19   `semantic_function.py`

```
@tool
def my_python_tool(
    input: str,
    input_node: int,
    history: str,
```

```
    semantic_function: str,
    evaluation_function: str,
    function_name: str,
    skill_name: str,
    max_tokens: int,
    temperature: float,
    deployment_name: str,
    connection: Union[OpenAIConnection,
                      AzureOpenAIConnection],
) -> str:
    if input is None or input == "":
        return ""

    kernel = sk.Kernel(log=sk.NullLogger())
    # code for setting up the kernel and LLM connection omitted


    function = kernel.create_semantic_function(
                    semantic_function,
                        function_name=function_name,
                        skill_name=skill_name,
                        max_tokens=max_tokens,
                        temperature=temperature,
                        top_p=0.5)
    evaluation = kernel.create_semantic_function(
                        evaluation_function,
                        function_name="Evaluation",
                        skill_name=skill_name,
                        max_tokens=max_tokens,
                        temperature=temperature,
                        top_p=0.5)

    async def main():
        query = f"{history}\n{input}"
        try:
            eval = int((await evaluation.invoke_async(query)).result)
            if eval > 25:
                return await function.invoke_async(query)
        except Exception as e:
            raise Exception("Evaluation failed", e)

    try:
        result = asyncio.run(main()).result
        return result
    except Exception as e:
        print(e)
        return ""
```

Uses a union to allow for different types of LLM connections

Checks to see if the input is empty or None; if so, the function shouldn't be executed.

Sets up the generation function that creates a plan

Sets up the evaluation function

Runs the evaluate function and determines if the input is good enough to continue

If the evaluation score is high enough, generates the next step

The semantic function tool is used in the tree's experts, nodes, and answer blocks. At each step, the function determines if any text is being input. If there is no text, the block returns with no execution. Passing no text to a block means that the previous block failed evaluation. By evaluating before each step, ToT short-circuits the execution of plans it deems as not being valid.

This may be a complex pattern to grasp at first, so go ahead and run the flow in VS Code. Listing 10.20 shows just the answer node output of a run; these results may vary from what you see but should be similar. Nodes that return no text either failed evaluation or their parents did.

Listing 10.20   Output from `tree-of-thought-evaluation` flow

```
{
    "answer_1_1": "",      ◁——    Represents that the first     The plan for node 2 and
    "answer_1_2": "",              node plans weren't valid     answer 2 failed evaluation
    "answer_1_3": "",             and not executed                      and wasn't run.
    "answer_2_1": "Alex spends a total of 29 days in the past before he
sees the end of the battle.",
    "answer_2_2": "",                                                              ◁——┐
    "answer_2_3": "Alex spends a total of 29 days in the past before he
sees the end of the battle.",
    "answer_3_1": "",                                                              ◁——┐
    "answer_3_2": "Alex spends a total of 29 days in the past before he
sees the end of the battle.",
    "answer_3_3": "Alex spends a total of 9 days in the past before he
sees the end of the battle.",
                                            The plan for this node failed
                                             to evaluate and wasn't run.
```

The output in listing 10.20 shows how only a select set of nodes was evaluated. In most cases, the evaluated nodes returned an answer that could be valid. Where no output was produced, it means that the node itself or its parent wasn't valid. When sibling nodes all return empty, the parent node fails to evaluate.

As we can see, ToT is valid for complex problems but perhaps not very practical. The execution of this flow can take up to 27 calls to an LLM to generate an output. In practice, it may only do half that many calls, but that's still a dozen or more calls to answer a single problem.

10.4   Exercises

Use the following exercises to improve your knowledge of the material:

- *Exercise 1*—Create Direct Prompting, Few-Shot Prompting, and Zero-Shot Prompting
  Objective—Create three different prompts for an LLM to summarize a recent scientific article: one using direct prompting, one with few-shot prompting, and the last employing zero-shot prompting.
  Tasks:
  – Compare the effectiveness of the summaries generated by each approach.
  – Compare the accuracy of the summaries generated by each approach.

- *Exercise 2*—Craft Reasoning Prompts
  Objective—Design a set of prompts that require the LLM to solve logical puzzles or riddles.

Tasks:

– Focus on how the structure of your prompt can influence the LLM's reasoning process.

– Focus on how the same can influence the correctness of its answers.

▪ *Exercise 3*—Evaluation Prompt Techniques

Objective—Develop an evaluation prompt that asks the LLM to predict the outcome of a hypothetical experiment.

Task:

– Create a follow-up prompt that evaluates the LLM's prediction for accuracy and provides feedback on its reasoning process.

Summary

▪ Direct solution prompting is a foundational method of using prompts to direct LLMs toward solving specific problems or tasks, emphasizing the importance of clear question-and-answer structures.

▪ Few-shot prompting provides LLMs with a few examples to guide them in handling new or unseen content, highlighting its power in enabling the model to adapt to unfamiliar patterns.

▪ Zero-shot learning and prompting demonstrate how LLMs can generalize from their training to solve problems without needing explicit examples, showcasing their inherent ability to understand and apply knowledge in new contexts.

▪ Chain of thought prompting guides the LLMs through a reasoning process step by step to solve complex problems, illustrating how to elicit detailed reasoning from the model.

▪ Prompt chaining breaks down a problem into a series of prompts that build upon each other, showing how to structure complex problem-solving processes into manageable steps for LLMs.

▪ Self-consistency is a prompt technique that generates multiple solutions to a problem and selects the most consistent answer through evaluation, emphasizing the importance of consistency in achieving reliable outcomes.

▪ Tree of thought prompting combines self-evaluation and prompt chaining to create a comprehensive strategy for tackling complex problems, allowing for a systematic exploration of multiple solution paths.

▪ Advanced prompt engineering strategies provide insights into sophisticated techniques such as self-consistency with CoT and ToT, offering methods to increase the accuracy and reliability of LLM-generated solutions.

11

Agent planning and feedback

This chapter covers

- Planning for an LLM and implementing it in agents and assistants
- Using the OpenAI Assistants platform via custom actions
- Implementing/testing a generic planner on LLMs
- Using the feedback mechanism in advanced models
- Planning, reasoning, evaluation, and feedback in building agentic systems

Now that we've examined how large language models (LLMs) can reason and plan, this chapter takes this concept a step further by employing planning within an agent framework. Planning should be at the core of any agent/assistant platform or toolkit. We'll start by looking at the basics of planning and how to implement a planner through prompting. Then, we'll see how planning operates using the OpenAI Assistants platform, which automatically incorporates planning. From there, we'll build and implement a general planner for LLMs.

Planning can only go so far, and an often-unrecognized element is feedback. Therefore, in the last sections of the chapter, we explore feedback and implement it within a planner. You must be familiar with the content of chapter 10, so please review it if you need to, and when you're ready, let's begin planning.

11.1   Planning: The essential tool for all agents/assistants

Agents and assistants who can't plan and only follow simple interactions are nothing more than chatbots. As we've seen throughout this book, our goal isn't to build bots but rather to build autonomous thinking agents—agents that can take a goal, work out how to solve it, and then return with the results.

Figure 11.1 explains the overall planning process that the agent/assistant will undertake. This figure was also presented in chapter 1, but let's review it now in more detail. At the top of the figure, a user submits a goal. In an agentic system, the agent takes the goal, constructs the plan, executes it, and then returns the results.

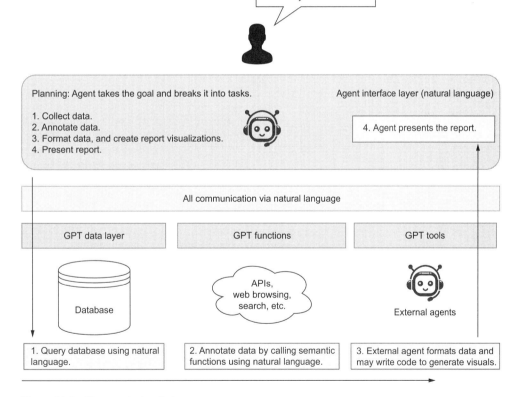

Figure 11.1   The agent planning process

Depending on your interaction with platforms such as ChatGPT and GPTs, Claude, and others, you may have already encountered a planning assistant and not even noticed. Planning is becoming ubiquitous and is now built into most commercial platforms to make the model appear more intelligent and capable. Therefore, in the next exercise, we'll look at an example to set a baseline and differentiate between an LLM that can't plan and an agent that can.

For the next exercise, we'll use Nexus to demonstrate how raw LLMs can't plan independently. If you need assistance installing, setting up, and running Nexus, refer to chapter 7. After you have Nexus installed and ready, we can begin running it with the Gradio interface, using the commands shown next.

Listing 11.1 Running Nexus with the Gradio interface

```
nexus run gradio
```

Gradio is an excellent web interface tool built to demonstrate Python machine learning projects. Figure 11.2 shows the Gradio Nexus interface and the process for creating an agent and using an agent engine (OpenAI, Azure, and Groq) of your choice. You can't use LM Studio unless the model/server supports tool/action use. Anthropic's Claude supports internal planning, so for the purposes of this exercise, avoid using this model.

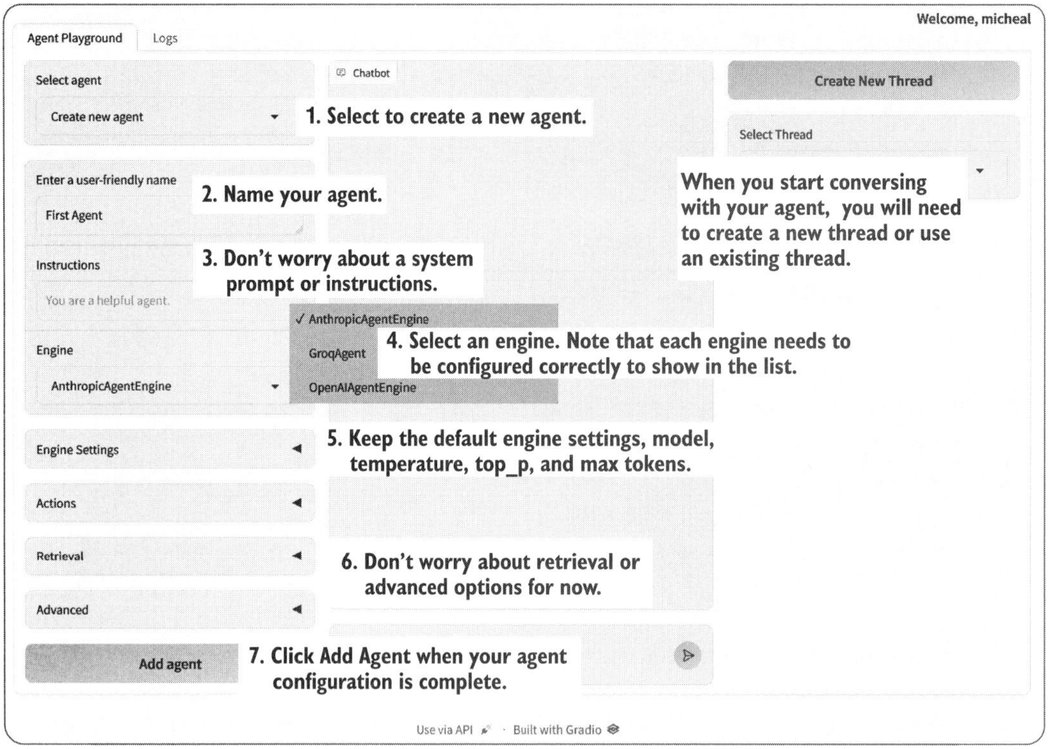

Figure 11.2 Creating a new agent in Nexus

After creating the agent, we want to give it specific actions (tools) to undertake or complete a goal. Generally, providing only the actions an agent needs to complete its goal is best for a few reasons:

- More actions can confuse an agent into deciding which to use or even how to solve a goal.
- APIs have limits on the number of tools that can be submitted; at the time of writing, hitting this limit is relatively easy.
- Agents may use your actions in ways you didn't intend unless that's your goal. Be warned, however, that actions can have consequences.
- Safety and security need to be considered. LLMs aren't going to take over the world, but they make mistakes and quickly get off track. Remember, these agents will operate independently and may perform any action.

WARNING While writing this book and working with and building agents over many hours, I have encountered several instances of agents going rogue with actions, from downloading files to writing and executing code when not intended, continually iterating from tool to tool, and even deleting files they shouldn't have. Watching an agent emerge new behaviors using actions can be fun, but things can quickly go astray.

For this exercise, we'll define the goal described in the following listing.

Listing 11.2 Demonstrating planning: The goal

```
Search Wikipedia for pages on {topic} and download each page and save it
to a file called Wikipedia_{topic}.txt
```

This goal will demonstrate the following actions:

- `search_wikipedia(topic)`—Searches Wikipedia and returns page IDs for the given search term.
- `get_wikipedia_page(page_id)`—Downloads the page content given the page ID.
- `save_file`—Saves the content to a file.

Set the actions on the agent, as shown in figure 11.3. You'll also want to make sure the Planner is set to None. We'll look at setting up and using planners soon. You don't have to click Save; the interface automatically saves an agent's changes.

After you choose the actions and planner, enter the goal in listing 11.2. Then click Create New Thread to instantiate a new conversation. Substitute the topic you want to search for in the chat input, and wait for the agent to respond. Here's an example of the goal filled with the topic, but again, use any topic you like:

```
Search Wikipedia for pages on Calgary and download each page and save it to
a file called Wikipedia_Calgary.txt.
```

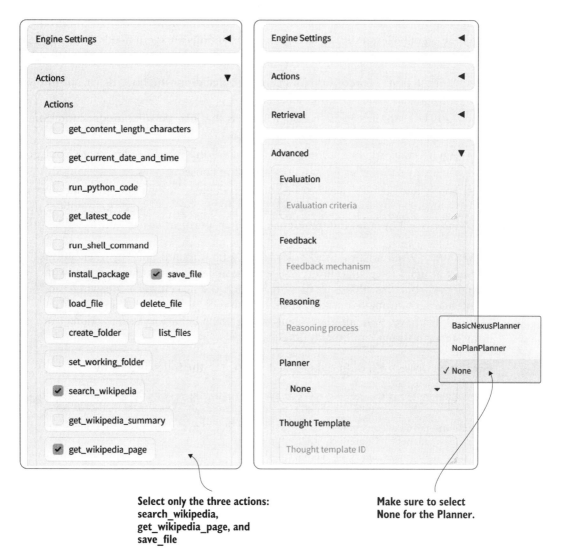

Figure 11.3 Selecting the actions for the agent and disabling the planner

Figure 11.4 shows the results of submitting the goal to the plain agent. We see the agent executed the tool/action to search for the topic but couldn't execute any steps beyond that. If you recall from our discussion and code example of actions in chapter 5, OpenAI, Groq, and Azure OpenAI all support parallel actions but not sequential or planned actions.

The LLM can answer reasonably well if you submit a goal with several parallel tasks/actions. However, if the actions are sequential, requiring one step to be dependent on another, it will fail. Remember, parallel actions are standalone actions that can be run alongside others.

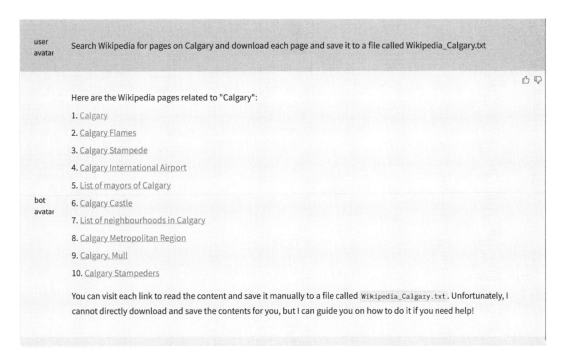

Figure 11.4   The results from trying to get the agent/LLM to complete the goal

Anthropic's Claude and OpenAI Assistants support sequential action planning. This means both models can be called with sequential plans, and the model will execute them and return the results. In the next section, we'll explore sequential planning and then demonstrate it in action.

11.2   Understanding the sequential planning process

In the next exercise, we'll ask an OpenAI assistant to solve the same goal. If you have Anthropic/Claude credentials and have the engine configured, you can also try this exercise with that model.

Figure 11.5 shows the difference between executing tasks sequentially (planning) and using iteration. If you've used GPTs, assistants, or Claude Sonnet 3.5, you've likely already experienced this difference. These advanced tools already incorporate planning by prompt annotations, advanced training, or combining both.

As LLM and chat services evolve, most models will likely natively support some form of planning and tool use. However, most models, including GPT-4o, only support action/tool use today.

Let's open the GPT Assistants Playground to demonstrate sequential planning in action. If you need help, refer to the setup guide in chapter 6. We'll use the same goal but, this time, run it against an assistant (which has built-in planning).

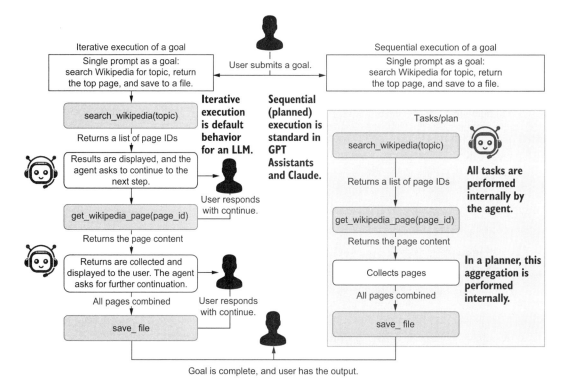

Figure 11.5   **The difference between iterative and planned execution**

After you launch the Playground, create a new assistant, and assign it the `search_wikipedia`, `get_wikipedia_page`, and `save_file` actions. Figure 11.6 shows the results of entering the goal to the assistant. As you can see, the assistant completed all the tasks behind the scenes and responded with the user's final requested output, achieving the goal.

To demonstrate the effectiveness of the OpenAI Assistant's planner, we added another task, summarizing each page, to the goal. The inserted task didn't have a function/tool, but the assistant was savvy enough to use its ability to summarize the content. You can see the output of what the assistant produced by opening the `[root folder]assistants_working_folder/Wikipedia_{topic}.txt` file and reviewing the contents. Now that we understand how LLMs function without planners and planning, we can move on to creating our planners in the next section.

11.3   *Building a sequential planner*

LLM tools such as LangChain and Semantic Kernel (SK) have many planners using various strategies. However, writing our planner is relatively easy, and Nexus also supports a plugin-style interface allowing you to add other planners from tools such as LangChain and SK, or your derivatives.

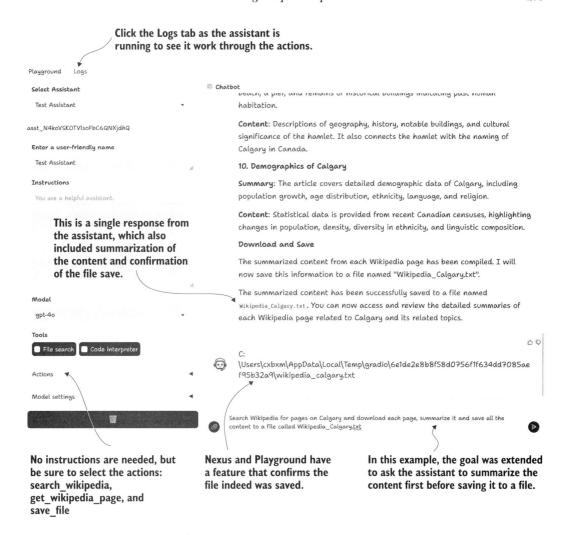

Figure 11.6 The assistant processing the goal and outputting the results

Planners may sound complicated, but they are easily implemented through prompt engineering strategies that incorporate planning and reasoning. In chapter 10, we covered the basics of reasoning and deriving plans, and now we can put those skills to good use.

Listing 11.3 shows a sequential planner derived from the SK, which is extended to incorporate iteration. Prompt annotation planners like those shown in the listing can be adapted to fit specific needs or be more general like those shown. This planner uses JSON, but planners could use any format an LLM understands, including code.

Listing 11.3 `basic_nexus_planner.py`

> **The preamble instructions telling the agent how to process the examples**

You are a planner for Nexus.
Your job is to create a properly formatted JSON plan step by step, to
satisfy the goal given.
Create a list of subtasks based off the [GOAL] provided.
Each subtask must be from within the [AVAILABLE FUNCTIONS] list. Do not
use any functions that are not in the list.
Base your decisions on which functions to use from the description and the
name of the function.
Sometimes, a function may take arguments. Provide them if necessary.
The plan should be as short as possible.
You will also be given a list of corrective, suggestive and epistemic
feedback from previous plans to help you make your decision.
For example:

[SPECIAL FUNCTIONS]
for-each- prefix
description: execute a function for each item in a list
args:
- function: the function to execute
- list: the list of items to iterate over
- index: the arg name for the current item in the list

> **Beginning of the three (few-shot) examples**

[AVAILABLE FUNCTIONS]
GetJokeTopics
description: Get a list ([str]) of joke topics

EmailTo
description: email the input text to a recipient
args:
- text: the text to email
- recipient: the recipient's email address. Multiple addresses may be
included if separated by ';'.

Summarize
description: summarize input text
args:
- text: the text to summarize

Joke
description: Generate a funny joke
args:
- topic: the topic to generate a joke about

[GOAL]
"Get a list of joke topics and generate a different joke for each topic.
Email the jokes to a friend."

[OUTPUT]
    {
        "subtasks": [
            {"function": "GetJokeTopics"},

```
        {"function": "for-each",
         "args": {
                "list": "output_GetJokeTopics",
                "index": "topic",
                "function":
                        {
                            "function": "Joke",
                            "args": {"topic": "topic"}}}},
        {
         "function": "EmailTo",
          "args": {
                "text": "for-each_output_GetJokeTopics"
                ecipient": "friend"}}
    ]
  }
# 2 more examples are given but omitted from this listing

[SPECIAL FUNCTIONS]                                    ◁┐  Adds the for-each
for-each                                                 │  special iterative
description: execute a function for each item in a list  │  function
args:
- function: the function to execute
- iterator: the list of items to iterate over            Available functions are
- index: the arg name for the current item in the list   autopopulated from the
                                                         agent's list of available
[AVAILABLE FUNCTIONS]                                ◁┘  functions.
{{$available_functions}}

[GOAL]
{{$goal}}                                    ◁─── The goal is inserted here.

Be sure to only use functions from the list of available functions.
The plan should be as short as possible.
And only return the plan in JSON format.
[OUTPUT]                                     ◁─┐  Where the agent is expected
                                               │  to place the output
```

Figure 11.7 shows the process of building and running a planning prompt, from building to execution to finally returning the results to the user. Planners work by building a planning prompt, submitting it to an LLM to construct the plan, parsing and executing the plan locally, returning the results to an LLM to evaluate and summarize, and finally returning the final output back to the user.

It's essential to notice a few subtle details about the planning process. Typically, the plan is built in isolation by not adding context history. This is done to focus on the goal because most planning prompts consume many tokens. Executing the functions within the executor is usually done in a local environment and may include calling APIs, executing code, or even running machine learning models.

Listing 11.4 shows the code for the `create_plan` function from the `BasicNexus-Planner` class; tools such as LangChain and SK use similar patterns. The process loads the agent's actions as a string. The goal and available functions list are then inserted into the planner prompt template using the `PromptTemplateManager`, which is just a wrapper

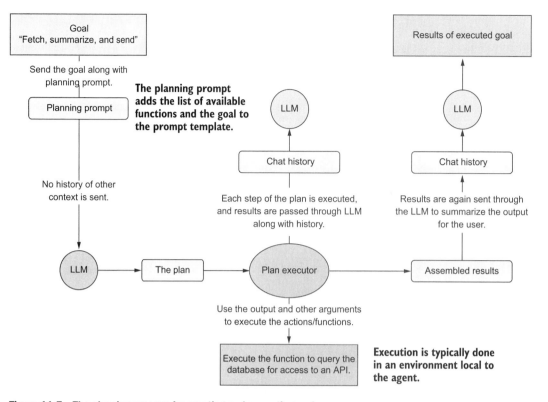

Figure 11.7   The planning process for creating and executing a plan

for the template-handling code. Template handling is done with simple regex but can also be more sophisticated using tools such as Jinja2, Handlebars, or Mustache.

Listing 11.4   `basic_nexus_planner.py (create_plan)`

```
def create_plan(self, nexus, agent, goal: str, prompt: str = PROMPT) -> Plan:
    selected_actions = nexus.get_actions(agent.actions)
    available_functions_string = "\n\n".join(
        format_action(action) for action in selected_actions
    )

    context = {}
    context["goal"] = goal
    context["available_functions"] = available_functions_string
```

The context will be injected into the planner prompt template.

Loads the agent's available actions and formats the result string for the planner

```
ptm = PromptTemplateManager()
prompt = ptm.render_prompt(prompt, context)

plan_text = nexus.execute_prompt(agent, prompt)
return Plan(prompt=prompt,
            goal=goal,
            plan_text=plan_text)
```

◁ **A simple template manager, similar in concept to Jinja2, Handlebars, or Mustache**

◁ **Sends the filled-in planner prompt to the LLM**

The results (the plan) are wrapped in a Plan class and returned for execution.

The code to execute the plan, shown in listing 11.5, parses the JSON string and executes the functions. When executing the plan, the code detects the particular `for-each` function, which iterates through a list and executes each element in a function. The results of each function execution are added to the context. This context is passed to each function call and returned as the final output.

Listing 11.5 basic_nexus_planner.py (execute_plan)

```
def execute_plan(self, nexus, agent, plan: Plan) -> str:
    context = {}
    plan = plan.generated_plan
    for task in plan["subtasks"]:
        if task["function"] == "for-each":
            list_name = task["args"]["list"]
            index_name = task["args"]["index"]
            inner_task = task["args"]["function"]

            list_value = context.get(list_name, [])
            for item in list_value:
                context[index_name] = item
                result = nexus.execute_task(agent, inner_task, context)
                context[f"for-each_{list_name}_{item}"] = result

            for_each_output = [
                context[f"for-each_{list_name}_{item}"]
                for item in list_value
            ]
            context[f"for-each_{list_name}"] = for_each_output

            for item in list_value:
                del context[f"for-each_{list_name}_{item}"]

        else:
            result = nexus.execute_task(agent,
                                        task,
                                        context)
            context[f"output_{task['function']}"] = result

    return context
```

◁ **Iterates through each subtask in the plan**

◁ **Handles functions that should be iterated over and adds full list of results to the context**

◁ **Removes individual for-each context entries**

◁ **General task execution**

◁ **Returns the full context, which includes the results of each function call**

The returned context from the entire execution is sent in a final call to the LLM, which summarizes the results and returns a response. If everything goes as planned, the LLM will respond with a summary of the results. If there is an error or something is missing, the LLM may try to fix the problem or inform the user of the error.

Let's now open Nexus again and test a planner in operation. Load up the same agent you used last time, but select the planner under the Advanced options this time, as shown in figure 11.8. Then, enter the goal prompt as you did before, and let the agent take it away.

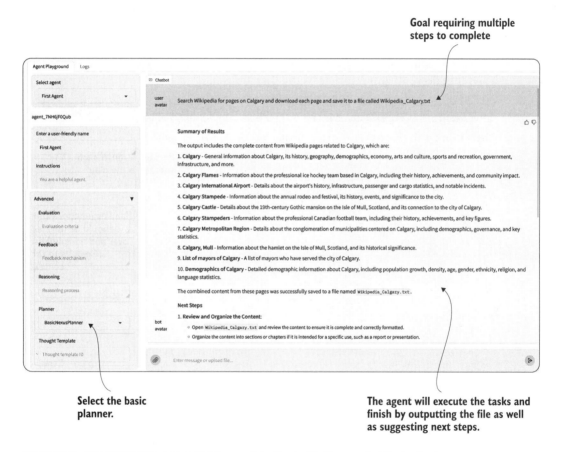

Figure 11.8   The results from requesting to complete the goal in Nexus using the basic planner

After a few minutes, the agent returns with the saved file, and in some cases, it may provide extra information, such as the next steps and what to do with the output. This is because the agent was given a high-level overview of what it accomplished. Remember, though, that plan execution is done at the local level, and only context, plan, and goal were sent to the LLM.

This means that plan execution can be completed by any process, not necessarily by the agent. Executing a plan outside the LLM reduces the tokens and tool use the agent needs to perform. This also means that an LLM doesn't need to support tools usage to use a planner.

Internally, when a planner is enabled within Nexus, the agent engine tool is bypassed. Instead, the planner completes the action execution, and the agent is only aware of the actions through the passing of the output context. This can be good for models that support tool use but can't plan. However, a planner may limit functionality for models that support both tool use and planning, such as Claude.

In general, you'll want to understand the capabilities of the LLM you're using. If you're unsure of those details, then a little trial and error can also work. Ask the agent to complete a multistep goal with and without planning enabled, and then see the results.

Planning allows agents to complete multiple sequential tasks to achieve more complex goals. The problem with external or prompt planning is that it bypasses the feedback iteration loop, which can help correct problems quickly. Because of this, OpenAI and others are now directly integrating reasoning and planning at the LLM level, as we'll see in the next section.

11.4 Reviewing a stepwise planner: OpenAI Strawberry

The release of the o1-preview model, code named Strawberry, introduced a dramatic shift in the type of LLMs becoming available for agentic systems. Strawberry was not only proclaimed to be more efficient at math, science, and general calculation tasks but also able to engage in reasoning, planning, evaluation, and feedback directly in the LLM.

Consider our time travel problem from chapter 10 and shown again in figure 11.9. If you recall, this problem was difficult to solve using GPT-4 and other similar LLMs. However, with the application of reasoning and feedback, we were able to produce output that was occasionally correct.

As an experiment, enter this problem into ChatGPT using the o1-preview model, as shown in listing 11.6. Sit back for a few seconds and wait for the answer. Yep, the model still gets it wrong.

> **Listing 11.6   Time travel reasoning/planning problem**

```
In a sci-fi film, Alex is a time traveler who decides to go back in time
to witness a famous historical battle that took place 100 years ago,
which lasted for 10 days. He arrives three days before the battle starts.
However, after spending six days in the past, he jumps forward in time
by 50 years and stays there for 20 days. Then, he travels back to
witness the end of the battle. How many days does Alex spend in the past
before he sees the end of the battle?
```

While it may be somewhat disappointing to see the model get the wrong answer, it does, however, do a far better job of breaking down the problem and demonstrating

The problem statement:

> In a sci-fi film, Alex is a time traveler who decides to go back in time to witness a famous historical battle that took place 100 years ago, which lasted for 10 days. He arrives three days before the battle starts. However, after spending six days in the past, he jumps forward in time by 50 years and stays there for 20 days. Then, he travels back to witness the end of the battle. How many days does Alex spend in the past before he sees the end of the battle?

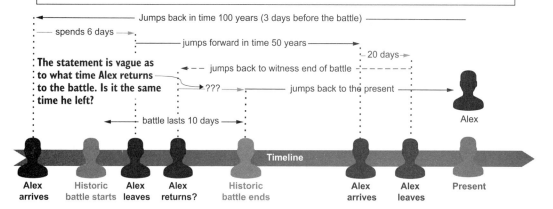

Figure 11.9   The time travel problem, revisited

its answer. Listing 11.7 shows the sample output from posing the problem in listing 11.6 to the Strawberry model. Note, you may get a different answer because of the stochastic nature of the LLM.

Listing 11.7   o1-preview response to time travel problem

To determine how many days Alex spends in the past before witnessing the end of the battle, let's reconstruct the timeline step by step:
Arrival in the Past:
Alex arrives 3 days before the battle begins.
He spends these 3 days waiting for the battle to start.
During the Battle:
The battle starts, and Alex experiences the first 3 days of it.
At this point, he has spent a total of 6 days in the past (3 days before the battle and 3 days during the battle).
Time Jump Forward: ⟵ ⌐ It becomes obvious
After these 6 days, Alex jumps 50 years forward in time.   where the model is
He spends 20 days in this future time.   making the error.
Return to the Past:
Alex then returns to the past to witness the end of the battle.
Since the battle lasts 10 days and he left after day 3 of the battle, there are 7 days remaining in the battle.
However, because he was away for 20 days, which is longer than the remaining 7 days of the battle, he must return to a point in time before the battle ends to witness its conclusion.
To see the end of the battle, he returns to the past on the last day of

```
the battle.
Final Days Spent Before the Battle Ends:
Upon returning, he spends 1 more day in the past to witness the battle's
end.
Total Days Spent in the Past Before Seeing the End:
6 days before jumping forward in time.
1 day after returning to the past.
Total: 6 + 1 = 7 days.
Answer: 7
```

Because we know the right answer is 27, we know the LLM is wrong, but if we didn't, we could just as easily assume that the work and reasoning were all correct. Problems like this can happen when we remove feedback in LLM interactions and agentic systems. Feedback can guide the model to correct itself.

However, what if we didn't know the correct answer was 27 (26, if you assume he doesn't spend the day to witness the battle) and assumed the LLM or agent was correct? Well, this is a problem we can rectify with a couple of simple prompts that can engage the LLM in reasoning and planning feedback. However, these techniques are more effective with LLMs or wrappers such as the OpenAI Assistants, which provide reasoning and planning within the model.

What we want to do is provide feedback to the LLM, but understanding what that feedback is will likely be difficult for us. Fortunately, we can elicit feedback directly from the LLM, provided we give the correct answer. Listing 11.8 shows how to generate constructive feedback from the LLM concerning our time travel problem.

Listing 11.8   Generating feedback

```
the correct answer is 27, please review what you did wrong and suggest
feedback you could give yourself when trying to solve similar future problems
```

Entering this after the model answers the question wrong will generate feedback that you can use to guide the model through prompting or as part of system instructions. Listing 11.9 shows an example of the feedback provided by o1-preview. You can then extract this feedback and augment the instructions the next time you want to tackle complex time travel problems.

Listing 11.9   Generated feedback

```
Feedback for Future Problems
Understanding Time Frames in Time Travel:
Relative Time Frames: Always consider the time periods relative to the
original point of reference. In this problem, even though Alex jumps
forward 50 years, he is still in the past relative to his original
present time.
Including All Relevant Periods:
Ensure that all time periods spent in the past (or future) are included
in the total calculation, even if they involve moving to different
points in time.
Time Continuity:
```

```
Remember that while the traveler moves through time, events in other
time periods continue to progress unless specified otherwise.
Application:
Careful Reading:
Pay close attention to the details provided, such as the durations and
the sequences of time jumps.
Visualization:
It may help to draw a timeline to visualize the sequence of events and
time periods involved.
Double-Checking Calculations:
After solving, revisit each step to ensure all time periods are
accounted for correctly.
```

This feedback technique will consistently work on models such as o1-preview, but other models may still struggle to answer correctly, even given this feedback. Over time, as models become smarter, this technique will likely generally work on most models. However, this feedback mechanism will likely be essential even as models get progressively brighter. because language is nuanced, and not every problem we challenge LLMs with may have an obvious absolute answer. Take our example problem, for instance. This problem is an excellent example of requiring the problem solver to make assumptions and draw correlations from the question. There are still plenty of areas in science, from geology to behavioral science, where answering the same problem may yield a range of answers. Let's look next at a few techniques for how the application of reasoning, planning, evaluation, and feedback can be applied to agentic systems.

11.5 Applying planning, reasoning, evaluation, and feedback to assistant and agentic systems

In recent chapters, we've examined how the agentic components of planning, reasoning, feedback, and evaluation can be implemented. Now we look at how, when, and where those components can be integrated into assistant and agentic systems for real-time production, research, or development.

While not all of these components may fit the same into every application, it's useful to understand where and when to apply which component. In the next section, we look at how planning can be integrated into assistant/agentic systems.

11.5.1 Application of assistant/agentic planning

Planning is the component where an assistant or agent can plan to undertake a set of tasks, whether they are in series, parallel, or some other combination. We typically associate planning with tool use, and, rightfully, any system using tools will likely want a capable planner. However, not all systems are created equally, so in table 11.1, we'll review where, when, and how to implement planners.

Table 11.1   When and where planning is employed and used in various applications

Application	Implemented	Environment	Purpose	Timing	Configuration
Personal assistant	At or within the LLM	Personal device	Facilitate tool use	During the response	As part of the prompt or LLM
Customer service bot	Not typical; restricted environment	Restricted environment, no tool use			
Autonomous agent	As part of the agent prompt and within the LLM	Server or service	Facilitate complex tool use and task planning	As part of constructing the agent and/or during the response	Within the agent or LLM
Collaborative workflows	As part of the LLM	Shared canvas or coding	Facilitate complex tool use	During the response	Within the LLM
Game AI	As part of the LLM	Server or application	Complex tool use and planning	Before or during the response	Within the LLM
Research	Anywhere	Server	Facilitate tool use and engage in complex task workflows	Before, during, and after response generation	Anywhere

Table 11.1 shows several varied application scenarios in which we may find an assistant or agent deployed to assist in some capacity. To provide further information and guidance, this list provides more details about how planning may be employed in each application:

- *Personal assistant*—While this application has been slow to roll out, LLM personal assistants promise to surpass Alexa and Siri in the future. Planning will be essential to these new assistants/agents to coordinate numerous complex tasks and execute tools (actions) in series or parallel.
- *Customer service bot*—Due to the controlled nature of this environment, it's unlikely that assistants engaged directly with customers will have controlled and very specific tools use. This means that these types of assistants will likely not require extensive planning.
- *Autonomous agent*—As we've seen in previous chapters, agents with the ability to plan can complete a series of complex tasks for various goals. Planning will be an essential element of any autonomous agentic system.
- *Collaborative workflows*—Think of these as agents or assistants that sit alongside coders or writers. While these workflows are still in early development, think of a workflow where agents are automatically tasked with writing and executing test code alongside developers. Planning will be an essential part of executing these complex future workflows.

- *Game AI*—While applying LLMs to games is still in early stages, it isn't hard to imagine in-game agents or assistants that can assist or challenge the player. Giving these agents the ability to plan and execute complex workflows could disrupt how and with whom we play games.
- *Research*—Similar to collaborative workflows, these agents will be responsible for deriving new ideas from existing sources of information. Finding that information will likely be facilitated through extensive tool use, which will benefit from coordination of planning.

As you can see, planning is an essential part of many LLM applications, whether through coordination of tool use or otherwise. In the next section, we look at the next component of reasoning and how it can be applied to the same application stack.

11.5.2 *Application of assistant/agentic reasoning*

Reasoning, while often strongly associated with planning and task completion, is a component that can also stand by itself. As LLMs mature and get smarter, reasoning is often included within the LLM itself. However, not all applications may benefit from extensive reasoning, as it often introduces a thinking cycle within the LLM response. Table 11.2 describes at a high level how the reasoning component can be integrated with various LLM application types.

Table 11.2   When and where reasoning is employed and used in various applications

Application	Implemented	Environment	Purpose	Timing	Configuration
Personal assistant	Within the LLM	Personal device	Breaking down work into steps	During the response	As part of the prompt or LLM
Customer service bot	Not typical; usually just informational	Limited tool use and need for composite tool use			
Autonomous agent	As part of the agent prompt and within the LLM	Server or service	Facilitate complex tool use and task planning	As part of LLM, external reasoning not well suited	Within the agent or LLM
Collaborative workflows	As part of the LLM	Shared canvas or coding	Assists in breaking work down	During the response	Within the LLM
Game AI	As part of the LLM	Server or application	Essential for undertaking complex actions	Before or during the response	Within the LLM
Research	Anywhere	Server	Understand how to solve complex problems and engage in complex task workflows	Before, during, and after response generation	Anywhere

Table 11.2 shows several varied application scenarios in which we may find an assistant or agent deployed to assist in some capacity. To provide further information and guidance, this list provides more details about how reasoning may be employed in each application:

- *Personal assistant*—Depending on the application, the amount of reasoning an agent employs may be limited. Reasoning is a process that requires the LLM to think through a problem, and this often requires longer response times depending on the complexity of the problem and the extent of the prompt. In many situations, responses intended to be closer to real-time reasoning may be disabled or turned down. While this may limit the complexity at which an agent can interact, limited or no reasoning can improve response times and increase user enjoyment.
- *Customer service bot*—Again, because of the controlled nature of this environment, it's unlikely that assistants engaged directly with customers will need to perform complex or any form of reasoning.
- *Autonomous agent*—While reasoning is a strong component of autonomous agents, we still don't know how much reasoning is too much. As models such as Strawberry become available for agentic workflows, we can gauge at what point extensive reasoning may not be needed. This will surely be the case for well-defined autonomous agent workflows.
- *Collaborative workflows*—Again, applying reasoning creates an overhead in the LLM interaction. Extensive reasoning may provide benefits for some workflows, while other well-defined workflows may suffer. This may mean that these types of workflows will benefit from multiple agents—those with reasoning and those without.
- *Game AI*—Similar to other applications, heavy-reasoning applications may not be appropriate for most game AIs. Games will especially require LLM response times to be quick, and this will surely be the application of reasoning for general tactical agents. Of course, that doesn't preclude the use of other reasoning agents that may provide more strategic control.
- *Research*—Reasoning will likely be essential to any complex research task for several reasons. A good example is the application of the Strawberry model, which we've already seen in research done in mathematics and the sciences.

While we often consider reasoning in tandem with planning, there may be conditions where the level at which each is implemented may differ. In the next section we consider the agent pillar of evaluation of various applications.

11.5.3   *Application of evaluation to agentic systems*

Evaluation is the component of agentic/assistant systems that can guide how well the system performs. While we demonstrated incorporating evaluation in some agentic workflows, evaluation is often an external component in agentic systems. However, it's also a core component of most LLM applications and not something that should be overlooked in most developments. Table 11.3 describes at a high level how the evaluation component can be integrated with various LLM application types.

Table 11.3   When and where evaluation is employed and used in various applications

Application	Implemented	Environment	Purpose	Timing	Configuration
Personal assistant	External	Server	Determine how well the system is working	After the interaction	Often developed externally
Customer service bot	External monitor	Server	Evaluate the success of each interaction	After the interaction	External to the agent system
Autonomous agent	External or internal	Server or service	Determine the success of the system after or during task completion	After the interaction	External or internal
Collaborative workflows	External	Shared canvas or coding	Evaluate the success of the collaboration	After the interaction	External service
Game AI	External or internal	Server or application	Evaluate the agent or evaluate the success of a strategy or action	After the interaction	External or as part of the agent or another agent
Research	Combined manual and LLM	Server and human	Evaluate the output of the research developed	After the generated output	Depends on the complexity of the problem and research undertaken

Table 11.3 shows several varied application scenarios in which we may find an assistant or agent deployed to assist in some capacity. To provide further information and guidance, this list provides more details about how evaluation may be employed in each application:

- *Personal assistant*—In most cases, an evaluation component will be used to process and guide the performance of agent responses. In systems primarily employing retrieval augmented generation (RAG) for document exploration, the evaluation indicates how well the assistant responds to information requests.
- *Customer service bot*—Evaluating service bots is critical to understanding how well the bot responds to customer requests. In many cases, a strong RAG knowledge element may be an element of the system that will require extensive and ongoing evaluation. Again, with most evaluation components, this element is external to

the main working system and is often run as part of monitoring general performance over several metrics.

- *Autonomous agent*—In most cases, a manual review of agent output will be a primary guide to the success of an autonomous agent. However, in some cases, internal evaluation can help guide the agent when it's undertaking complex tasks or as a means of improving the final output. Multiple agent systems, such as CrewAI and AutoGen, are examples of autonomous agents that use internal feedback to improve the generated output.
- *Collaborative workflows*—In most direct cases, manual evaluation is ongoing within these types of workflows. A user will often immediately and in near real time correct the assistant/agent by evaluating the output. Additional agents could be added similarly to autonomous agents for more extensive collaborative workflows.
- *Game AI*—Evaluation will often be broken down into development evaluation—evaluating how the agent interacts with the game—and in-game evaluation, evaluating how well an agent succeeded at a task. Implementing the later evaluation form is similar to autonomous agents but aims to improve some strategies or execution. Such in-game evaluations would also likely benefit from memory and a means of feedback.
- *Research*—Evaluation at this level generally occurs as a manual effort after completing the research task. An agent could employ some form of evaluation similar to autonomous agents to improve the generated output, perhaps even contemplating internally how evaluation of the output could be extended or further researched. Because this is currently a new area for agentic development, how well this will be executed remains to be seen.

Evaluation is an essential element to any agentic or assistant system, especially if that system provides real and fundamental information to users. Developing evaluation systems for agents and assistants is likely something that could or should have its own book. In the final section of this chapter, we'll look at feedback implementation for various LLM applications.

11.5.4   Application of feedback to agentic/assistant applications

Feedback as a component of agentic systems is often, if not always, implemented as an external component—at least for now. Perhaps confidence in evaluation systems may improve to the point where feedback is regularly incorporated into such systems. Table 11.4 showcases how feedback can be implemented into various LLM applications.

Table 11.4   When and where feedback is employed and used in various applications

Application	Implemented	Environment	Purpose	Timing	Configuration
Personal assistant	External or by the user	Aggregated to the server or as part of the system	Provides means of system improvement	After or during the interaction	Internal and external
Customer service bot	External monitor	Aggregated to the server	Qualifies and provides a means for system improvement	After the interaction	External to the agent system
Autonomous agent	External	Aggregated at the server	Provides a means for system improvement	After the interaction	External
Collaborative workflows	While interacting	Shared canvas or coding	Provides a mechanism for immediate feedback	During the interaction	External service
Game AI	External or internal	Server or application	As part of internal evaluation feedback provided for dynamic improvement	After or during the interaction	External or as part of the agent or another agent
Research	Combined manual and LLM	Server and human	Evaluate the output of the research developed	After the generated output	Depends on the complexity of the problem and the research undertaken

Table 11.4 shows several application scenarios in which we may find an assistant or agent deployed to assist in some capacity. To provide further information and guidance, this list provides more details about how feedback may be employed in each application:

- *Personal assistant*—If the assistant or agent interacts with the user in a chat-style interface, direct and immediate feedback can be applied by the user. Whether this feedback is sustained over future conversations or interactions, it usually develops within agentic memory. Assistants such as ChatGPT now incorporate memory and can benefit from explicit user feedback.
- *Customer service bot*—User or system feedback is typically provided through a survey after the interaction has completed. This usually means that feedback is regulated to an external system that aggregates the feedback for later improvements.
- *Autonomous agent*—Much like bots, feedback within autonomous agents is typically regulated to after the agent has completed a task that a user then reviews. The feedback mechanism may be harder to capture because many things can

be subjective. Methods explored in this chapter for producing feedback can be used within prompt engineering improvements.

- *Collaborative workflows*—Similar to the personal assistant, these types of applications can benefit from immediate and direct feedback from the user. Again, how this information is persisted across sessions is often an implementation of agentic memory.
- *Game AI*—Feedback can be implemented alongside evaluation through additional and multiple agents. This feedback form may again be single-use and exist within the current interaction or may persist as memory. Imagine a game AI that can evaluate its actions, improve those with feedback, and remember those improvements. While this pattern isn't ideal for games, it will certainly improve the gameplay experience.
- *Research*—Similar to evaluation in the context of research, feedback is typically performed offline after the output is evaluated. While some development has been done using multiple agent systems incorporating agents for evaluation and feedback, these systems don't always perform well, at least not with the current state-of-the-art models. Instead, it's often better to isolate feedback and evaluation at the end to avoid the common feedback looping problem.

Feedback is another powerful component of agentic and assistant systems, but it's not always required on the first release. However, incorporating rigorous feedback and evaluation mechanisms can greatly benefit agentic systems in the long term concerning ongoing monitoring and providing the confidence to improve various aspects of the system.

How you implement each of these components in your agentic systems may, in part, be guided by the architecture of your chosen agentic platform. Now that you understand the nuances of each component, you also have the knowledge to guide you in selecting the right agent system that fits your application and business use case. Regardless of your application, you'll want to employ several agentic components in almost all cases.

As agentic systems mature and LLMs themselves get smarter, some of the components we today consider external may be closely integrated. We've already seen reasoning and planning be integrated into a model such as Strawberry. Certainly, as we approach the theoretical artificial general intelligence milestone, we may see models capable of performing long-term self-evaluation and feedback.

In any case, I hope you enjoyed this journey with me into this incredible frontier of a new and emerging technology that will certainly alter our perception of work and how we undertake it through agents.

11.6 Exercises

Use the following exercises to improve your knowledge of the material:

- *Exercise 1*—Implement a Simple Planning Agent (Beginner)

  Objective—Learn how to implement a basic planning agent using a prompt to generate a sequence of actions.

  Tasks:

  - Create an agent that receives a goal, breaks it into steps, and executes those steps sequentially.
  - Define a simple goal, such as retrieving information from Wikipedia and saving it to a file.
  - Implement the agent using a basic planner prompt (refer to the planner example in section 11.3).
  - Run the agent, and evaluate how well it plans and executes each step.

- *Exercise 2*—Test Feedback Integration in a Planning Agent (Intermediate)

  Objective—Understand how feedback mechanisms can improve the performance of an agentic system.

  Tasks:

  - Modify the agent from exercise 1 to include a feedback loop after each task.
  - Use the feedback to adjust or correct the next task in the sequence.
  - Test the agent by giving it a more complex task, such as gathering data from multiple sources, and observe how the feedback improves its performance.
  - Document and compare the agent's behavior before and after adding feedback.

- *Exercise 3*—Experiment with Parallel and Sequential Planning (Intermediate)

  Objective—Learn the difference between parallel and sequential actions and how they affect agent behavior.

  Tasks:

  - Set up two agents using Nexus: one that executes tasks in parallel and another that performs tasks sequentially.
  - Define a multistep goal where some actions depend on the results of previous actions (sequential), and some can be done simultaneously (parallel).
  - Compare the performance and output of both agents, noting any errors or inefficiencies in parallel execution when sequential steps are required.

- *Exercise 4*—Build and Integrate a Custom Planner into Nexus (Advanced)

  Objective—Learn how to build a custom planner and integrate it into an agent platform.

  Tasks:

  - Write a custom planner using prompt engineering strategies from section 11.3, ensuring it supports sequential task execution.
  - Integrate this planner into Nexus, and create an agent that uses it.

- Test the planner with a complex goal that involves multiple steps and tools (e.g., data retrieval, processing, and saving).
- Evaluate how the custom planner performs compared to built-in planners in Nexus or other platforms.

- *Exercise 5*—Implement Error Handling and Feedback in Sequential Planning (Advanced)

  Objective—Learn how to implement error handling and feedback to refine sequential planning in an agentic system.

  Tasks:

  - Using a sequential planner, set up an agent to perform a goal that may encounter common errors (e.g., a failed API call, missing data, or invalid input).
  - Implement error-handling mechanisms in the planner to recognize and respond to these errors.
  - Add feedback loops to adjust the plan or retry actions based on the error encountered.
  - Test the system by deliberately causing errors during execution, and observe how the agent recovers or adjusts its plan.

Summary

- Planning is central to agents and assistants, allowing them to take a goal, break it into steps, and execute them. Without planning, agents are reduced to simple chatbot-like interactions.
- Agents must differentiate between parallel and sequential actions. Many LLMs can handle parallel actions, but only advanced models support sequential planning, critical for complex task completion.
- Feedback is crucial in guiding agents to correct their course and improve performance over time. This chapter demonstrates how feedback mechanisms can be integrated with agents to refine their decision-making processes.
- Platforms such as OpenAI Assistants and Anthropic's Claude support internal planning and can execute complex, multistep tasks. Agents using these platforms can use sequential action planning for sophisticated workflows.
- Properly selecting and limiting agent actions is vital to avoid confusion and unintended behavior. Too many actions may overwhelm an agent, while unnecessary tools may be misused.
- Nexus allows for creating and managing agents through a flexible interface, where users can implement custom planners, set goals, and assign tools. The chapter includes practical examples using Nexus to highlight the difference between a raw LLM and a planner-enhanced agent.
- Writing custom planners is straightforward, using prompt engineering strategies. Tools such as LangChain and Semantic Kernel offer a variety of planners that can be adapted or extended to fit specific agentic needs.

- Models such as OpenAI Strawberry integrate reasoning, planning, evaluation, and feedback directly into the LLM, offering more accurate problem-solving capabilities.
- Evaluation helps determine how well an agentic system is performing and can be implemented internally or externally, depending on the use case.
- As LLMs evolve, reasoning, planning, and feedback mechanisms may become deeply integrated into models, paving the way for more autonomous and intelligent agent systems.

appendix A
Accessing OpenAI
large language models

Although several commercial large language model (LLM) services are available, this book recommends using OpenAI services directly or through Azure OpenAI Studio. To access either service, you must create an account and register a payment method not covered in this appendix. The GPT-4 family of LLMs is considered best in class and better suited for agent development. Using open source and alternative services is always an option but generally only advisable after you've worked with GPT-4 for some time.

A.1 Accessing OpenAI accounts and keys

The following general steps can help you quickly set up using OpenAI LLMs for agent development. Though using OpenAI and other commercial LLMs comes at a price, you can expect to pay less than US$100 to complete all the exercises in this book:

1 Go to https://openai.com and log in, or register for an account and log in. If this is your first time creating an account, you'll likely be given free credit in some amount. If you already have an account, you must register a payment method and type. It's generally better to purchase a number of credits at a time. This will allow you to manage the costs better and avoid overruns.

2 After logging in to the platform, select ChatGPT or the API, as shown in figure A.1. Choose the API.

Select the API

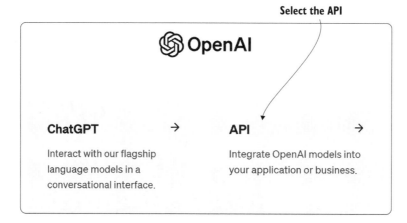

Figure A.1   Selecting the API section of the OpenAI platform

3   Open the left menu, and select the API Keys option, as shown in figure A.2.

Select the API Keys

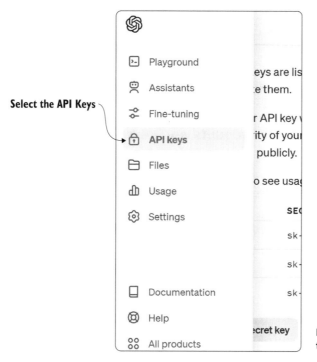

**Figure A.2   Selecting
the API Keys option**

4 Click the Create button to create a new key, enter a name for the key, and click the Create Secret Key button, as shown in figure A.3.

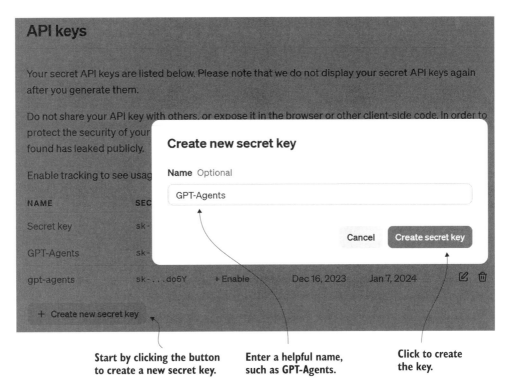

Figure A.3 Creating the secret API key

5 Copy and paste the key to a notepad or another area for safekeeping using the Copy button, as shown in figure A.4. Keep this key secret, and ensure it remains only on your development machine.

After generating a key, you can continue to use it within an .env configuration file or through other means of registering an OpenAI key. For most of the packages used in this book, configuring OpenAI will generally only require the key. Other services, such as Azure OpenAI, will require the configuration of a model deployment and a base URL as covered in the next section.

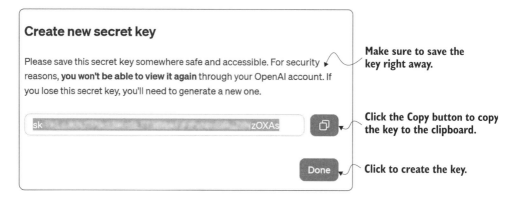

Figure A.4   Copying and pasting the key to a well-known safe location

A.2   *Azure OpenAI Studio, keys, and deployments*

Through its ongoing relationship with OpenAI, Microsoft hosts the same models at the same price within Azure OpenAI Studio. Occasionally, Azure may be a model version behind, but Microsoft generally keeps current with the latest OpenAI models.

These guidelines will be more general because there are several ways to access Azure and methods of creating accounts and accessing the studio (for specific instructions, refer to Microsoft documentation):

1   Log in to your Azure portal account subscription.
2   Create a new Azure OpenAI Studio resource in a region that makes sense to you. At the time of writing, not all regions provided access to all models. You may need to check which models are available for your region first. This will also be specific to your account and usage.

    Within Azure OpenAI, models are exposed through a resource allocation called a *deployment*. Deployments wrap a model, such as GPT-4, and provide access to the resource. Figure A.5 shows an example of various models being exposed through deployments.

3   Click the Create New Deployment button to create a new deployment, and then select the model you want to deploy.

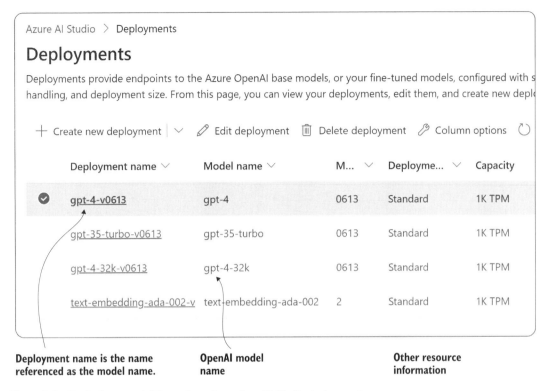

Figure A.5 **Deploying a model through an Azure OpenAI Studio deployment**

4 After the model is wrapped in a deployment, you must access the parent Azure
   OpenAI resource. From there, you can access the key, endpoint, or base URL
   needed to configure your connection, as shown in figure A.6.

Again, if you get stuck, the Microsoft documentation can guide you in the right direction. The three critical differences to remember when connecting to a resource such
as Azure OpenAI Studio or another LLM using the OpenAI tooling are listed here:

- The `api key` to access the model
- The base `url` or `endpoint` where the model is located
- The name of the `model` or `deployment` name

If you can't access a model for whatever reason, a good alternative is open source
models. Setting up and consuming open source LLMs is covered in chapter 2.

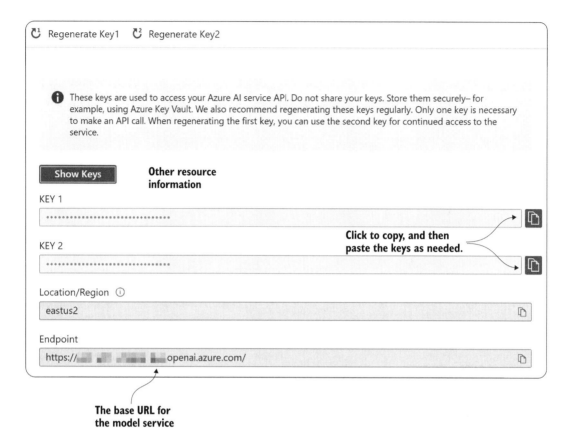

The base URL for
the model service

appendix B
Python development environment

While this book assumes readers are experienced Python developers, this could mean many different things. In this appendix, we look at configuring a Python development environment that will function with the code examples in this book. You can use other integrated development environments (IDEs), but not all tooling, especially extensions, will work in all IDEs.

B.1 Downloading the source code

To download and run the source code, install Git, and then pull the repository locally. Here are the high-level steps to pull the code from the book's GitHub repository:

1. Install Git if you need to. Git can be installed from multiple sources, but a good option is the main release, found here: https://git-scm.com/downloads. Follow the instructions to download and install the tool for your operating system.

2. Open a terminal in a folder you want to download the source to, and then enter the following command:

   ```
   git clone https://github.com/cxbxmxcx/GPT-Agents.git
   ```

3. After the code is downloaded, you can begin by opening the chapter folder that you're working on in Visual Studio Code (VS Code). If you need to

install VS Code or understand how to load a chapter folder as a workspace, consult section B.5 in this appendix.

B.2   Installing Python

Python is provided through different versions and deployments. This book relies on the standard Python installation, version 3.10. Anaconda is another deployment of Python that is very popular and could be used. However, all the material in this book has been run and tested with a Python 3.10 virtual environment:

1 Go to www.python.org/downloads/.
2 Locate and download the latest release of Python 3.10 for your operating system.
3 Install the release on your machine using the instructions for your operating system.
4 To confirm your installation, open a terminal, and execute the following command:

```
python --version
```

The version should be 3.10, but if it isn't, don't worry. You may have multiple Python versions installed. We'll also confirm the installation when setting up VS Code.

B.3   Installing VS Code

Installing VS Code is relatively straightforward and can be done in just a few steps:

1 Go to https://code.visualstudio.com.
2 Download a stable release of VS Code for your operating system.
3 After the release is downloaded, follow the installation instructions for your operating system.
4 Launch VS Code for your operating system, and make sure no warnings or errors appear. If you encounter problems, try to restart your computer and/or reinstall.

With VS Code running, we can install the necessary extensions. We'll cover those extensions next.

B.4   Installing VS Code Python extensions

Thousands of extensions for VS Code can provide an excellent Python coding environment. The recommended ones are only the start of what you can explore independently. Beware, though, that not all extensions are created equally. When installing new extensions, look at the number of installs and ratings. Extensions with fewer than four stars are generally to be avoided. To install the extensions, follow these steps:

1 Launch VS Code, and open the Extensions panel, as shown in figure B.1.

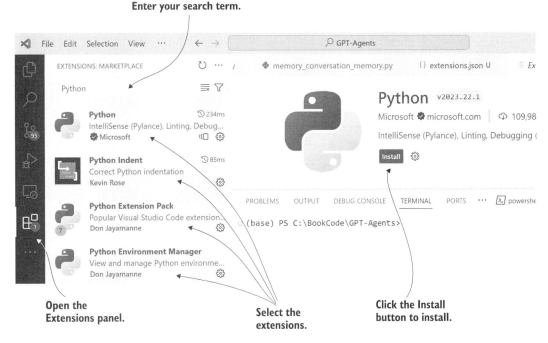

Figure B.1 Installing VS Code extensions

2 Install the following list of extensions:
- Python, for environment and language support
- Python Extension Pack, for covering other extensions
- Python Environment Manager, for managing environments
- Python Indent, for code formatting
- Flake8, for code formatting/linting
- Prompt Flow, for testing LLM prompts
- Semantic Kernel Tools, for working with the Semantic Kernel framework
- Docker, for managing Docker containers
- Dev Containers, for running development environments with containers

You'll only need to install the extensions for each VS Code environment you're running. Typically, this will mean installing for just your operating system installation of VS Code. However, if you run VS Code in containers, you must install extensions for each container you're running. Working with Python in the Dev Containers extension will be covered later in this appendix.

B.5   *Creating a new Python environment with VS Code*

When developing Python projects, you often want to create isolated virtual environments. This will help in managing multiple package dependencies across various tasks and tools. In this book, it's recommended that a new virtual environment be created for each new chapter. VS Code can help you create and manage multiple Python environments quickly and efficiently via the following steps:

1 Press Ctrl-Shift-P (Cmd-Shift-P) to open the command panel, and select Python: Create Environment, as shown in figure B.2.

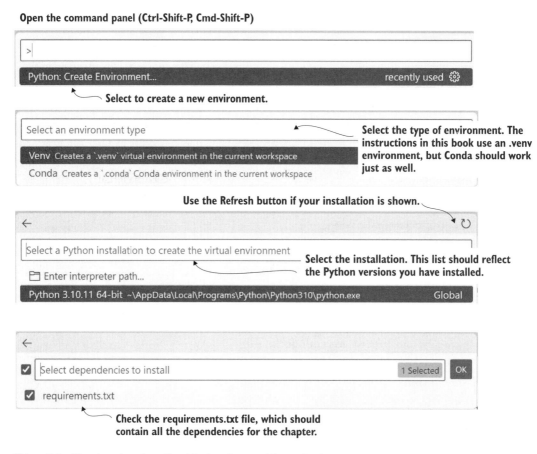

Figure B.2   The steps to set up the virtual environment for a chapter

2 Select the environment type, either Venv or Conda. This book demonstrates Venv but Conda should also work.

3   Select the Python installation. The code in this book has been run with Python 3.10 at a minimum. The agent tools and frameworks featured in this book are cutting edge, so they should support later versions of Python.

4   Check that the `requirements.txt` file in the chapter folder is selected. This will install all the requirements for the current chapter.

You should complete these steps for each new chapter of the book. The alternative is to use VS Code development containers, which will be covered in the next section.

B.6   Using VS Code Dev Containers (Docker)

When working with advanced agents and agents that can generate and execute code, running them in isolated containers is generally recommended. Container isolation prevents operating system disruption or corruption and provides a base for deploying agents.

Getting familiar with containers and platforms such as Docker can be an extensive undertaking to grasp everything. Fortunately, it takes very little knowledge to start using containers, and VS Code extensions make this even more accessible.

You'll first need to install a container toolset. Docker is free (provided you use the tool as a hobby or you're a student) and the most accessible. Follow these instructions to install Docker and get started working with containers:

1   Go to the Docker Desktop download page at www.docker.com/products/docker-desktop.

2   Download and install Docker for your operating system. Follow any other instructions as requested.

3   Launch the Docker desktop application. Completing this step will confirm you have Docker installed and working as expected.

4   Open VS Code, and confirm that the Docker extensions listed in section 1.4 are installed.

With Docker and VS Code configured, you can move on to using Dev Containers by following these steps:

1   Open a new instance of VS Code.

2   Select to open a remote window, as shown in figure B.3.

3   Select Open Folder in Container to start a container from a folder, or select New Dev Container to start without a folder.

After the container is launched, your VS Code environment will be connected. This allows you to develop code on the container without worrying about dependencies not working.

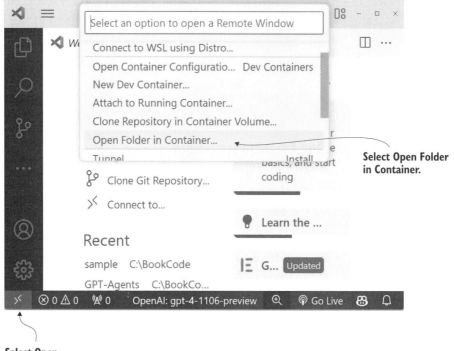

**Select Open Folder
in Container.**

**Select Open
Remote Window.**

Figure B.3   Opening a remote window to a container in VS Code

index

RELATED MANNING TITLES

Multi-Agent Systems with AutoGen
by Victor Dibia

ISBN 9781633436145
325 pages (estimated), $59.99
Spring 2025 (estimated)

Generative AI for the IT Pro
by Chrissy LeMaire and Brandon Abshire

ISBN 9781633436428
350 pages (estimated), $49.99
Spring 2025 (estimated)

The Complete Obsolete Guide to Generative AI
by David Clinton

ISBN 9781633436985
240 pages, $39.99
July 2024

Generative AI in Action
by Amit Bahree
Foreword by Eric Boyd

ISBN 9781633436947
464 pages, $59.99
September 2024

For ordering information, go to www.manning.com

The Manning Early Access Program

Don't wait to start learning! In MEAP, the Manning Early Access Program, you can read books as they're being created and long before they're available in stores.

Here's how MEAP works.

- **Start now.** Buy a MEAP and you'll get all available chapters in PDF, ePub, Kindle, and liveBook formats.

- **Regular updates.** New chapters are released as soon as they're written. We'll let you know when fresh content is available.

- **Finish faster.** MEAP customers are the first to get final versions of all books! Pre-order the print book, and it'll ship as soon as it's off the press.

- **Contribute to the process.** The feedback you share with authors makes the end product better.

- **No risk.** You get a full refund or exchange if we ever have to cancel a MEAP.

Explore dozens of titles in MEAP at www.manning.com.

A new online reading experience

liveBook, our online reading platform, adds a new dimension to your Manning books, with features that make reading, learning, and sharing easier than ever. A liveBook version of your book is included FREE with every Manning book.

This next generation book platform is more than an online reader. It's packed with unique features to upgrade and enhance your learning experience.

- Add your own notes and bookmarks
- One-click code copy
- Learn from other readers in the discussion forum
- Audio recordings and interactive exercises
- Read all your purchased Manning content in any browser, anytime, anywhere

As an added bonus, you can search every Manning book and video in liveBook—even ones you don't yet own. Open any liveBook, and you'll be able to browse the content and read anything you like.*

Find out more at www.manning.com/livebook-program.

*Open reading is limited to 10 minutes per book daily